# The Vegetarian Alternative

# The Vegetarian Alternative

A Guide to a Healthful and Humane Diet

Vic S. Sussman

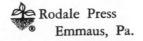
Rodale Press
Emmaus, Pa.

*Printed in the United States of America on recycled paper contain-
ing a high percentage of de-inked fiber.*

**Library of Congress Cataloging in Publication Data**

Sussman, Vic S.
    The vegetarian alternative.

    Bibliography: p.
    Includes index.
    1. Vegetarianism.   I.   Title.
TX392.S9      613.2'6      78-2755
ISBN 0-87857-227-9  paperback


8      10      9      7                    paperback

This one is for Lora and Betsy.

# ✿ Contents

# Acknowledgments

This book couldn't have been written without a lot of help from friends, family, and experts in specialized fields. I am especially grateful to my wife, Betsy Millmann Sussman. Her love, advice, and support helped make dreams into reality. Thanks also to my cousin, Robin Levine, who gave instruction, counsel, and warm encouragement right from the start; Marilyn Mower, who gave unselfishly of her expertise as a nutritionist (any errors are my own, however); Steve and Diane Isaacs, who read, edited, and discussed early chapters and put up with my one-subject ramblings at dinner; Pat Brett Pollock, who cried when she read about veal calves; Bill and Kathy Wahl, who reviewed the rough draft and good-naturedly endured my evangelistic fervor; Don Stallone, itinerant Viking, who gave unstintingly of his time and other people's money; Tommy Dowd, who generously gave me legal advice; Paul Weisenfeld, who did the same; Bob and Stephanie Harris, who answered my endless store of questions; Judy Cottman, who helped with proofreading; and George Chornesky, M.D., without whose help this book would never have been written.

Thanks also to Alex Hershaft, Vegetarian Information Service; Nellie Shriver, American Vegetarians; Roger Glenn Brown, Inscape Publishers; the Center for Science in the Public Interest; the information staffs of the Food Safety and Quality Service (FSQS) and the Animal and Plant Health Inspection Service

(APHIS) of the United States Department of Agriculture; the information officers of the Food and Drug Administration; and the staff of the National Medical Library.

Special thanks to my close friend Alan M. Pollock, who always wanted to see his name in a book. And my gratitude to Roger B. Yepsen, Jr. of Rodale Press for his editorial judgment, encouragement, and patience.


Vic S. Sussman
Travilah, Maryland
Winter, 1977

# Introduction

I became a vegetarian because of a white rabbit. Her name was Lora and she was a pet in a first grade class my wife taught. Lora couldn't be left at school on weekends or vacations, though, so she became a frequent houseguest. Eventually she came to mean more to us than to the school children—who moved on to gerbils and hermit crabs anyway.

People will tell you that rabbits are dumb, that they have no personality, that they're dirty. But Lora was at least as bright as most dogs (and some people) I've known. She possessed definite moods and prejudices and was as clean as a cat. Fully house-broken, Lora ran free in our home.

She met me at the door when I came home from work and greeted me by loudly thumping a hind foot and bounding over to lie at my feet. She slept at the end of our bed—though often we'd awake to find her snoring on the pillows above our heads. She also developed a taste for Tiger's Milk Cookies and would snarl and rip the box out of your hand if you didn't offer her one fast enough.

Lora was affectionate, bossy, and sometimes pixilated. She'd often race and leap about the house out of sheer exuberance. No animal before or since has taught me more about the narrowness of judging other life forms according to our own parochial standards and traditions.

Lora was only two years old when she died in my hands one night in May. She had been ill with enteritis. My wife Betsy and I had struggled for two months to nurse her back to health. Because she was unable to eat, we force fed her four times a day with a special veterinary food paste. We fed her liquids with an oven baster. Lora recovered from her initial illness and seemed her old self for a month. Then she fell ill again and died quickly.

The evening after her death we sat down to a subdued dinner. I looked down at my plate, at the piece of meat lying there, and suddenly said to Betsy, "I don't think I can eat this."

"I know what you mean," she said, pushing her own plate to one side, "I had trouble preparing it." We ate around the meat that night, had noodles and cheese the next night, and began discussing the possibility of doing without meat altogether.

Neither of us had thought much about becoming vegetarians before—we had been raised in meat-and-potatoes families. But Lora's life and death had triggered something in us. I am not overly sentimental about animals. I know Lora was "only a rabbit"—just as we are "only human." But I also know that this fragile creature brought us joy and made us think more deeply about the value and meaning of existence and love and compassion.

And because Lora's life had touched us so deeply, it seemed somehow inconsistent at her death to go on eating other animals possessed of the same vitality we celebrated in her. This hesitation about eating meat—plus our already well-developed preference for natural living and chemical-free foods—pushed us toward experimenting with meatless meals.

We changed our diet slowly, carefully, because we realized our new direction was based largely on intuitive and still unclear notions. Our knowledge of nutrition, we soon discovered, was shaky at best. We were still very much part of what Frances Moore Lappé calls "The Great American Steak Religion." Nutritional apostasy didn't come easily to us. We had yet to discover the important health and economic benefits of a vegetarian or low meat diet. Nor were we in a hurry to dub ourselves vegetarians.

Most people think vegetarians are a little weird. It's one thing to tell your friends and family that you're cutting back on meat to save money, or that your doctor put you on a prudent diet free of beef, milk fat, and eggs.

That's okay.

You can even get away with saying that you won't eat fish because you hate looking into their glassy eyes. But see what happens when you announce to the world that you're swearing off *all* meat, fowl, and fish—that you'll no longer eat foods of animal origin—that you've decided to become a (gasp!) *vegetarian.*

Even the word sounds alien and threatening. Its staccato consonants have the ring of ideology and fanaticism. Speak the word softly and it still comes out too loudly, a verbal raised fist, a warning that you've become a dietary Bolshevik about to overturn the dinner table and garrote the guests' with their own gravy-stained napkins. Become a vegetarian and the curious will crowd around you at lunch. "So what *do* you eat?" they will ask, peering deeply into the recesses of your brown bag, trying to divine its mysteries, wrinkling their noses as though the sack held fresh buffalo dung or live snakes.

"What's *that?*" they'll ask, bending low over your sandwich. "Does it taste good?"

"Yes. And wipe your feet off before you jump in."

Friends and acquaintances will ask detailed questions about what, how, and why you eat the way you do. They'll express concern about your children's health. Strangers will stop you in elevators or at parties, challenging your beliefs:

"I hear you don't eat meat."
"That's right."
"But you wear leather shoes."
"I don't eat shoes, either."

What is a vegetarian, anyway? Everyone has his or her own idea:

A vegetarian is a kook, a health food store habitué, a fanatic passing out leaflets—CLOSE THE SLAUGHTERHOUSES—or bearing bumper stickers—LOVE ANIMALS/DON'T EAT THEM.

A vegetarian is a leathery old man doing push-ups in the park, endlessly telling you how healthy he is and how his aunt was cured of cancer by drinking carrot juice.

A vegetarian is a flaky, frizzy, New-Age-Human-Potential-Be-Here-Now-Aquarian-Person who says that, y'know, vegetarianism is the only way to get your act together, karma-wise.

A vegetarian is a health-conscious, compassionate person who refuses to participate in the needless killing of innocent creatures.

All of the above?

And yet—its loony image aside—vegetarianism has been making converts faster than the best of the beatific gurus promising salvation. Old and young, rich and poor—vegetarianism's appeal cuts across all social lines, drawing its adherents from every level and for every reason: ethics, ecology, economics, religion, health, and aesthetics. That a movement the news media still regard as a novelty should make such inroads into a meat-centered society is amazing. Yet bubbling starlets tell us vegetarianism is the Now Diet. Futurists warn that it's the Survival Diet. Consumerists advise that it's the Cheap and Nourishing Diet.

Newspaper columns ply us with meatless recipes that foil high prices. Vegetarian athletes come out of the closet, revealing their herbaceous tendencies. TV sitcoms feature vegetarian characters. Conservative nutritionists and medical experts—who might have condemned vegetarianism as faddism only a few years ago—now hint that a sensible meatless or low-meat diet may decrease the incidence of cancer, heart disease, hypertension, and other ills.

But what do vegetarians eat, anyway?

They eat fish.
They don't eat fish.
They eat eggs and drink milk.
They use no animal products whatever.
They live on brown rice and green tea.
They only eat raw vegetables.
None of the above.

What should you believe? Parents and educators are confused and concerned because young people have been embracing vegetarianism with the fervor they usually reserve for rock stars and skateboards.

> My son came home from school, and as he sat at the dinner table, he cast a disdainful eye on the roast and announced he had become a vegetarian. . . . We told the boy to stop being ridiculous and to eat his meat. He responded by declaring that only insensitive persons . . . with the grossest type of sensuality . . . would eat meat. All he wanted was some rice or nuts or beans. Isn't there anything we can do to change his attitude? *

One of my motivations for writing this book was the number of misguided vegetarians I met while I was a college instructor. During the years I taught, I met scores of young people who had either discarded meat eating or planned to do so. Most of them leaped into their version of vegetarianism with less thought than they'd have given to buying a new pair of jeans. Their renunciation of flesh was usually spurred by compassion for other creatures, an often-confused involvement with Asian mysticism, or a desire to discard the culture of the establishment. But their ideologically directed diet, while rich in good intentions, was a model of poor nutrition: meals of meat, milk, cheese, and eggs

---

\* From Dr. Jean Mayer's *A Diet for Living* (New York: David McKay Co., Inc., 1975), p. 183.

were abandoned, to be replaced by soft drinks, candy, and junk foods. Twinkies and Pepsi Cola were somehow less culturally threatening than hamburgers or pepperoni pizzas.

I met some of the worst advertisements for a vegetarian life: fat vegetarians, skinny ones, pale ones, weak and sickly ones. I spoke with parents, (usually other faculty members), who feared that their kids were on the road to the intensive care unit. And I met dozens of failed vegetarians: people who had tried what they thought was a vegetarian diet for weeks, months, or years and had given it up because they became sick, run-down, or simply hungry all the time. Many were demoralized by their failure to adapt to a regimen advocated by the likes of Da Vinci, Emerson, Thoreau, Gandhi, Schweitzer, and others. I met people who had turned to vegetarianism out of a sense of spiritual awareness or a quest for better health who then had their compassion and concern rewarded with illness or lassitude. They discovered, to their dismay, that virtue and good intentions have no nutritional value.

Vegetarianism, like any ism too quickly snapped up by an enthusiastic audience, is suffering from an information gap. Too many vegetarians, would-be vegetarians, and their critics are full of beans, literally, because they mistakenly believe only a daily dose of beans can replace meat, and figuratively, because myths and misconceptions about vegetarianism are bandied about as facts.

Is a vegetarian diet good, bad, healthy, unhealthy, energizing, debilitating, cheap, or even necessary? Will a nonmeat diet make you thin, fat, anemic, vibrant, sexy, impotent, mellow, or sappy? Everybody has a different idea. The result is total confusion.

Vegetarian cookbooks keep appearing, filled with recipes that range from gloppy to glorious. But most cookbooks only tell how to prepare food. They don't discuss those things potential vegetarians really need to know:

What do vegetarians eat, anyway?

Can a vegetarian be well nourished?

Will a vegetarian diet change you emotionally or physically?

Is it safe to raise an infant or teenager as a vegetarian?

What is the ethical and moral basis for a nonflesh diet?

How should you shift to a vegetarian diet:
   gradually, or—pardon the expression—cold turkey?

So here's a book that explains the fundamentals of a *sensible* vegetarian diet. Covering nutrition, health, ethics, philosophy, and kitchen techniques, this book is a guide for those who merely want to back away from the Western world's overemphasis on flesh foods and animal fat—the occasional meat eater; for potential vegetarians pondering how best to make the shift to a meatless regimen; for parents agonizing over their child's refusal to eat traditional foods; and for established vegetarians wondering how to accurately answer the endless questions asked about their diet and beliefs.

# ✿ ONE ✿

# *Vegetus,*
# *Vegetabilis,*
# Vegetarian

What is a vegetarian?

The word has been used to describe everything from health food freaks and ascetics to the starving peoples of the world. I've met people who told me they ate fish, but no meat; ate pork and chicken, but no beef; ate no meat, fowl, or fish, but used eggs and milk; ate no animal origin foods whatever; ate meat once in a while or on social occasions. And every one of these people claimed to be a vegetarian.

Now either the word vegetarian means anything anyone wants it to mean—in which case it means nothing—or an accurate definition of the word has been lost somewhere along the way. *Webster's Third International Dictionary* defines vegetarian as "vegetable+arian." Since the suffix "-arian" means believer or advocate, a vegetarian is one who believes in or advocates vegetables—which makes vegetarians sound like lobbyists for a produce stand. *Webster's* also defines vegetarianism as "the theory or practice of living solely upon vegetables, fruits, grains, and nuts." Both definitions are wrong.

Rather than being a combination of "vegetable+arian," vegetarian is a word purposely created by a group of people who tried to correct what they saw as a deficiency in the language. Geoffrey L. Rudd, former secretary of the British Vegetarian

Society, explains: "English vegetarians, finding the terms 'vegetable diet' and 'nonmeat eating' both inadequate and misleading . . . first coined the word 'vegetarian' in 1842." (These same people went on in 1847 to found the still influential British Vegetarian Society.)

"Vegetarian" wasn't created from *vegetable,* though both words share a common etymological history. Vegetable comes from Middle English via Medieval Latin: *vegetabilis,* meaning having the power to grow (as with plants); and *vegetare,* meaning to grow. "Vegetarian," however, was derived from the Latin word *vegetus,* meaning "whole, sound, fresh, or lively," as in the ancient Latin term *homo vegetus*—a mentally and physically vigorous person. Thus, the English vegetarians were trying to make a point about the philosophical and moral tone of the lives they sought to lead. They were not simply promoting the use of vegetables in the diet.

And, as the British Vegetarian Society emphasizes, the meaning of vegetarian doesn't depend on what people *think* it means, but on its original meaning. Those who coined the word took pains to define a vegetarian as "one who abstains from flesh,* fish, and fowl, and who may or may not use milk, eggs, and cheese."

A vegetarian who uses milk is called a lacto-vegetarian or lactarian. One who uses both milk and eggs is termed a lacto-ovo-vegetarian or lactovarian. And a vegetarian eating no foods of animal origin is called a vegan or pure or total vegetarian.

To assume, then, that a vegetarian is really a "vegetable-arian" living solely on a monotonous diet of vegetables and fruit is not only erroneous, but it misses the point as well. Unfortunately, most of the nonvegetarian public make this mistake, including many otherwise knowledgeable physicians, nutritionists, and lexicographers. And since vegetables are almost always considered a side dish—an accessory to the main course of meat, poultry, or fish—anyone in the United States who appears to live on vege-

---

* The words flesh and meat are used interchangeably in this book. While meat originally meant *any* food of whatever origin, it has become a euphemism for flesh or animal tissue.

tables and other plant foods (with or without eggs and milk) is apt to be condemned as a faddist, fanatic, or oddball.

Of course, like any philosophy or system, vegetarianism does have its crackpots and fanatics. They make good copy, so the media traditionally present them as representative of a kinky subculture. But while ascetic or flamboyant vegetarians get most of the media coverage, the vegetarian middle ground remains largely unknown. This group is more health-conscious than the general public, more concerned with proper nutrition and whole foods. Vegetarianism is to them less of a burning cause or ego trip and more a freely adopted lifestyle. They select their foods from a wide range of sources, enjoy their meals, and perpetually wonder why the general public regards them as penitents.

There is nothing crackpot about a philosophy that suggests humans can live healthy lives while staying low on the food chain and high on an ethical scale. When judged according to its original meaning—not the inaccurate image held in the public mind—vegetarianism is anything but a limited or ill-conceived lifestyle. Let's examine the several reasons why people choose to become vegetarians.

*Ethics and Morality.* An ethical aversion to flesh eating is probably the oldest form of vegetarianism. Sensitive people have argued and wondered for centuries about the morality of killing other creatures. "Why kill animals for food?" they ask, citing the wealth of alternative foods available. This ethical stance may grow out of a religious orientation, as with Hinduism, Jainism, and Buddhism. But most ethical vegetarians are opposed to the unnecessary destruction of life, independent of their religious affiliation or lack of same.

While various spiritual movements practice abstention from flesh foods, vegetarianism *per se* is a secular philosophy based on the idea that nonhuman animals deserve the same compassion and respect due humans. No amount of chatter about meat's wholesomeness or nutritive value will sway ethical vegetarians. They simply don't eat animals (nor will vegans eat any animal products), no matter how the animals were raised, what they were fed, or how they were killed.

Those who become vegetarians for humanitarian reasons believe that an ethical aversion to killing other creatures is at the core of vegetarianism. Compassion for life is the one issue unaffected by the price of meat, the methods used to produce it, or the ultimate wholesomeness of meat reaching the marketplace.

*Aesthetics.* George Bernard Shaw was an aesthetically minded vegetarian, though health and economic reasons also influenced him. Shaw wasn't particularly outraged that animals or humans were killed for various legitimate reasons, but he drew the line, he said, at "eating corpses."

Like Shaw, some people become vegetarians because they're troubled by the idea of eating the bodies of other creatures. Aesthetically minded vegetarians point out that a bowl of fruit is pleasing to the eye and mouth-watering in its natural state, while the smell and sight of dead animals is repugnant to most people.

Fresh vegetables and fruits need no embellishment, but the carcass of a cow or pig depends on the meatcutter's deft hand to disguise its reality. Even the terms used to describe meat—sirloin, cutlets, brisket—are euphemisms designed to further obscure their origins. (The Academy Award in this class goes to Rocky Mountain oysters—pig testicles.)

Aesthetics play an important role in food choices. Many people wouldn't enjoy meat eating if they had to do their own killing and butchering. And many who do their own slaughtering freely admit its unpleasantness.

*Health.* Health and hygienic concerns have been traditional reasons for adopting a meatless diet and continue to attract people today as we discover more about the effects of toxic chemicals in our food and environment. The vegetarian movement in England and the United States, which began in the 1840s, actually grew out of the dietary teachings of three people: Rev. Sylvester Graham, the inventor of graham crackers; Ellen White, one of the founders of the Seventh-Day Adventist Church; and Dr. John Harvey Kellogg of breakfast cereal fame.

Like White and Kellogg, many nineteenth century converts and reformers were Seventh-Day Adventists committed to the Biblical injunction that the human body is "the temple of God." As such, the body was not to be defiled by an unwholesome diet, flesh foods, alcohol, tobacco, or other stimulants and adulterants. Adventists today continue to promote lacto-ovo-vegetarianism and health consciousness throughout the world. (Their chief concern, however, remains centered more on health and theological issues than on the ethics or aesthetics of killing animals for food.)

The health food movement (or diet reform) was tied in with vegetarianism during the mid-1800s. Diet reformers believed, as health-oriented vegetarians believe today, that a vegetarian diet was more natural and hygienic than one based on flesh foods. They warned that meat consumption leads to disease, digestive problems, and general ill health. Many contemporary vegetarians agree, pointing out that commercially produced flesh foods contain everything from pesticides, hormones, antibiotics, and assorted toxins, to harmful bacteria and viruses.

The largest organized group of health-oriented vegetarians are the Natural Hygienists. With headquarters in Chicago and adherents all over the world, Hygienists advocate regular fasting, a vegan diet centered around raw (or lightly steamed) vegetables, fruits, juices, and seeds; periodic colonic irrigation (enemas) and exercise to promote internal cleanliness. Many Hygienists claim to have had their health restored—including remission of cancer, arthritis, and other diseases—through their diet and lifestyle.

*Ecology and Economics.* These are two of the more modern reasons for avoiding flesh foods. The ecological argument attracts those people committed to eating lower on the food chain. They want to avoid participating in a national food pattern that wastes and exploits land, water, air, and energy at a staggering rate. They realize that a plant-based diet is kinder to our fragile environment than an omnivorous one based on an enormous centralized meat and agriculture industry.

The economic concern focuses on the fact that commercial meat production feeds very few people at the expense of many. Grain that might feed humans directly is fed instead to livestock. Carcasses return only a fraction of the protein fed the animal; the rich end up eating more than a fair share of the world's resources.

One may become a vegetarian for any or all of these reasons. And sometimes you can't tell the players without a scorecard. Vegans won't eat or use any animal product they can avoid. But hygienic vegetarians may have no qualms about using animal by-products—like leather—as will some lacto-ovo-vegetarians. There are also ethical fruitarians concerned about "plant consciousness." They won't eat vegetables whose harvest causes the destruction of the entire plant such as carrots, beets, and turnips, but will eat fruits like tomatoes, legumes, apples, and melons.

On the outer fringes are the vegetarian extremists who make the newspapers and wind up as kickers on the end of newscasts: "sproutarians," who center their diets and lives around sprouted alfalfa, wheat, beans, and a dozen other seeds; "vitarians," who *won't* eat seeds, nuts, or grains, believing them unfit for human consumption for philosophic and religious reasons; and the so-called "breathatarians," who claim to have given up not only animals foods but *all* foods. Breathatarians supposedly live on nothing but sunlight, pure water, and clean air—a noble aspiration.

These are the extremes, however. Most vegetarians fit somewhere in the middle, eating a lacto-, lactovarian, or diversified vegan diet—which brings us to what a vegetarian *isn't*. Followers of a macrobiotic diet are often called vegetarians. They are not. Macrobiotics devotees often eat fish and may eat meat or fowl as they progress through the various levels of their system. Macrobiotics puts its stress on the spiritual qualities of certain foods, substances, and practices rather than on the ethics of taking life or the health benefits of a meatless diet.

The macrobiotic system divides food into two categories based on the ancient principle of yin-yang: the balance of universal feminine (yin) and masculine (yang) forces. The object of macrobiotics is to reach a personal balance of yin-yang as a means of getting into harmony with the universe, which is already harmonious.

Critics of macrobiotics, and there are many, say that the system violates most of the commonly held principles of nutrition and that its followers are flirting with everything from anemia and scurvy to death from malnutrition. The bulk of criticism is directed at macrobiotics' seventh and highest dietary level—a regimen of *only* grain and a little liquid.

Although such a diet is certainly fleshless, it's inaccurate to dub it vegetarianism since the focus is on the macrobiotic system itself and not on abstinence from flesh foods for its own merits. Followers of the macrobiotic system and other unorthodox diets believe that principles higher than those expressed in modern science or nutrition govern an organism's well-being. They eat according to cosmic principles rather than medical dicta.

That there appear to be healthy and hearty people on strange diets proves once again that humans are unique in their ability to adapt to various regimens, and that nutrition is an art as well as a science. Appearances may also be deceiving. Obvious symptoms of some dietary deficiencies may take years or decades to fully reveal themselves. Today's enthusiastic zealot may be tomorrow's patient. The point of this book, however, is to demonstrate that there is nothing extreme or risky about following a well-planned, balanced vegetarian diet—*sensible vegetarianism.*

What about the so-called part-time or semivegetarian who only eats meat infrequently or on social occasions? The original definition of vegetarian contains the word abstains, implying a deliberate, *permanent* renunciation of flesh foods. A teetotaler abstains from alcohol; someone who only drinks on weekends can't be called a semiteetotaler. Vegetarianism, by a strict definition, is an all-or-nothing proposition. You either abstain or you don't.

But many people who begin a long evolution toward vegetarianism or veganism do so by dropping flesh foods gradually or in fits and starts. A good friend of mine eats no meat, fish, or poultry at home, yet he eats whatever is served when dining at his parents' home. That includes a turkey at Thanksgiving. He's been influenced by the various questions raised by vegetarianism— the ethics, health, and hygienic concerns—but he's not yet ready to go all the way toward a fleshless diet.

Similarly, many people have drastically cut back on the amount of flesh foods they eat but still eat meat occasionally. Are they "part-time" vegetarians? Well, while some vegetarians have organized into clubs and organizations, vegetarianism itself is anarchistic. There are no rules and regulations beyond the confines of the original definition. The key issues in my view are to develop a greater sense of our ethical relationship to the natural world; to become more aware of how, why, and what we eat; and to eventually stop eating flesh foods.

Thus, while the idea of semivegetarianism is rhetorically and historically incorrect, the concept has some practical value.

That is, if referring to yourself as a part-time vegetarian makes it easier for you to become sensitized to the issues above and to move away from flesh foods, then do it. It's not what you call yourself that matters, after all, but what you do.

Some people are aided by giving a name to the issues that confront them. Labels like vegetarian or environmentalist or natural living often help us focus on concepts. Labels also help to set us apart from the crowd. They act as a kind of shorthand by letting our peers know how we stand on an issue. Vegetarianism is more acceptable today than ever before, but calling yourself a vegetarian or semivegetarian will still make you stand out in this meatball society—if that's what you want.

If you hate labels, however, believing that they limit you and color other people's perceptions of you, then don't call yourself anything. As my grandmother used to say, "Just eat your food and keep your mouth shut."

Protein-deficient or malnourished people are sometimes referred to as vegetarians or as being on a vegetarian diet. This is as inaccurate and unwarranted as calling starving people "dieters." A vegetarian regimen grows out of a calculated decision; it is not the result of deprivation imposed by economics or environment. One doesn't become a vegetarian by default. (Many people don't eat pork; not all of them are kosher.)

Even nonflesh-eating animals are sometimes called vegetarians. It's more accurate to call them herbivorous (plant eating) or frugivorous (fruit eating) or even phytophagous—if you're a show-off. A cow doesn't *abstain* from eating other cows any more than a lion freely *chooses* a diet of blood and flesh. Only humans have the cerebral power to make philosophical or moral choices.

It may strike you as splitting hairs to dwell on the meaning of words, but why offer a book on so maligned a subject as vegetarianism without giving a clear definition of the terms used? Understanding exactly what we mean by vegetarian and vegetarianism is important since most antivegetarian criticism is based on fuzzy or incorrect definitions of these words. So, as you read, bear in mind that this book assumes throughout that:

> Vegetarianism is a voluntary *self-imposed* dietary choice.
>
> A vegetarian is one who *abstains* from the eating of meat, fowl, or fish. (In the unforgettable words of Dr. Kellogg, "If it runs away, don't eat it.")
>
> Vegetarians *may or may not* use milk, eggs, or cheese.
>
> Vegans avoid all foods of animal origin.

Beyond these commonly held principles, there is no such thing as a typical vegetarian. Because there is no central authority and no rigid dogma, no one vegetarian can be representative of the entire group. Vegetarians reflect the same range of aberrations, foibles, and temperaments as the rest of the human race. There are vegetarian gourmands and gourmets in search of new and exotic foodstuffs; vegetarian ascetics living on a narrow range of legumes and fruits; and vegetarian junk food junkies who have cut flesh foods out of their diets and replaced them with a shopping cart full of soda pop and cupcakes.

But this book is concerned with *sensible* vegetarianism: *a nonflesh regimen (with or without milk and eggs) that relies on a variety of natural, unfabricated foods and adheres to commonly accepted principles of nutrition.* Neither attempting to live only on soybeans or brown rice nor stoking up on TV dinners, sugar-coated breakfast cereals and pastries can be termed sensible vegetarianism—or sensible at all.

This book also tilts toward lacto- or lacto-ovo-vegetarianism and is biased toward ethical reasons for avoiding flesh foods. Most people find it easier, emotionally and nutritionally, to start out by giving up those products directly linked to slaughter (meat, fowl, and fish), while continuing to use milk products and eggs. And a majority of vegetarians seem to remain committed to a lacto-ovo diet. While veganism may be the ideal, especially for ethical vegetarians, it's an advanced system that should be adopted only after one has gained some reasonable and practical experience and nutritional awareness as a lacto- or lacto-ovo-vegetarian.

# TWO

# The Queen of the Table and Other Myths

The prejudice against a vegetarian alternative dies hard. While establishment nutritionists and government agencies now admit, at least, that vegetarianism isn't as bad as leprosy, they do so through gritted teeth. The National Academy of Sciences, for example, says in a report that "vegetarian diets can be adequate." The report acknowledges this adequacy in a curiously backhanded manner, dwelling largely on the possibilities of nutritional deficiencies and other dangers. The tone of the report incorrectly suggests that a vegetarian diet is feasible but risky.[1]

A study by the USDA Consumer and Food Economics Institute takes a similar attitude. Suggesting that vegetarians are an oddity and a challenge to nutrition educators, the report thinks teachers should help vegetarians "upgrade their often limited diets."[2] And a nongovernment consumer publication is even more darkly ominous. Calling vegetarianism a "practice of self-imposed limited choices," it emphasizes that "many vegetarian diets have serious shortcomings."

> They tend to be very bulky diets. If most of the needed calories are obtained from unrefined grains, legumes, nuts and nutlike seeds, these foods would need to be accompanied by the consumption of a wide variety of vegetables, especially green leafy ones, and a good deal of fruit.

What's so bad about a high roughage diet rich in unrefined foods, "a wide variety of vegetables . . . and a good deal of fruit"? The article doesn't explain. It does go on to say that a vegetarian diet

> requires effort, familiarity with the complex data on food composition, and diligent study and application . . . and will demand far more time and study than many people are willing to give.[3]

The article concludes by listing the grave consequences of veganism, while failing to explain that the horrors described are easily avoidable.

Each of these reports lies by omission. They never define exactly what they mean by vegetarian; they never admit that a fleshless diet can be excellent and satisfying, not just adequate. They speak of limited choices as though vegetarians cut themselves off from the majority of worthwhile and tasty menu selections. They hint of diseases and deficiency symptoms, never acknowledging the superior health record of various vegetarian groups studied over the past decades.

The reports also use guilt-by-association. The National Academy of Sciences report was prepared by its Committee on Nutritional Misinformation, a study group that investigates food fads and fallacies. The USDA report was included in a series attacking quick-weight-loss diets, macrobiotic diets, and other dietary extremes. Vegetarianism has no relationship to these subjects. Its inclusion shows that many nutrition authorities still consider vegetarianism a quack diet or fad.

There *are* vegetarian quacks and those eating poor diets, but the same can be said of meat eaters. A report issued by the Center for Science in the Public Interest says these typical indictments of vegetarianism describe

> possible problems of inadequate protein in vegetarians, never once mentioning that many Americans consume two to three times their Recommended Daily Allowance for protein . . . that the typical American diet is far from ideal, and that vegetarians may actually enjoy certain health benefits.[4]

Vegetarianism isn't as negative as its popular image implies.

Every lifestyle involves some denials and limitations, of course. We all draw the line somewhere, whether it's about food, morals, clothing, or the kind of people with whom we prefer to associate. Vegetarianism, however, seems an especially restrictive choice in the United States because Americans are such avid meat eaters that anyone *not* gobbling up chops and burgers is unique. Maybe even a little suspicious. Yet even meat eaters draw a line, don't they?

Not all meat eaters will eat all meats. North Americans are particularly finicky about what cuts and kinds of meat they'll consume, sticking to a narrow range of choices. Cows, steers, and pigs are eaten more than any other animals and their muscle meats predominate. Steaks, chops, roasts, and ground meat variations are preferred over organs. Ethnic and racial groups may eat hearts, brains, eyeballs, intestines, and feet, but most North Americans blanch at the thought.

Of fowl, chicken is the bird of choice. Americans eat five times more chicken than turkey, their next choice. And seafood, the most diverse of flesh foods, is the least consumed of the major animal foods. The USDA says that the average American annually eats about:

93 pounds of beef

57 pounds of pork

45 pounds of chicken

9 pounds of turkey

12.5 pounds of seafood [6]

In 1977, Americans ate a per capita yearly total of 155 pounds of beef, veal, lamb, and pork. They ate very little goat, horse, rabbit, pigeon, dog, or cat, though a supply of these animals is plentiful and relatively cheap. And how was this limited selection of flesh foods prepared? The typical U.S. mealtime pattern is to serve the meat, poultry, or fish as a main dish or entree, using vegetables as a side order. Even these vegetables are of a limited selection, according to the USDA. Carrots, corn, peas, and potatoes top the list year after year, though instant, precooked convenience and snack foods may soon replace them. But side dishes aren't that important anyway, right? Meat is what matters. As the Iowa Beef Council asked in a series of radio commercials, "Without beef on the table, is it really a meal?"

Our earliest ancestors never had the luxury of gathering meat as easily as they picked berries or dug roots. Hunting with primitive weapons was dangerous for the hunter as well as the hunted. Primitive hunters possessed skill, courage, and a deep understanding of their prey. The animals they sought were more than abstractions; they were beings with measurable qualities of bravery, genius, and treachery. Animals were worshipped and feared. Their characteristics were studied, their histories and habits were charted and cataloged, and the accumulated wisdom was passed on to the group through songs and stories and myths.

Consider the insane fury of a primitive hunt: a flash of tawny fur, hooves and antlers slashing out at tormentors, choking dust and guttural shouts, a flurry of rocks and jabbing spears, blood spurting out over hunters and prey, screams of death agony and triumph. The sky turned upside down.

Compare this with the modern supermarket "hunters" searching for bargains at meat counters: bending over refrigerated showcases, they nonchalantly select plastic-wrapped packages computer-labeled loin, flank, and leg. Then, absentmindedly, they toss their prey into waiting shopping carts. Once in a while, a droplet of blood may seep through the package to smear a finger or dot a skirt—the closest the modern meat eater ever gets to the reality of slaughter.

But to our forebears, the process of the hunt was governed by more than mere physical prowess. The hidden forces and secret principles that caused one hunt's success and another's failure might be understood only by careful study and acts of ritual and ceremony. In time, concern for these unseen forces gave flesh eating an importance far beyond that of any other dietary staple.

Hunting prey and eating meat became at once acts of magic and the precursors of religion and science. A mouthful of raw brains or heart allowed the eater to consume the spirit of the slain creature. Cracking out and eating an animal's marrow let one merge with that beast's power. Eating flesh was a way to swallow another being's strength and stealth and wisdom.

Even when early agriculture freed many humans from the insecurity and fickleness of nomadic life, their reliance on the mysteries of flesh continued. Babylonian priests tried to divine their god's secrets by examining a sheep's liver; the priests believed that the Powers had selected that organ alone as a mirror of destiny. Later, the more civilized Greeks called on Demeter, the earth mother, to insure a full harvest. They bribed her by sowing bits of pork among the seeds, eating handfuls themselves as a sacrament. By the fifth century B.C., the Buddha and other holy men of India were warning their disciples of the karmic dangers of killing and eating animals; while in China of the same period, Confucius was giving explicit directions for the correct kitchen preparation of meat, poultry, and fish.

So it continued. Down through the ages and within each society and group, humans developed contrasting sets of laws, customs, and attitudes about the food they ate. Flesh foods gathered about them a huge body of symbolism and folklore. Depending on the society or subculture, meat was (and is) seen as necessity, luxury, perversion, taboo, medicine, or poison. And, as pointed out by Mark Graubard in *Man's Food, Its Rhyme or Reason*, no flesh has gone untasted:

> Monkeys, carnivorous and herbivorous four-legged animals, snakes, reptiles, turtles and frogs, birds of all kinds, all fish of rivers and oceans, sea mammals, insects, spiders, shellfish, clams and cuttlefish . . . everything living was eaten whether it walked, crawled, climbed, flew, or swam . . . all flesh was eaten regardless of the appearance, nature, or habits of the animal.[6]

"All flesh" includes, of course, human flesh—eaten both as a ritual act and for its aesthetic qualities. (One group of South Pacific cannibals referred to their human prey as "long pig.") No matter whether a society depended on the hunt or the harvest, the mythical notions about meat persisted and were universally passed on to succeeding generations. Today, in our own relatively well-educated society, the ancient romance and lore of flesh foods holds as much sway as in any hunt-centered group of "primitives." Meat is a sacred, traditional food in the United States. To give up meat is to give up part of America: the two-inch steak, red-rare and marbled with fat; the hamburger, hot dog, Thanksgiving turkey and Easter ham; the odor of breakfast bacon wafting up through bedroom floorboards; ham hocks, chitlins, pickled pigs' feet, chicken livers, gefilte fish, veal parmigiana, sweet and sour pork, lamb chops, and brook trout sizzling in a frying pan.

Most people still believe eating meat of some kind is the only way to insure a healthy diet and a sound body. Coaches still stuff their gladiators with red meat and name their teams after carnivores: Tigers, Lions, Bears. (There are teams less ferociously symbolized, but rest assured the Cardinals and Orioles don't train on sunflower seeds.)

The myth making starts in infancy when mothers feed their babies strained and pureed beef, chicken, and fish, confident that such ingredients are absolutely essential to proper growth. When the child matures, he or she moves on to a life measured out in Big Macs, Roy Rogers' Roast Beef, and Colonel Sanders' finger-lickin' good white meat.

Meat's importance as a social symbol in the United States surpasses even the ownership of expensive cars or big houses. You can get by with a little car and an apartment to match, but no meat on the table means poverty, debasement, and lurking hunger. Those at the top of the social scale eat the symbols of their success: filet mignon, lobster, caviar. Those at the bottom eat cat and dog food.

That pet food has become a staple for some of the poor— especially the elderly poor—shows the power of both meat myth and propaganda. The message that meat is a *required* food is so strong that these poor souls spend their limited cash on Ken-L-Ration and Friskies, passing by the cheaper and more nutritious dried beans and rice in the next aisle. Ignorance, more than hunger, drives them to this embarrassment. But what else can we expect? They spent their lives in a society that constantly told them:

Meat makes the meal.

Meat sticks to your ribs.

Meat builds blood.

They lived in a society where meat on the table was worshipped and rhapsodized as "the queen of the table," as described by Thomas P. Ziegler in *The Meat We Eat:*

It transcends all other foods in aroma, causing a watering of the mouth and a conscious glow in the most bulbous organ of the gastrointestinal tract. It is a psychological stimulus that causes a flow of saliva and gastric juice, preparing the food chamber for the royal guest. And it does not beguile us; it satisfies . . . as we crunch its juicy fibers between permanent or removable ivories, we receive our first pleasant realization . . . we begin to radiate satisfaction in our eyes, in our speech, and in our actions. We become more amiable, more clear-minded, and more reasonable.[7]

Now what vegetarian praising lentils or celery could match such orgasmic adoration? But notice that this worshiper's praise goes not to meat's strictly nutritive qualities—its protein, vitamins, and minerals—but to its sensual delights and tactile richness. He dotes on the "crunch" and "juicy fibers." Who can argue with poetic images? Yet often the scientific arguments for meat's necessity are couched in equally vague language, sometimes even by those who should know better.

When an experienced and skillful doctor learned that my wife was both pregnant and a vegetarian, he became agitated. "She should eat *some* meat," he told me.

"Why?"

"Because animal tissue is a natural food for humans."

"So are plant foods," I said. "Why do you see meat as a necessity?"

"Man has always been a hunter. Meat is a natural food for . . ."

"Do you hunt?"

"That's beside the point. The fact is, meat has always been an essential part of the human diet. A pregnant woman should be getting a little bit of meat every day."

"How much is a 'little bit'? An ounce? Two ounces? What special power is there in that dab of flesh? You talk like meat was a magic potion."

"Look," he said, rising in anger, "I just don't think it's right for an expectant woman to do without at least *some* meat in her diet."

The conversation—or debate—ended at that point, having come full circle. I have yet to discover what mystical forces dwell in a "little bit" of meat, or what, beyond the nutritive qualities widely available in other foods, recommends meat as an absolute essential in the human diet. The answer resides neither in science nor in nutrition. The worship of meat is pure atavism. Meat is part of our collective unconscious. For most people, no matter what the level of their education or their access to information, the idea of doing without meat of some sort produces a vague sense of guilt and apprehension, as though they were breaking an ancient taboo.

For all their adoration of meat, however, most meat eaters would prefer to remain ignorant of the reality of flesh foods. They'd rather keep their illusions and continue to think of meat as an inert, abstract substance. All of us have seen the hit-and-run carcasses of cats, dogs, and wildlife strewn along the roadsides. Most people avert their eyes as they pass by. Most swerve to avoid running over the flyblown body, as though twice maiming the carcass would add insult to fatal injury.

Yet those same sensitive souls who swoon at the sight of a crushed rabbit may well be driving to the supermarket to visit a showcase of glassy-eyed fish. As they casually look on, a white-coated clerk deftly guts and fillets their supper, carelessly tossing the slippery entrails into a barrel. Then our shoppers may linger at the meat counter to pick up some chicken livers, beef kidneys, and a package of tongue.

If they return home by the same route, they'll again drive

over the mangled creature and again carefully keep the carcass between their vehicle's wheels. Should they be accompanied by a child, the comment "YEGGH!" is sure to echo loudly as they roll over the corpse. Then they'll all go home and eat dinner. Isn't it ironic that meat eaters are offended by a dead body on the road yet don't mind eating one for dinner? Some vegetarians like to point this irony out—often in a loud voice—in restaurants, at private dinners, and in crowded buses, none of which makes vegetarians popular. It's a wonder more of them aren't found dead on the road with the rabbits and squirrels.

A friend of mine was having dinner with his in-laws. A newly converted vegetarian, he was eating a macaroni salad while his mother-in-law sat across from him working on a steak. Predictably, the conversation drifted around to food and eating habits. My friend said something about "Americans who eat mostly muscle meats." His mother-in-law, lip curling in disgust, said, "Muscles? Who eats muscles?"

"What do you think *you're* eating?"

"Steak," she said.

"But, steak is a cow's muscle."

"N–no," she said, bewildered, looking down at her plate. "Steak is . . . *steak.*"

Even those people made uncomfortable by meat's origins rationalize with the thought that animals were put here for us to use. And while most urbanized people wouldn't dream of killing anything larger than a mouse (if that), they have little difficulty buying and eating the end result of the abattoir's violence. I once interviewed a woman who was the director of a large organization devoted to the preservation of the world's wildlife. We talked for an hour about the plight of whales, the death agonies of poisoned coyotes, and the nobility of the California condor. Listening to her plead for the lives of black-footed ferrets and prairie dogs was like hearing Sister Theresa bearing witness for the lepers and beggars of Calcutta. She was so fervent about the sanctity of animal life and liberty that I naturally assumed she was a vegetarian.

"Oh no," she explained, "I eat meat."

"But doesn't it bother you that millions of cows, pigs, chickens, and lambs are slaughtered every year?"

"No," she said. "Those animals are raised to be killed."

She would eat beef, but not whale; chicken, but not bald eagle; pork, but not wild mustang. Her compassion was selective. She was opposed to the wanton slaughter of rare and endangered animals; she was not bothered by slaughter and killing *per se.*

Vegetarians make no such convenient distinctions. Whether a carcass hangs in a butcher's freezer or is sprawled along a highway makes no difference. Whether the beast is plentiful—raised to be killed—or near extinction, matters not. Whether the substance is called steak, hock, or tripe, in the vegetarian's book it's still muscle, leg, and stomach.

The sudden realization that meat is an animal's flesh creates a lot of instant vegetarians. When children and adults make the connection that meat isn't simply some packaged stuff from the supermarket—that steak isn't just steak—they often give up meat eating on the spot, sometimes for life. An acquaintance of mine had one of these instant conversions as a teenager. She sat down one evening to eat a turkey dinner with her family. Suddenly, it dawned on her that those golden brown drumsticks were, as she put it, "a Goddamn turkey's *legs!*" She swore off flesh foods from that moment forward, much to her family's anguish. Her mother begged her for years afterward to "at least have a little tuna fish so you won't get sick."

I remember my own childhood realization that the meat on

my plate had once been a live chicken. We had recently visited a farm where my parents, who loved animals and hated hunting, introduced me to Bossy and Henny Penny. Some nights later I sat down to find Henny Penny all brown and basted on a platter. I asked my parents to explain this contradiction. Why was it wrong for us to hunt and kill, but okay to eat animals somebody else killed?

"But that's different," they explained. "These animals are raised for food. They give their bodies to us."

Somehow that explanation sufficed. I must have believed that cows and chickens acted like Shmoos, those plump, lovable animals created by cartoonist Al Capp. Shmoos periodically invade L'il Abner's world where they joyfully drop dead when anyone thinks of eating them. They also yield eggs, quarts of milk (in the bottle), and anything else humans desire. Living only to satisfy our needs, Shmoos jump happily into the frying pan or stew pot.

For years, I accepted the Shmoo Theory of Animal Husbandry, applied to all the bodies and parts thereof in the supermarket. I went along with the idea that they're raised for this purpose, that humane slaughter covers a multitude of sins, that meat is a basic and indispensable food. Only when I got to college (ironically to a campus awash in cheeseburgers, hot dogs, and pastrami sandwiches) did I begin to question the sense and value of meat eating.

But such dinner table insights and conversions are rare in the United States, where all manner of food and nonfood is witlessly shoveled down collective throats like coal sliding down a chute. Meat is meat. Most Americans have always eaten it and always will.

A deep-seated belief in the supremacy of flesh foods is what blocks most people from seeing the potential rewards of vegetarian meals. Suggest vegetarianism to the average meat eater and he instantly visualizes his dinner plate. He sees his salad, mashed potatoes, and peas. He sees his mashed potato dam burst and flood gravy onto the peas. But there—where the meat should be—is a big empty space. No meat? Potatoes and peas and limp lettuce night after night? And he shakes his head and whistles a low whistle and says, "Boy, I just couldn't live that way." Vegetarians don't necessarily live "that way" either, but who can blame him for thinking so?

Yet think about it. Is the vegetarian more limited in choice than the meat eater? Of the more than two million species of animals in the world, only about 250 are domesticated and eaten. Of mammals and poultry, only nine species make up 100 percent of the world's meat protein: cattle, chickens, ducks, geese, goats, pigs, sheep, turkeys, and water buffaloes. And of these, beef and pork—in approximately equal amounts—make up 90 percent of the world's nonpoultry production.

Now consider the plant kingdom. There are roughly 250,000 vegetable and fruit species. Of these, 600 are cultivated and eaten, including 50 different vegetables, two dozen varieties of beans and peas, 20 different fruits, 9 varieties of grains, and more than a dozen types of seeds and nuts. Many of these hundreds of nourishing plant foods are relatively inexpensive and plentiful throughout the United States and other Western nations. The most common problem surrounding vegetarianism, then, isn't a lack of resources but a lack of understanding.

Meat eaters keep seeing that empty space on their plates. They say to vegetarians, "I admire your courage," as though meatless meals involve a constant recommitment to a life of denial and pain, as though vegetarians must daily dig their nails into their palms, praying for the strength to carry them through yet another anchorite's sparse meal.

Most Americans don't realize that vegetarians aren't suffering. Far from it. Freed from thinking of flesh foods as the focal point of menu planning, and unfettered by the traditional main dish concept, vegetarians may create delicious, healthy meals. Foods may be prepared and combined in an infinite variety of ways never imagined by the cook chained to a meat-makes-the-meal mentality. Vegetarian cookery can also be as fast and as simple as a meat-based diet and just as nutritious—perhaps *more* nutritious, considering the way most North Americans eat.

The truth is that flesh foods are not required in the human diet, nor are they essential for proper nutrition. Not only can we "get along" without meat eating, but we can also as vegetarians maintain or improve our health, save money, put less strain on our planet's resources, and sit down to eat knowing that we have minimized our participation in the needless suffering and death of our fellow creatures. If meat is the "queen of the table," vegetarians are culinary anarchists and happy to be so.

*Chapter Two notes.*

1. National Academy of Sciences, "Vegetarian Diets" (Washington, D.C.: Committee on Nutritional Misinformation, 1974), p. 1.
2. USDA, *Nutrition Program News,* "Vegetarian Diets," Nancy R. Raper and Mary M. Hill (Washington, D.C.: Consumer and Food Economics Institute, Agricultural Research Service, July-August 1973), p. 4.
3. *Consumers Research Magazine,* October, 1974, p. 65.
4. Patricia Hausman, "Vegetarianism: Out of the Closet," *Nutrition Action* (Center for Science in the Public Interest, Washington, D.C. February 1976), p. 5.
5. Economic Research Service, USDA, Washington, D.C.
6. Mark Graubard, *Man's Food, Its Rhyme or Reason* (New York: Macmillan Co., 1943), p. 92.
7. Thomas P. Ziegler, *The Meat We Eat* (Danville, Illinois: The Interstate Printers and Publishers, Inc., 1968), pp. 6-7.

# How to Be a Vegetarian without Being Full of Beans

"How do I become a vegetarian?"
"Just place your right hand on this sack of garbanzos
and repeat after me. . . ."

There's no formal vow of abstinence involved in becoming a vegetarian. Since a vegetarian is one who eats no meat, fish, or fowl, the answer to the question "How do I become one?" seems to be simple: just stop eating flesh foods. That's accurate, but abrupt. If you've been a meat eater for several decades, your body, taste buds, and emotions may be rigidly tied to a particular set of aromas, textures, and flavors. An acute change could be an unpleasant shock to your system. Some people fired by passionate feelings of ethical awareness do drop all animal-origin foods at once and are happy with their decision. But sweeping, overnight changes in one's diet are generally not advisable. Most people do best with a gradual, sensible withdrawal—one that allows them time to adjust physically and emotionally to a new regimen.

Before you begin phasing out flesh foods, however, be sure you understand the principles of sound nutrition (covered later in this book). Good intentions or compassion for animals will nourish your soul, but not your body. While vegetarians don't need an extraordinary knowledge of nutrition, as many critics have claimed, they should be clear about the basics. *The single most important nutritional guideline is to eat from a wide variety of foods.* Don't rely on one or two foods to supply all your nutritional needs.

Neophyte vegetarians often make the mistake of abandoning flesh eating without trying to expand their circle of foods to make up for missing nutrients. However healthful the dropping of flesh foods may be in theory, it still results in forsaking an entire class of foods, including dairy products and eggs for vegans. If you're going to do without animal foods, you must provide for good nutrition by turning to a variety of other foods. Unfortunately, misinformed critics of vegetarianism make this sound like an impossible task. It isn't, as I'll stress throughout this book. There are hundreds of different, inexpensive, good-tasting foodstuffs waiting on the shelves of supermarkets, grocery stores catering to ethnic groups, specialty shops, farmers' markets, and natural food stores. And there are an equal number of vegetarian cookbooks available with detailed instructions for using this variety of nonflesh foods.

Does this sound staggering, like learning a new language? Then think of it in terms of adding only one new recipe or food each week. Within six months you'll have a collection of table-tested meatless recipes that rivals the best of the vegetarian restaurants. Meat and potatoes as a steady diet may be dull, but so are rice and beans or cottage cheese and peanut butter. Don't let breaking away from flesh eating throw you into a nutritional rut. Slowly expanding your range of foods and recipes will add a sense of excitement and discovery to meals, while ensuring that more of your nutritional bases are covered. (Detailed nutritional data will be found in subsequent chapters; specific food suggestions and recipes are in the last chapter.)

You may want to taper off flesh eating by adopting one or two meatless days the first week, substituting egg- and cheese-based or grain and legume recipes. Add several more meatless days the next week and continue cutting back until you're no longer using flesh foods. This method has the advantage of allowing alternate meals of meat and nonmeat; your palate will have the chance to acclimate to new food combinations. A gradual phaseout of meat may also help family groups by avoiding impulsive changes—often the precursors of dinner table riots and uproars.

The disadvantages of this alternating plan, however, fall heaviest on new ethical vegetarians. The realization that one is eating the flesh of slaughtered creatures hits some people hard, jolting them out of their complacency. They don't want to abstain one day and eat flesh the next, once they know what they're eating. If this is your attitude, you may wish to use the method my wife and I adopted.

While we were committed to the ethical basis of vegetarianism, we were—when we first thought about the change—unsure of the nutritional and health aspects of meatless living. Many of the same questions answered in this book plagued us. How will we get enough protein? Will this make us sick? Will we change physically or emotionally? Visions of pasty-faced vegetarians danced in our heads.

We were so propagandized and brainwashed about the traditional importance of meat in the diet that we made half-jokes about keeping an open line to our family doctor during "the experiment." We were prepared to give vegetarianism a try, but only by plotting our way through this unknown territory with a menu map.

We spent several days going through vegetarian and general cookbooks looking for recipes that appealed to us. Then we devised a plan of daily menus, charting out breakfast, lunch, and dinner for the week. We also listed a variety of wholesome snacks for nibbling between meals. We then went shopping and bought all the ingredients and produce we needed at once, stocking the kitchen fully for the weeklong trial.

The menus we created weren't fancy, just useful, simple, and (we hoped) good tasting. Without giving specific recipes, here's a basic lacto-ovo menu for three days:

---

### Breakfast
Apple juice (or juice of one lemon in cup of hot water)
Yogurt with cold, cooked brown rice, chopped fruit and nuts

## Lunch
Vegetable soup
Whole grain rolls or bread
Fruit salad with sunflower seeds

## Dinner
Rice patties*
Baked winter squash
Green beans
Tossed green salad with chopped nuts and raisins

## Breakfast
Grapefruit juice
Hot or cold whole grain cereal with fruit and milk or yogurt
Whole grain bread, lightly toasted, spread with
    peanut butter, tahini (sesame butter), or margarine

## Lunch
Sandwich of soybean pâte,* sliced tomato, and lettuce
Vegetable salad with vinegar and oil
Yogurt and fruit

## Dinner
Nut loaf * (nuts, eggs, cottage cheese, chopped vegetables,
    onions, oats, etc.)
Steamed kale or collards
Stewed or fresh tomatoes
Fruit salad

## Breakfast
Orange juice
Whole grain pancakes topped with plain yogurt
Quartered apples or other fruit

* See last chapter for recipe.

## Lunch
Sprout salad (sprouted alfalfa, lentils, and/or mung beans
 mixed with shredded carrot, tomatoes, etc., and dressing)
Cottage cheese and fruit (if you're still hungry)

## Dinner
Deep-fried tofu (bean curd)
Steamed brown rice
Mixed stir-fried vegetables (cabbage, tomato, garlic, onion,
 sprouts, snow peas or green beans)
Applesauce

Your daily menus should be built around regular servings of
these foods: grains, seeds, nuts, beans, peas, and lentils; milk,
cheese, yogurt, and eggs; green and yellow vegetables, root
vegetables, and fruits. (More about basic foods for vegetarians later.)

---

This is obviously just a bare outline. I haven't said anything
about seasoning, specific ingredients, or preparation because such
matters are best worked out in your own kitchen.* Some people
may find the above menu too spartan. Others may gain weight on
so much food. Work out your own menus and food creations
using any of several excellent cookbooks listed at the end of this
book. Take the time to create a framework of attractive meals
made with foods you already enjoy. Experiment, but don't add
too many new foods or attempt more than a few complicated
recipes the first week. The object is to ease into vegetarianism
or meatless cookery with as little disruption to your accustomed
tastes as possible.

This approach worked well for us. Having each meal plotted
out beforehand left nothing to chance. Meals were never haphazard, never thrown together at the last desperate moment. We
never had to stand peering into the refrigerator and ask, "What'll

* You'll find more specific nutritional information, however, in Chapters
Five and Six.

we eat tonight?" The menu plan gave us a sense of continuity and calmness.

Almost every meal was a pleasing or unusual (to us) mixture of foods and tastes. Since both of us had been raised as two- and three-times-a-day meat eaters, we had gotten used to a limited range of acceptable foods served in a familiar routine. So our menu plan nourished us while challenging our preconceptions. We started the week with a sense of self-denial, but by midweek we were congratulating each other at every meal, immensely enjoying what had become a grand adventure. We approached each meal with positive expectations. Thoughts of asceticism never entered our minds. We were too busy enjoying the food.

At the end of the week we compared notes. Both of us had dropped several pounds of excess weight. Neither of us felt weak or malnourished by our "sparse" diet. If anything, we felt lighter and more energetic than before. And we made several pleasant discoveries about vegetarian cooking:

1. It was cleaner: little or no grease to clean up on pots, stove, oven, or kitchen counters.
2. It was as quick as the meat-centered, noninstant meals we'd been eating.
3. It left us satisfied without feeling stuffed.
4. Neither of us missed flesh foods at any time during the week.

We pronounced the weeklong experiment a success, and we decided to repeat it with a new set of menus. The second week produced similar results. That's how Betsy and I eventually became vegetarians. We kept repeating our menu-planned week over and over until the weeks became months and then years. We never swore an oath of abstinence. We never suffered withdrawal symptoms. We simply took it one day at a time, let a new way of eating unfold by itself, and woke up one day to find ourselves vegetarians. This is probably the best way to make the change— evolution rather than revolution.

Even our approach may seem drastic because it drops all flesh foods at once; but it's really quite gentle. Using small amounts of eggs, cheese, and milk the first few weeks considerably eases the transition. (You needn't—indeed you shouldn't—replace meat ounce-for-ounce with milk and eggs.) While you may miss some tastes and textures at first, the fat content and familiarity of these foods will carry you past any major feeling of dislocation. A lot depends, of course, on your sense of commitment to a nonmeat diet. The more you want to change, and the more time you spend organizing that change, the easier the transition will be.

Some people have reported experiencing various withdrawal symptoms during this phase, though accounts of these reactions have generally been exaggerated. Quitting meat is not as difficult as quitting tobacco or nail biting. Meat does have several prominent physical and psychological qualities, however, and if it's been a staple in your diet, its disappearance may produce a reaction. Some new vegetarians have reported feelings of lassitude during the first few weeks of the change. This condition may be largely emotional. Giving up steaks and chops in the United States is like becoming an atheist in Vatican City. No matter one's enthusiasm, the real and imagined social significance of such a renunciation may weigh heavily on the psyche. That's enough to make anyone tired.

Fatigue may also stem from a loss of meat's stimulative qualities. Whether this has to do with a lowering of one's fat intake, a decrease in the amount of hormones (natural and synthetic) ingested, or changes in one's balance of fluids and nutrients is unknown. Not everyone experiences withdrawal-related fatigue, but enough new vegetarians have reported the condition to suggest that you should proceed slowly and with nutritional awareness.

Others have experienced the opposite—that is, feelings of great physical and emotional energy, a rush of euphoria, a natural high. Is this also psychological, related to a release from one's suppressed guilt over flesh eating? Is it physical, due to freeing the body from heavy daily doses of animal fats and toxins? No one knows as yet, but both conditions—fatigue and euphoria— are temporary. Most people eventually settle down to a more balanced state, assuming they were balanced to begin with.

A more immediate and permanent change you may notice on quitting flesh eating is a decrease in body odor. Americans are fanatics about disguising or obliterating all traces of body odor, so this should come as a delight to some. Though not everyone notes this phenomenon, one scientific explanation for the change is that meat fat contains butyric acid. This chemical is excreted through the pores of heavy meat eaters, giving them a relatively stronger body odor than low or nonmeat eaters.

One of the most widely observed changes in some new vegetarians is a condition known as *vegetarianus evangelicus*. This malady may attack all ages from adolescence on, but is most virulent among the college-aged. Symptoms include a holier-than-thou attitude (sometimes called veggier-than-thou), shouted debates with meat-eating dinner guests, philosophical discussions with strangers in health food stores, and a compulsion to talk endlessly of protein and nutrition. The condition is cured or diminished by the passage of time and a few swift kicks under the dinner table.

Knocking flesh foods out of the diet may produce one common reaction: hunger, sometimes ravenous. This is a normal and temporary condition akin to the sensation some people have after eating Chinese food; they eat a large, multicourse meal, and fifteen minutes later they're hungry again. The type of Chinese cuisine favored by most Americans is based largely on vegetables and rice, with flesh foods used as condiments. As nourishing as the meals are, they may leave the habitual meat eater—who's gotten used to that overstuffed sensation—feeling only half-full. Vegetarian meals may leave you feeling the same way, particularly during the first week or two of your change in diet.

A diet centered around animal fat is also higher in calories than a regimen based on plant foods. Excluding meat means you may have to make up some of that missing food energy. Don't compensate by stoking up on empty calories. Avoid added sugar, whether it be white, brown, raw, or table syrup. Don't replace white sugar with brown, thinking you're getting a better deal; brown sugar is white sugar colored with molasses. Don't replace table sugar with honey; a little honey in recipes is okay, but sugar is sugar.

Stay away from fabricated and highly refined foods. Giving up junk foods and beverages may be harder than giving up meat. Center your diet around whole grains, whole-grain yeast-raised bread, legumes, vegetables, and fruits. Snack on fresh or dried fruit, unsalted nuts, or plain yogurt with sliced fruit. Eat smaller meals more frequently rather than three big meals. Nibbling throughout the day tends to spread out your hunger debt, while keeping your energy level on a more even line. (Tell that to your boss when he asks why there are sunflower seeds scattered all over your desk.)

"Wait a minute," you might say, "Look at all those carbohydrates! Beans, fruit, nuts, bread. Why I'd blow up like a balloon!" Are you overweight? Losing weight has replaced baseball as America's national pastime. But the charge that a vegetarian diet is fattening is untrue.

Carbohydrates aren't the problem,* nor are so-called fattening foods. Nutritionists will tell you that no food is specifically fattening. The fault, dear Brutus, lies in ourselves, not our food. If you eat more calories than you burn up, you'll gain weight. Where those calories come from is basically irrelevant.

Unfortunately, the causes of obesity aren't quite that simple. Only a profound change in lifestyle and attitude can really keep you trim and in good health. Many people with weight problems achieve these changes only through various forms of therapy and behavior modification—obviously beyond the scope and purpose of this book.

The point is that it's unfair to condemn a vegetarian diet as fattening; it's equally misleading to suggest that you'll automatically lose weight as a vegetarian. No matter what your diet, you'll lose or gain weight in direct proportion to the amount of food you eat, how much exercise you get, and the workings of your metabolism. A sensible health-oriented vegetarian diet, low in fats and free of fabricated and junk foods, will be of great help in any weight loss or weight maintenance program. But the ultimate solution to obesity, as with many health problems, rests with the person wielding the fork.

The most important aid to your transition will be a relaxed mind and patience with yourself. Vegetarianism is supposed to be a simplification of your habits, a discarding of excess baggage. So, if your first trials with a nonflesh diet leave you with a slightly

---

* There is, however, a difference between the potentially harmful *refined* carbohydrates in overprocessed foods and the nutritious whole carbohydrates in grains, legumes, and vegetables. (More on this in Chapter Six.)

empty feeling, enjoy it. It beats bloat. Remember Ben Franklin's warning: "A full belly is the mother of all evil."

Whether or not vegetarianism affects you physically, it will definitely have an impact on your social life. The number of dinner invitations you receive may dwindle as people discover your new preferences. An old friend called to ask us to dinner shortly after we changed our diet. "Sure," said Betsy, "but we're vegetarians now."

"Oh," said our friend, "the hell with it then. We're still meat eaters."

The situation is better now, thanks to the public's raised consciousness about food and the general upsurge in vegetarianism. High meat prices have also forced many families to adopt meatless days—just the days you'll probably be invited. You can help your friends by offering them recipes or gift cookbooks, or by inviting them to dinner at your house.

People with busy social lives, those used to eating out frequently, or those forced to eat away from home because of their jobs, may find vegetarian eating a hardship unless they're willing to make adjustments. Vegetarian restaurants are easier to find now than they were even a few years ago. Most large cities and college communities have natural food or vegetarian establishments, and more are appearing every day. While such places may not have the ambience of a classy French restaurant, the not-just-for-a-profit atmosphere, good food, and generally cheerful service make up for the unadorned surroundings.

But even the swankiest restaurants have nonmeat selections. Just don't believe everything you read on the menu. Unless you clearly specify your preferences, your spaghetti may arrive with meat sauce or your egg drop soup may have a chicken broth base. Ask questions. I once ordered the bean soup in a small, exclusive restaurant. After I quietly told the waitress that I was a vegetarian, she assured me that the soup was "just beans." When the soup arrived, however, there were several suspicious pink chunks peeking out between the beans. I inquired. The manager identified the blobs as pork.

"But I explained to the waitress that I was a vegetarian."

"So what?" the manager asked innocently. "I'm a vegetarian too, and I eat this soup all the time."

"You're a *what?*" I sputtered. "And you eat *what?*"

I never got the rest of the story. My luncheon companion, a nonvegetarian magazine editor with a low embarrassment threshold, gave me an Oh-My-God-What-Did-I-Do-To-Deserve-This look. I sank down and ordered a salad. See what I mean about making adjustments? Your idea of vegetarianism may not be everybody's.

Most people seem to prefer starting off as lacto-ovo-vegetarians and the majority of them tend to remain as such. Some, however, graduate to veganism, avoiding all foods of animal origin, including milk, eggs, gelatin, and honey. If this is your preference, go slowly. An all-plant diet is a sharp change from the way most Americans are used to eating. Veganism demands more attention to nutrition and food choices. A diet relying solely on plant foods will be nourishing and beneficial if you're willing to educate yourself and exert control over what and how you eat.

Vegans who eat a variety of whole foods will probably have little problem meeting their protein needs, but all-plant diets may be short in calcium, riboflavin, and vitamin $B_{12}$. Vegans can obtain calcium from fortified soy milk, fortified brewer's yeast, unhulled sesame seeds, tahini (sesame paste or butter), sunflower seeds, and certain leafy greens (those free of calcium-binding oxalic acid: collards, kale, and dandelion greens, for example). Riboflavin can be found in leafy greens, other vegetables, wheat germ, almonds, and brewer's yeast. Vitamin $B_{12}$ can be added to the vegan diet by vitamin pills, fortified brewer's yeast, fortified soy milk, and other soy products.

Many good vegan cookbooks are available (see Bibliography) and new vegans would be wise to work out several weeks of all-plant food menus.* Those who find veganism a satisfying, healthy way of life generally adhere to principles of sound nutrition. A *haphazard* approach to veganism may be dangerous, however, especially for children and pregnant women.

What about vegetarian children? At certain stages, children and adolescents may develop perverse food habits due to glandular and emotional changes or peer pressure—or both. Getting young-sters to eat properly can be hard enough without the added diffi-culty of converting the family to a lacto-ovo or vegan regimen, diets their peers may think unorthodox and strange. And unfor-tunately, when some adults choose to become vegetarians, it is often their children who wind up the losers.

Americans usually take better care of their cars than their bodies. While adults may be able to get away with this for a time, children have special dietary needs that must be met if their rapid development is to proceed normally. Nutritional ne-glect isn't an exclusive vegetarian problem, of course. Most of the studies of malnourished children, both poor and affluent, have been done on those eating a normal U.S. diet heavy in mixed animal proteins and refined sugar. Vegetarians, though, do have a special responsibility for their children.

First, vegetarian adults usually choose a fleshless regimen out of a sense of compassion for their fellow creatures. What better example of misplaced affection than those vegetarians who, while concerned about the well-being of cows and pigs, forget their children's welfare in the process?

Second, while a diet rich in flesh foods may be potentially dangerous (or at the least, less healthful than vegetarian fare), foods of animal origin do provide certain key nutrients that may be lacking in a *random* selection of plant foods.

And third, because society always has its collective eye on those who diverge from the status quo, vegetarians are obligated to prove, to their children as well as to society, that their rebellion

* The American Vegan Society (Malaga, N.J. 08328) can supply you with preplanned vegan menus.

stems from a search for a greater good. Of what value is any philosophy if it penalizes the innocent?

In recent years, vegetarianism has been mixed in with various esoteric philosophies. Many seem to think the good vibrations accruing to a vegetarian diet have a magical or cosmic immunological effect. This leads to a laissez faire attitude about food. "The Universe will provide" is a nice slogan, but it may be disastrous if applied to a child's eating patterns. Children left to compound their own meals with no knowledgeable guidance are neglected children, nothing more.

Much of the criticism directed at vegetarianism is due to the behavior of careless zealots more committed to a cause than their own health or the well-being of their children. A 1971 study of several hundred counterculture vegetarians, fruitarians, and macrobiotics in the Berkeley, California, area focused only on the "better-nourished groups who could afford to eat in restaurants and usually ate well." Yet, the researcher reported: "The infants I came in contact with were given watery gruel or unpasteurized whole Guernsey milk formulas. This makes them susceptible to scurvy and general malnutrition." [1]

Being in harmony with the universe and going with the flow is too often construed to mean doing nothing. Vegetarians cannot afford to be lackadaisical about nutrition, especially if they're parents of growing children.

*The vegetarian baby.* Child care begins in the womb. A good diet is crucial to normal fetal development. If the mother's diet is poor, particularly between the second week and the second month of pregnancy, the fetus may then be permanently damaged. Fetal development during this time is comparatively rapid, demanding a constant flow of essential nutrients.

Good prenatal care is a must. The pregnant vegetarian should find an obstetrician or nurse-midwife who understands and supports the basic soundness of a sensible vegetarian diet. Don't believe anyone who says you must eat meat or fish in order to produce a healthy baby; you need good nutrition, not meat. And neither you nor your baby needs the hormones, pesticides, additives, and adulterants commonly found in much commercially available flesh foods and overprocessed foods. The ultimate effects of toxic residues on fetal and genetic health are still unknown. (You'd be wise, in addition, to give up smoking, drinking, prolonged fasting, and *all* drug use—at least during your pregnancy.)

Pregnancy increases one's need for protein. The Recommended Daily Dietary Allowance (RDA) for protein for pregnant North American women eating a mixed animal-plant diet—*this includes lacto-ovo-vegetarians*—is 30 grams a day more protein than normal. (A 128-pound woman 19 or older has a protein RDA of 46 grams per day. If pregnant, her RDA would be 76 grams daily.)

This increase doesn't mean you must run out and buy a can of protein supplement. Many of these supplements are highly refined products themselves. They're not only expensive but may actually lack nutrients other than protein. You'd be better off increasing your protein intake by any of several ways. Lactovarians can simply increase their use of milk and eggs; skim milk powder is inexpensive, low-fat, and easy to add to almost any dish or liquid. (Noninstant milk powder contains about 8 grams of usable protein per one-quarter cup.) Only a few ounces of cheese can also go a long way to increase your protein intake. (One-half cup of uncreamed cottage cheese has about 25 grams of usable protein— almost your entire daily RDA increase.)

You can also add full-fat soy powder (not flour) to blender drinks, cereals, breads, soups, and casseroles. Soy flour can be used to boost the protein content of breads and muffins. Protein sources other than grains, legumes, and nuts include brewer's yeast (50 percent usable protein and a storehouse of vitamins and minerals) and tofu or soybean curd (a food of infinite uses, 65 percent protein, and highly digestible).

Don't worry too much about weight gain during pregnancy. Restricting your diet—much less actually reducing—may be harmful to your baby's development. A weight increase of up to 30 pounds during pregnancy isn't unusual.

Pregnant vegans have the same net protein needs (30 grams additional) as nonvegetarians or lactovarians, but vegans need more *gross* protein to compensate for their diet of less-concentrated plant foods. (See Chapter Five for more details.) Soy powder, high-protein bread, grain-legume and seed-grain dishes, brewer's yeast, and tofu can help expectant vegans to comfortably make up the difference. (Needless to say, the "empty" calories of junk and fabricated foods should be avoided during pregnancy, if not as a general rule.)

You may want to add up your daily intake of protein for several days to determine your range of protein intake; [2] but don't stuff or starve yourself according to a chart and a column of numbers. Eat a sensible diet drawn from a variety of sources.

Calcium needs also increase during pregnancy and lactation, from the usual RDA of 800 milligrams to 1,200 milligrams daily. But these figures are for those on a typically high-protein U.S. diet. Your calcium RDA as a pregnant vegetarian may be closer to 800 milligrams a day. But don't try to limit your calcium intake; you'll need all the calcium a good diet supplies. Excess dietary calcium will be stored by your body as a reserve during nursing.

More iron-bearing foods should be included in the diet during pregnancy. Although pregnancy tends to increase a woman's ability to absorb iron from food, the extra iron intake suggested by the Food and Nutrition Board cannot easily be obtained from an ordinary meat-based or vegetarian diet. Your obstetrician or nurse-midwife may suggest a daily iron supplement if your hemoglobin is low.

Increase your consumption of iron-rich foods: whole-grain leavened breads (yeast-raised), legumes (especially soybeans), and dark green vegetables. Cooking in cast iron pots adds significant traces of iron to the diet. Vitamin C also helps increase your ability to absorb iron.

For vegetarians and meat eaters alike, pregnancy and lactation also increase the need for calories, vitamins A, C, $B_6$, $B_{12}$, E, folacin, niacin, thiamin, and riboflavin. One's need for phosphorous, iodine, magnesium, and zinc also increases. Obstetricians generally meet these increased needs by prescribing supplemental vitamins, but this hardly minimizes your need for conscientious meal planning and food selection.

*The vegetarian infant.* When an infant is born, it comes into the world with few nutritional reserves. All its essential nutrients must come from food, and they must come without fail. Babies make extraordinary growth during their first year, generally tripling their weight at birth and growing one-and-a-half times their length at birth. Development like that needs solid nutrition. But should it be breast or bottle? You'll have to make up your own mind about this controversy. There are dozens of books on nursing, infant nutrition, and allied subjects at your library. You might also contact the La Leche League (9616 Minneapolis Avenue, Franklin Park, Illinois 60131) for literature on breast feeding.

Breast feeding is the perfect choice for vegans, of course, as they want to avoid cow's milk—though soy milk formulas are available. Critics of formula feeding say cow's milk is fine for raising calves and the soybean is a wonderful plant, but human milk is *human* milk. Anything else is a poor substitute. As Karen Pryor says in *Nursing Your Baby:*

> Breast milk is the only completely adequate food for the first six months, and forms a splendid addition to the diet there-after. In a reasonably healthy mother, breast milk has all the needed nutrients. . . . [T]he best food for a human baby is its mother's milk.[3]

Objections to breast feeding have traditionally centered around its aesthetics and supposed inconvenience to the mother. The U.S. Environmental Protection Agency and the nonprofit private Environmental Defense Fund, however, have raised some disturbing questions about the safety of breast feeding infants.

In 1976, the EPA analyzed samples of breast milk taken from 1,400 women in 46 states. The analysis disclosed widespread contamination of human milk by DDT, dieldrin, PCBs, and similar chemicals linked to cancer and other illnesses. Because the contaminants accumulate in body fat, nursing infants end up ingesting ten times the acceptable * level of PCBs, twice the acceptable level of DDE, and more than nine times the acceptable level of dieldrin.

That same year, EDF asked EPA to conduct a similar breast milk analysis of vegetarian women to determine if dietary patterns influenced the accumulation of pesticides in fatty tissues. The results of this second test showed that women on a vegetarian diet had levels of pesticides in their milk that were *two to three times lower* than women eating a standard diet.

Because of an earlier less-thorough French study, the EDF had already been cautioning women planning on nursing to restrict or eliminate meat, some kinds of fish, and whole-fat dairy products. Now EDF's Stephanie Harris advises:

> If you're a heavy meat consumer we recommend you nurse once a day and supplement with bottle feeding. But if your diet is— and has been—very low in animal fats, one can assume that the residues in your body will be lower; the benefits of breast feeding will then outweigh the risks. . . . If you're planning on becoming pregnant and especially if you plan on nursing, then become a vegetarian or reduce your consumption of animal fats by other dietary methods.[4]

Your baby is ready for solid food any time after the sixth month. Some parents start feeding much earlier than this, often feeding cereals at two weeks. This may be convenient for the parents—it fills the baby up and keeps him quiet—but a too-early introduction to solid food isn't in the infant's best interests.

A baby's system is brand new and sensitive to sudden changes in diet and environment. The undeveloped digestive system, for example, can't handle starch at first. Starches pass through in the feces. Besides, the older a baby is before the introduction of food other than mother's milk, the less likely are the chances of allergies developing.[5]

---

* Acceptable to whom? According to the EDF and other watchdog environmental groups, acceptable daily intakes of pesticides and industrial wastes are set by the FDA on the basis of preliminary evidence and political judgments. Not enough is known about the short- and long-range effects of these chemicals on humans or the environment. The only really acceptable level of a known or suspected carcinogen or mutagen should be zero.

The first solids may be either cereals * or fruit. Try rice as a first cereal. Grind it finely and cook to a smooth paste, or cook the grains first and then puree in a blender or food mill. Add a little water to form a semiliquid and offer your baby a tiny mouthful. No more than two or three baby-sized spoonfuls should be offered at the start. Babies need time to adjust to new tastes and the strange feeling of solid food in their mouths.

Introduce your baby to *one* food per week. If allergies erupt you'll be able to pinpoint which food caused the problem. After the introduction of rice you can move on to other cereals prepared the same way: oats, barley, and millet (but hold off on offering wheat for a while, as wheat is the cereal most likely to foment allergic reactions).

Bananas are a good first fruit. They should be fully ripe— skin flecked with dark spots, tan-colored and soft inside. Mash well and mix with a little water. Avocado is also a good first fruit. Other fruits may be introduced in succeeding weeks; apples, apricots, peaches, and pears should be stewed and pureed.

Vegetables are next and the mild-flavored ones should be offered first: carrots, beets, string beans, peas, squash, and tomatoes. When the baby has become used to handling solids you may move on to the mineral-rich greens so important to vegetarians: kale, mustard greens, turnip tops, collards, cabbage, and dandelion greens.

Milk other than breast milk may be added after the eighth month. North Americans have been raised to believe that milk is an indispensable, "perfect" food to be religiously consumed. But some pediatricians, nutritionists, and researchers now express doubts about the ultimate value of milk in the diet. Milk can produce allergies in infants and children; some adults have a lactose intolerance and can't digest milk at all. More conservative pediatricians recommend that milk not be introduced until after the fifteenth month.

Yogurt comes under less fire than milk. The bacterial action that produces yogurt predigests the lactose and reduces milk's

* Organically grown cereals and grains are available through natural food stores, food co-ops, and by mail.

allergenic effect. The same is so for most cheeses.

Eggs can also lead to allergic reactions and should be introduced late—after the first year to 18 months of life. Egg yolk is a good source of iron; it can be pureed or mashed and mixed with liquids and fed with other foods.

What about raising an infant as a vegan? Most nutritionists would warn against this, and with good reason. Adequate nutrition and those elements most likely to be missing in a vegan diet—calcium, riboflavin, zinc, iron (but not $B_{12}$)—can be derived from an all-plant regimen, but it takes considerable and sophisticated nutritional knowledge to plan meals correctly. Infant feeding is tricky enough and far more crucial than adult nutrition. Adults may be able to get away with short-term deficiencies, but infants may be permanently damaged.

A recent limited study compared children on vegan, lacto-vegetarian, and omnivorous diets. The vegan children received adequate calories but derived significantly less calcium, riboflavin, and protein than the other children. Vegan children also had significantly lower serum $B_{12}$ and folate levels. Most important was the determination that the vegan children weighed less and were shorter than the other children.[6]

One study isn't proof positive, nor does it mean that it's impossible to raise a healthy infant or child on a well-balanced vegan diet. But the findings do underscore the need for parents to have a thorough grounding in nutrition and food preparation. Unless you have an overriding reason for not using milk, milk products, yogurt, and/or eggs in a child's diet, and unless you've been a longtime, healthy, *informed* vegan yourself, then you're better off raising your infant and young child as a lactarian or lactovarian.

As for the rest of your baby's diet, avoid feeding *anything* that isn't a wholesome, nourishing food. Preferably, use only foods from a known, chemical-free source or your own kitchen. Avoid adding salt or excessive sugar to the baby's diet. Too much sugar develops a sweet tooth early on and contributes to future problems of both obesity and tooth decay. All the salt (actually, sodium) a child or adult needs can be derived from grains, vegetables, and fruits as they are. Iodine, the only truly valuable component of table salt (assuming it's iodized salt), can be supplied by a pinch of powdered kelp used as a condiment.

Those readers committed to natural foods should make their own baby foods. Commercial baby foods are more expensive and energy-intensive than homemade products. (What do you do with all those little jars, anyway?) There are several books available on making baby food, though there's nothing complex about it.

You'll need a blender, an inexpensive hand-cranked baby food grinder, or a small food mill to puree the baby's food. For convenience, larger amounts of food can be prepared, divided into baby-sized portions, and frozen for future use. And why not give your child the best start by preparing food from your own organic garden? If you can't maintain a large enough garden, buy locally grown produce to provide your youngster with fresh, unsprayed vegetables and fruits.

*The vegetarian preschooler.* Children from two to six years grow more slowly than infants, but they should gain weight continuously at their own rate. Their arms, legs, and necks will lengthen during this time, as they change from potbellied toddlers into more physically mature children. Preschoolers are obviously going to need adequate calories and sufficient vitamins and minerals during this period. Once past early infancy, children normally follow the dietary patterns set by the family. If the parents are eating a well-balanced, junk-free lacto- or lacto-ovo diet, the preschooler should have no trouble deriving adequate nutrients for growth and development.

Those who insist upon vegan children should be sure to provide them with adequate calcium, riboflavin, iron, zinc, and especially $B_{12}$. Using $B_{12}$-enriched brewer's yeast, $B_{12}$-fortified soy milk (which will probably contain additional calcium, riboflavin, and iron), or $B_{12}$ tablets matters less than that *something* is done to insure adequate $B_{12}$ in the vegan child's diet. A $B_{12}$ deficiency is a biological time bomb. Symptoms, some irreversible, may not become apparent for years.

Why gamble with the life and health of a growing child? Non-animal-origin $B_{12}$ tablets cost only pennies a day, brewer's yeast is cheap and nutritious at any price, fortified soy milk is widely available, and no $B_{12}$ toxicity symptoms have been reported by researchers. Why not be conscientious about providing adequate $B_{12}$ in the diet? Your children are worth it. Youngsters on a lacto-ovo diet will derive enough $B_{12}$ from milk and eggs, but vegan children *must* have a sure, regularly ingested source of this vitamin.[7]

Providing good nutrition for the child two to six, vegetarian or not, is usually complicated by this age group's fickle eating habits. Many parents suffer anxiety during these years, convinced their child faces starvation, "She eats like a bird," though no child ever starved when good food was available. Family attitudes toward food and feeding are a crucial matter in child care, and authorities agree that it's best not to force children to eat when they say they're not hungry.

But vegetarian parents should be doubly careful not to shoehorn food and morality down their child's throat. Mixing food and guilt isn't restricted to vegetarians, of course, but this group tends to have a reservoir of self-righteousness, often propagandizing their own captive children. Small, wiggly children are usually more fascinated with their surroundings and the sound of their own voices than they are with what's on their plates anyway. Why compound the difficulties of dealing with a normal developmental stage by bringing ethical arguments and ego trips to the table? Please—no dining room lectures, no slaughterhouse descriptions, no aren't-we-lucky-we're-vegetarians monologues.

Exercise the same or greater care with your child's dietary

needs that you do with your own, but be gentle. Some brands of brewer's yeast, for instance, taste terrible. Few children are going to happily down a glass of yeast and fruit juice, any more than you will on your first try. Yeast is an acquired taste. When you force your child to take his yeast or wheat germ or kelp, food becomes medicine and punishment. Why not use a sneaky approach? A variety of foods your child may not eat directly can be added to soups, sandwich spreads, snacks, casseroles, pancakes, blender drinks, and bread dough. The whole family gets a nutritional boost this way, and it saves you telling your child, "This is good for you," thus ensuring his or her eternal hatred of whatever it is that you're pushing.

Fortunately, there's no lack of help in this area. Vegetarian and health food cookbooks are filled with ideas for nutritious meals, snacks, and drinks—even healthful sugar-and-additive-free "candy." Small children also have an instinctive taste for various kinds of fruit and raw vegetables. Why not provide them with carrot sticks, celery, cucumbers, apple and orange slices, dried fruit, nuts, and other finger foods?

*The vegetarian school child and adolescent.* Although the specific nutritional needs of children from 5 to 12 and adolescents from 13 to 18 differ from the preschooler's needs, the vegetarian parent's task remains the same—to provide tension-free, nourishing, good-tasting meals drawn from sources containing essential nutrients.

Teenagers do have special problems; they experience growth spurts that may double their body weight between the years 8 and 14 for girls and 10 and 17 for boys. These spurts will mean increased caloric and protein needs. A teen's appetite tends to be enormous and every bit as unpredictable and bizarre as the preschooler's. If your refrigerator and pantry are full of junk food, that's what your offspring will eat. A vegetarian teenager's nutritional needs are essentially the same as an adolescent on an animal foods regimen; only the source of their nutrients is really that different. Refer to the food suggestions in the next chapter, consult vegetarian and natural foods cookbooks, and let your gangling teen eat heartily from only the best.

What about peer pressure? ("All the other kids eat Twinkies and fried chicken. Why can't I?") These problems will be no different for vegetarian parents than for their omnivorous counterparts. Adolescence is a time of tears, trauma, and rebellion no matter what the family's diet. But if you push vegetarianism too hard while your child is struggling with pimples, sex, and independence, there's every chance you'll find your teen sneaking off to McDonald's or hiding a salami under the pillow.

Those parents who become vegans in midstream, dropping all animal products from a family diet previously dependent on dairy and flesh foods, may have more difficulties than those who go the lacto- or lacto-ovo route. But a total family commitment to any form of vegetarianism may just be impossible if it involves an adolescent already devoted to a thick-shake-and-cheeseburger diet. Vegetarianism cannot be successfully forced on people, whether children or adults. The best approach is to make changes gradually and logically, while respecting the preferences of other family members.

Some families eventually wind up with split allegiances; several members become vegetarians, while others continue to eat flesh. This presents obvious culinary and aesthetic difficulties, but it's preferable to forcing family members to eat under threat of exile. Parents who discuss issues and solicit opinions from children will have an easier time with a vegetarian change than those who do things by executive order.

A friend asked me recently, "Doesn't that turn kids into freaks—making them vegetarians, sending them out as 'different'?" It can. Raise a child to wear his parents' beliefs on his sleeve, to carry a sign, to yap about his superior diet at the drop of a fork, and you have produced a pariah—if not an obnoxious child. But unless you make it into an issue, vegetarianism needn't be all that obvious. Beyond its philosophy, abstinence from flesh foods is only a dietary preference like eating kosher food or not drinking coffee.

When people do discover that you or your children are vegetarians, they're usually more curious than hostile. Children generally are fascinated by those who eat no meat. Most children love animals and have a difficult time understanding why it's necessary to kill and eat them. The questions they ask are usually born of curiosity, not sarcasm. But your children will be teased by their classmates, of course. They'll get razzed about the clothes they wear, the way they comb their hair, and, no doubt, their eating habits. Children and teenagers do tease one another, and everything is fair game. That's why it's so important to keep vegetarianism in perspective. Parents who push too hard—teaching their children that meat eaters are gross or bloodthirsty—may end up raising herbivorous bigots who *invite* anger and ridicule.

"But how can I make sure my children will stay vegetarians?" a mother asked me. You can't, no more than you can insure their absolute adherence to your religious beliefs or moral values. I know a woman who's raised four children, now all away in college. She's not a vegetarian, but she raised her family on whole foods. No junk or convenience foods ever sullied her kitchen. She and her husband maintained a big garden and produced most of their own food. They bought grain by the hundredweight, ground their own flour, and baked whole-grain loaves by the dozens every week. From kindergarten through high school, everything served or put into lunch boxes was fresh, homemade, and nourishing.

Now, with her children scattered, out in the Real World of college cafeterias, fast food joints, and vending machines, I asked her what—after all her hard work—would prevent her brood from backsliding into nutritional hell. "Look," she said, "you don't own your children. You give them the best foundation you can, help them to develop a taste for what's good, and then you let them go. That's the best you can do."

There is one other problem involving vegetarian parents

and children: what about the adolescent who wishes to become a vegetarian while his or her parents are still committed to flesh foods? This is now a common situation as more young people adopt meatless diets. Obviously, the suggestions given above pertain here also; family members are going to have to discuss the implications of a vegetarian diet, with respect for individual opinions and accepted scientific facts.

Today's adolescents have an advantage over the teenage vegetarians of just a few years ago, as vegetarianism is losing its kook image. There is now virtually no orthodox nutritionist or modern nutrition textbook still opposed to a sensible lacto-ovo-vegetarian diet. Parents may prefer their wards not to become vegetarians for various reasons—because they think that it will complicate family life, that it's just a fad, or that the neighbors will talk. But assuming the children are willing to adhere to standard nutritional principles, parents cannot argue that vegetarianism is unhealthy. Indeed, parents might rejoice that their children show a concern for ethics and nutrition, even if the ideas expressed don't match their own.

All too common are cases like Jill's, a teenager whose family greeted her vegetarian leanings with derision and anger. "If you think I'm going to spend one extra minute in the kitchen for you," said her mother, "you're crazy." Jill knew nothing of vegetarian theory or nutrition, only that she wanted—for vague reasons—to stop eating meat. She did stop, but in the worst way: dinner at home found her eating around the meat, picking at the vegetables and salad, and filling up on desserts. Since neither she nor her parents could discuss the issue intelligently, and because no dietary alternatives were arranged for, mealtimes became nutritionally and emotionally unsound. Eventually, Jill got tired of eating under siege and gave up on vegetarianism.

Contrast this with Dave, the oldest of three teenagers. Dave chose a vegetarian regimen, though his brother, sister, and parents remained on a mixed diet. But Dave took time to read about vegetarian nutrition. He shared these ideas with his parents; they expressed their fears, science and statistics aside, that such a diet might be unsafe. All agreed to a trial period during which Dave would help his mother prepare his meals. That was several years ago. There was never any rancor about Dave's decision, and he's still the only vegetarian in the family. His mother, who now has a collection of vegetarian cookbooks, enjoys preparing meatless meals as a change of pace for the entire family. And Dave's father says his son's choice has enriched the family's life by introducing them to new, sometimes exotic foods and recipes.

Not all young people have parents as reasonable as Dave's, but they can minimize the impact of their vegetarianism on family life by doing the following:

1. Discuss only the *facts* about a vegetarian diet. Avoid mysticism and spiritually oriented arguments. Your parents will likely be more worried about your physical health than the strength of your soul.

2. Don't try to convert your family. Don't pontificate or threaten.

3. Don't dump the initial problems of vegetarian cookery into either parent's lap. Learn to prepare your own meals.

4. Wear your vegetarian mantle lightly; it is a way of eating born of a gentle philosophy. It needn't be a flaming revolutionary cause.

The spirit of this advice pertains to all family members, whatever their ages. Children and adults participating in a vegetarian conversion can probably bear with withdrawal symptoms, occasional kitchen disasters, and the strangeness of doing without a mealtime staple. But few people, no matter how close their personal or familial ties, can stand a steady diet of vegetarian campaign speeches and acrimonious debate.

Go easy. Let whatever delights there may be in a vegetarian existence reveal themselves as you proceed. And when you share these wonderful discoveries with those you love—please don't pound the table.

And finally, a kind word for our pets. Sometimes *vegetarianus evangelicus* even reaches out to snare the family dog or cat. It bothers some vegetarians to avoid flesh foods themselves, only to have to dump offal out of a can for Rex or Fifi. Some caution is advised here. The nutrition of dogs and cats is not the duplicate of human beings. Dogs can do quite well on dry meal formulations made primarily of soy meal and wheat. But even these commercial mixes contain bone meal and meat fat.

You can mix your own vegetarian dog food if you like. (And if the *dog* likes.) *Laurel's Kitchen,* an excellent vegetarian cookbook, contains a recipe for dog food made of egg, cooked vegetables, nutritional yeast, milk, and leftover bread, cereals, and beans. The authors report great success with two dogs on this diet. (Dog lovers, however, may have a hard time thinking of a canine without a bone to gnaw on.)

Cats are a different story. The mysteries of feline nutrition remain to be fully unraveled. Besides, unless a cat is permanently confined, it will—no matter what you feed it—happily busy itself bumping off birds, mice, moths and anything else that moves. This is what cats do and have always done.

Dr. Seth Koch, a veterinarian who specializes in ophthalmology, warns that on the basis of eye health alone, cats cannot do well on a restricted vegetarian diet. He told me of one case of a cat that had gone permanently blind because its owner had insisted on feeding it in all-plant diet. The blindness resulted from an amino acid deficiency in the cat's diet.[8]

If you feel so strongly about vegetarianism or nonviolence that it pains you to live with a carnivorous animal who, unlike humans, has no choice of lifestyle or moral values, then keep no pets. Or cultivate only "vegetarian" pets: a canary, a rabbit, a goat, or a hippo.

But again—go easy.

*Chapter Three notes.*

1. Darla Erhard, "Nutrition Education for the 'Now' Generation," *Journal of Nutrition Education,* Spring 1971, pp. 135-139.
2. See Frances Moore Lappé, *Diet for a Small Planet* (New York: Ballantine Books, 1975) for extensive NPU ratings.
3. Karen Pryor, *Nursing Your Baby* (New York: Harper and Row, 1963), p. 65.
4. Interview with Stephanie Harris, 11 October 1977. Ms. Harris is the coauthor of *Birthright Denied: The Risks and Benefits of Breast-Feeding.* Available from the Environmental Defense Fund, 1525 18th Street, N.W., Washington, D.C. 20036.
5. On the dangers of early feeding of solid food see E.F.P. Jelliffe, "Infant Feeding Practices: Associated Iatrogenic and Commerciogenic Diseases," *Pediatric Clinics of North America,* 24(1) February 1977, pp. 49-61.
6. "Vegan Child Seen Shorter, Lighter Than Others," *Pediatric News,* 11(4) April 1977, pp. 2, 41.
   For analysis of problems connected with infants on vegan diet (macrobiotic, in this case) see J.R.K. Robson, "Food Faddism," *Pediatric Clinics of North America,* 24(1):189-201, February 1977.
7. F.R. Ellis and P. Mumford, "The Nutritional Status of Vegans and Vegetarians," *Proceedings of the Nutrition Society,* 26:205, 1967 (Cambridge, England). "From our study of vegans it is clear that their diet is of satisfactory nutritional value for adult man, provided it is supplemented with vitamin $B_{12}$."
8. Interview with Dr. Seth Koch, V.M.D., 21 November 1976.

# ❧ FOUR ❧

# A New Look at Vegetarianism and Health

> It must be admitted that of the objections urged against vegetarianism, not one can withstand a loyal and scrupulous inquiry. I for my part can affirm that those whom I have known to submit themselves to this regimen have found its result to be improved or restored health, marked addition to strength, and the acquisition by the mind of a clearness, brightness, well-being, such as might follow the release from some secular, loathsome, detestable dungeon.
>
> Maurice Maeterlinck [1]

Will a vegetarian diet improve or restore health? Will it prevent certain diseases? Vegetarian advocates have claimed so for centuries. But because they had little solid scientific evidence to back their convictions, and because the public saw them as fanatics and crackpots—not a totally unjustified assessment—vegetarian claims were equally regarded as nonsense. After all, if a vegetarian diet was so healthy, why didn't more doctors and nutritionists recommend it instead of condemning it as faddism?

Yet now, toward the end of the twentieth century, when one startling medical and scientific advance follows another, vegetarianism and low-fat diets in general are getting another look from researchers. What they are discovering suggests that vegetarians haven't been so crazy after all.

The British blockade of the North Sea during World War I gives us an early example of how a balanced nonmeat diet can affect health positively. The blockade, staged to cut off Germany's access to supplies, also isolated Denmark. Warfare and starvation go together, and the Danes seemed ripe for tragedy when their ports were closed in 1917. Like many countries today, the Danes were dependent on imported grain, especially as livestock feed. The blockade shut off Danish supplies of American corn, Russian oil cake, and German rye. The situation was made even worse by a 1917 drought that further limited grain reserves.

Into this crisis stepped Dr. Mikkel Hindhede, appointed by the government to solve Denmark's food dilemmas. Hindhede, who had been researching the effects of a low-protein diet since 1895, saw that the Germans were already starving, though they normally harvested twice the grain and potatoes Denmark did. But Germany's chief nutritional policy makers were committed to a high-protein (meat) dietary.

So Germany, in an attempt to provide its population with regular rations of meat, fed much of its grain to livestock. The pigs thrived, Hindhede noted, while German adults and children died of malnutrition. Hindhede put Denmark on an opposite course. He diverted that country's stores of livestock feed to the human population. Potatoes, bran, and barley became the Danish staples along with plenty of greens, milk, and some butter. Hindhede had the bread enriched with bran and barley meal—items once considered only a by-product of milling, fit for pigs.

Pork was eaten mainly by farmers; city people got little or none. Beef was available only to the wealthy. The majority of Denmark, therefore, lived on a lacto-vegetarian regimen: milk, vegetables, and grain. "It was," wrote Hindhede, "a low-protein experiment on a large scale, about three million subjects being available." And the experiment was a success, though the Danes were not particularly happy about their forced conversion to a nonmeat diet.

When researchers computed the death rate in Copenhagen from October 1917 to October 1918—the period in which food restrictions were the most severe—they found that the overall mortality rate from disease was 10.4 deaths per thousand. It had never been lower than 12.5. This was a drop of 34 percent from the preceding 18 years, representing 6,300 fewer deaths than during prewar conditions. Hindhede wrote:

> It would seem then, that the principal cause of death lies in food and drink. It must be remembered in this connection that we took the cereals and potatoes from the distillers so that they could not make brandy, and one-half of the cereals from the brewers, so that the beer output was reduced one-half. Is it possible that this reduction in the output of alcoholic beverages is wholly responsible for the lower death rate? . . . . While the lessened alcohol consumption is a great contributing factor to the lowered death rate, it is not the only one.

Other factors may have contributed to these statistics—restricted use of tobacco, sugar, and spices; increased exercise—all balanced, perhaps, by the increased stress of wartime. But, said Hindhede, "I am convinced that overnutrition, the result of palatable meat dishes, is one of the most common causes of disease." Hindhede's conclusions, as we shall see, were strikingly accurate.[2]

During World War II, Norwegians were forced to adopt a diet similar to that followed by the Danes under Hindhede's direction. From 1940 to 1945, the Norwegian government was compelled to sharply reduce the amount of meat available to its citizens, while increasing the consumption of potatoes, fish, grain, and vegetables. Once again, the death rate from circulatory diseases dropped as it had during Hindhede's experiment. But more significantly, Norway's mortality figures shot right back to prewar levels as soon as its citizens returned to a richer postwar diet.[3]

Food consumption was also cut in Britain and Switzerland during World War II, with similar restrictions on animal foods. In both countries health was not only maintained, but improved. In Britain, infant and postnatal deaths dropped to their lowest levels. Instances of anemia were lower; children's growth rates and dental health were better than during peacetime. According to the Ministry of Health, Britain's general nutrition statistics showed an overall improvement despite—or because of—the severe wartime rationing.[4]

Those years between World War I and II have been called "The Golden Era of Vegetarianism," because a nonmeat diet no longer was thought to be a fad.[5] Vegetarianism was considered a sound, lifesaving regimen, far superior in health benefits and cost than a meat-based calorie-laden diet. The experience of food restrictions during two wars, in several countries, over a 30-year period, proved at least that the link between diet and disease was worth serious investigation, if not a drastic reappraisal of national food policies.

Nothing of the sort happened, of course. Vegetarianism was quietly handed back to the cultist. Few scientists pursued the lessons learned in Europe's kitchens. Postwar production and marketing was aimed at MORE and BIGGER. Rising affluence in Western Europe and North America saw people eating a diet even richer in animal foods than before both wars. A "chicken in every pot" became passé, replaced by "steak in every stomach." North Americans began gorging themselves on a collective diet that might have shamed Bacchus.

But the pendulum has swung back. Establishment scientists, government spokesmen, and conservative nutritionists are now issuing the same cautions the so-called health nuts were condemned for less than a decade ago. In July, 1976, Dr. Gio B. Gori, Deputy Director of the National Cancer Institute's Division of Cancer Cause and Prevention, went before the Senate Select Committee on Nutrition and Human Needs and said:

> Until recently, many eyebrows would have been raised by suggesting that an imbalance of normal dietary components could lead to cancer and cardiovascular diseases. . . . Today the accumulation of . . . evidence . . . makes this notion not only possible but certain. . . . [E]pidemiologic and laboratory data suggest that diet is an important factor in the causation of various forms of cancer, and that it is correlated to more than half of all cancers in women and at least one-third of all cancers in men.

While certain forms of cancer, heart disease, and digestive ailments may not be caused by dietary factors alone, nutrition plays a crucial if not fully understood role in disease resistance. As Dr. Gori told the Senate:

> Diet imbalances, perhaps coupled with other environmental hazards, may provide a continuous low-level insult that over a period would weaken the natural defenses of an organism, and produce the metabolic changes necessary to the appearance of

certain forms of cancer. . . . [P]resent knowledge provides provoking clues regarding those dietary factors that may be responsible, principally fat and meat intake, excessive caloric intake, and the hormonal and metabolic factors affected by nutrition.

With this in mind, consider the health record of the Seventh-Day Adventists. Unlike the short-term war experiences of the Danes and the English, the Adventists have advocated and followed a vegetarian diet for over 100 years. While adherence to the sect's dietary rules isn't a prerequisite for church membership, at least 50 percent of all Adventists are reported to be lacto-ovo-vegetarians. (There are roughly 2.5 million Adventists worldwide, with half a million in North America.)

Seventh-Day Adventists also abstain from smoking, alcohol, coffee, tea, spices, hot condiments, and highly refined products—factors that also affect disease occurrence and resistance. And while devotion to these rules may vary among members, a study published in *Cancer Research* demonstrates that the Adventists' lifestyle produces measurable benefits. Their rates of nutrition-related cancer, including colonic, rectal, and intestinal cancer, are *50 to 70 percent lower than the general population.* Statistical evidence, says the study, ". . . strongly suggests that the lacto-ovo-vegetarian diet may protect against colon cancer." [6]

British cancer researcher Dr. Denis Burkitt is more blunt. Intestinal cancer, he says, ". . . is a disease caused by the way we live." Burkitt and others strongly believe that bowel cancer, benign tumors, diverticular disease, and appendicitis are all directly linked to a diet low in fiber and high in refined foods. The typical U.S. diet—rich in animal fats, refined grains, sweets, snacks, and soft drinks—seems to be tailor-made for trouble. [7]

Scientists believe that a low-residue diet may allow carcinogens to be concentrated and held in contact with the bowel mucosa longer than a more fibrous diet would permit. The benefits of a fiber-rich diet have received much publicity in recent years, popularized by books suggesting that people can protect themselves against colonic cancer, heart disease, and a host of other ills by boosting their intake of dietary fiber. A diet containing plenty of green vegetables, legumes, fruits, and grains encourages more rapid passage of body wastes, helping to keep the colon clear of accumulated matter. Fiber advocates suggest Americans increase their roughage intake by avoiding fabricated foods, cutting back on alcohol and meat, using more grains and vegetables, and by consuming bran (about one to six teaspoonfuls a day). Good advice, but realize that several studies have shown that the typical vegetarian diet contains *two to four times more roughage* than found in a meat-based regimen.[8]

But fiber, as important as it is, may not be the whole story. Many scientists don't share the public's enthusiasm for the low-fiber theory of colonic cancer, believing such evidence is largely circumstantial. Studies by several researchers, including Dr. Michael J. Hill of the Central Public Health Laboratory, Colindale, London, suggest that fecal transit time may have less to do with cancer formation than what Hill calls the "physiological milieu in which the reactions take place." That is, the *speed* of waste movement through the intestines may not be as crucial as the concentrations of carcinogens already in the gut.

This conclusion favors a vegetarian diet even more than does the fiber theory, since there is evidence that a vegetarian's "physiological milieu" may be considerably different from a meat eater's. Numerous studies have demonstrated that bacterial action can convert bile acids in the human intestine into carcinogens. For example, certain kinds of *clostridia* (one of the bacteria found in the gut) are able to metabolize deoxycholic acid (a bile acid), converting it to 20-methylcholanthrene—a powerful carcinogen.

Exactly why and how this occurs is still being studied. But, say Dr. Hill and other scientists, food intake directly affects the output and concentration of both bile acids and intestinal bacterial flora. Thus, one's diet can directly influence the amount of carcinogens and cocarcinogens produced by the body.[9] Some studies have shown that meat fat tends to influence the production of carcinogens in the human intestine.

Dr. Gershon W. Hepner of Pennsylvania State University's Department of Medicine compared bile acid metabolism in controlled groups of lacto-ovo-vegetarians and meat eaters, and found that the vegetarians produced significantly less deoxycholic acid than the meat eaters. This study, Dr. Hepner reported,

indicates that meat may have an important effect on bile acid metabolism. The decreased deoxycholic acid pool size in the vegetarians may have important implications in connection with the prevalence of bowel cancer. . . . Previous efforts to link deoxycholic acid input and the diet have laid greater emphasis on dietary fiber content, but this study suggests that the effect of meat *per se* requires further investigation.[10]

Dr. Hill's research comes to the same conclusion. Writing in the *Lancet,* Dr. Hill noted that:

People living in the areas with a high recorded incidence of carcinoma of the colon tend to live on diets containing large amounts of fat and animal protein; whereas those who live in areas with a low incidence live on largely vegetarian diets with little fat or animal matter.[11]

Canadian researchers at the Ontario Cancer Institute have also raised questions about the influence of diet on the development of colonic cancer. Dr. William R. Bruce and his colleagues analyzed the feces of men eating a typical Western diet, finding mutagens that may be N-nitroso compounds—90 percent of which are carcinogenic. The fact that the food eaten by the test subjects contained little measurable nitroso or mutagenic activity indicated to the researchers that the body itself may produce certain carcinogens as by-products of the digestion of proteins and fats.

But the study also showed that the level of mutagens was sharply reduced when one tablespoon of bran fiber was added to the men's daily diet; that an even more significant decline in mutagens was achieved when the subjects cut their daily fat intake from 150 grams to 50 grams; and that mutagenic activity was also substantially cut when the subjects took a daily supplement of two grams of vitamin C.

If further research proves that nitroso compounds are indeed a cause of colonic cancer, then, says Dr. Bruce, "We should be able to predict changes in the diet which should lead to a reduction in the incidence of cancer of the colon." [12]

Several studies of the influence of diet on the development of colonic cancer tend to indict meat fat in particular. Milk and egg fats apparently don't cause the same bile acid effect. One scientist in Japan found a possible inverse relationship between stomach cancer and milk drinking. Japanese men who drank two glasses of milk daily had a lower risk of intestinal cancer than nonmilk drinkers. And nonsmokers who drank two glasses of milk daily had the lowest risk.[13]

There is also evidence that a diet heavy in animal fats may influence the incidence of breast cancer. The highest rates of breast cancer are found in those countries where people eat large amounts of animal fat: the United States, Canada, Argentina, Australia, New Zealand, and Great Britain. Rates are lowest in countries of the Far East and South America where less animal fat, particularly beef, is consumed. Japanese women have one of the lowest rates of breast cancer in the world, a statistic once attributed to racial or genetic factors. But Japanese women living in the United States, eating an American diet, are four times more likely to develop breast cancer than their counterparts in Japan. (Rates for cancer of the testis, prostate, and bowel are also higher among Japanese men in the United States than for those in Japan.)

Similarly, European Jewish women living in Israel are three times more prone to breast cancer than Asian or African Jews. Is the key to this disparity the comparatively high meat and caloric content of the European diet versus the simple fare of Asia, Africa, and poorer countries? Excessive consumption of animal fats (and excessive caloric intake in general) may somehow overstimulate breast development, creating overactive cancer-prone breast cells.

A similar relationship may exist between excessive fat intake and the development of cancer of the endometrium (uterus). Dr. Bruce Armstrong of the Perth Medical Centre in Australia cites five factors linked to a high risk of endometrial cancer: obesity, early puberty, late menopause, mild diabetes, and high blood pressure. Dr. Armstrong believes, however, that a "common mechanism" may be behind all five factors—excessive consumption of fat. Obesity, onset of puberty, and hypertension have been linked to fat consumption. Mild adult diabetes has been associated with obesity and total food intake. Too much dietary fat—converted to fatty tissue—may stimulate the production of estrogens that may then cause cancer directly or indirectly.

Dr. Armstrong's study made several key points related to vegetarianism:* U.S. women have higher rates of endometrial

* Note, however, that glandular disorder, previous ovarian or breast cancer, and radiation exposure are also associated with the development of endometrial cancer.

cancer than women of 23 other countries studied. Japanese and Nigerian women have the lowest rates. (Fat consumption in the United States is about 150 grams daily, about 40 grams per day in Japan and Nigeria.)

In addition, Seventh-Day Adventist women—half of whom are vegetarians—had lower blood pressure, earlier menopause, and a rate of endometrial cancer 40 percent lower than women in the general population.[14]

The human body is not entirely helpless against the activity of cancer-causing agents, whether naturally occurring or man-made substances. Just as our immunological defense mechanisms are able to battle bacteria and viruses, so can they neutralize carcinogens. Certain anticancer enzymes, for example, can be produced in the liver. But the ability to generate such substances may be linked to the components of one's diet.

Dr. Leo Wattenberg of the University of Minnesota School of Medicine demonstrated this in the laboratory by putting rats on a purified diet of a mixture of casein, starch, corn oil, and salt, with all vitamins and minerals furnished by a supplement. Although this fabricated diet was balanced in all essential nutriments, the rats were unable to produce the anticancer enzymes. However, when rats were fed an over-the-counter packaged rat feed, they *were* able to manufacture the enzymes.

Wattenberg isolated the dietary element that increased the animals' ability to produce the enzyme, discovering that ". . . considerable inducing activity was found in the vegetable component [of the packaged feed] which consists of alfalfa meal." And when alfalfa alone (grown without man-made chemicals) was added to the purified diet, the rats regained the ability to produce the cancer-fighting catalyst.

Wattenberg identified the agents (called indoles) in alfalfa that induced enzyme formation and found the same chemicals in other vegetables. Particularly potent sources were brussels sprouts, cabbage, turnips, broccoli, and cauliflower, their potency varying with harvesting practices and soil conditions; also spinach, dill, and celery. Citrus fruits were found to contain similar enzyme-inducing substances (flavones), and beans and seeds yield a type of plant protein (lectins) that also has demonstrated a positive effect on test animals' resistance to cancer.[15]

While we must be cautious about guessing at the ultimate implications of such data, and while it cannot be said that diet alone is the major cause of cancer ("cancer" is a generic term for a variety of conditions), many researchers are convinced that nutrition plays a fundamental causative and preventive role in the formation of several forms of cancer. Thus far the evidence is solidly against a life centered around the consumption of large amounts of meat, animal fats in general, table sugar, refined carbohydrates, alcohol, and tobacco.

A sensible vegetarian diet composed of unfabricated foods is naturally less concentrated in fat and sugar than the typical U.S. diet. A lunch of vegetable soup, whole-grain bread, and a salad is obviously lower in calories than a hamburger, french fries, and a thick shake. Well-chosen vegetarian food selections are filling and more difficult to wolf down and eat on the run. There is also evidence that a fibrous diet can actually limit the ability of the small intestine to absorb calories, while increasing the amount of fat excreted in the feces.

(Of course, nothing says that vegetarians can't stoke up on candy and cola, eating their way into corpulence; that most vegetarians don't do this probably says more about the kind of people they are than it does about a nonflesh diet per se.)

Vegetarians also eat considerably less cholesterol and saturated fats than most Americans, a fact that has attracted the attention of scientists investigating heart disease and related vascular problems. Cholesterol is normally produced by our bodies no matter what we eat. Found primarily in our blood, liver, nervous system, and brain, cholesterol is vital to the production of various body chemicals and sex hormones. Cholesterol becomes a problem, however, when an excess is deposited along the arterial walls. A buildup of this waxy material leads to circulatory blockages and thus to heart disease and stroke.

There is evidence that the higher a man's serum cholesterol level, the greater his risk of having a heart attack. (Women have a much lower rate of heart disease until after menopause.) Since eating foods rich in cholesterol and saturated fat raises one's serum cholesterol level, health authorities have been calling for a reduction in the amount of cholesterol and fat consumed by North Americans. (Heart disease is the number one cause of death in the United States.) The typical U.S. consumer eats about 500 to 700 mg or more of cholesterol daily. The American Heart Association, the Inter-Society Commission for Heart Disease Resources, and similar groups say Americans should reduce this intake to 300 mg a day. More conservative researchers have suggested that 200 mg daily would be even better.

The other dietary culprit is fat. Excessive amounts of fat, particularly saturated and hydrogenated fat, also raise serum cholesterol levels. (Saturated fat is found primarily but not exclusively in animal origin foods; hydrogenated fat is found in commercially prepared foods; cholesterol is found *only* in animal foods.)

The U.S. diet is high in total fat intake. Most Americans derive almost half—40 to 45 percent—of their caloric intake from fat. Health authorities believe this should be reduced to about 30 to 35 percent, with saturated fats comprising no more than 10 percent of one's daily caloric intake. (Ideally, polyunsaturated fats from plant sources should be consumed in amounts roughly equal to saturated fat intake.) Polyunsaturates tend to have a lowering effect on plasma cholesterol levels. On the other hand, too much polyunsaturated fat can be dangerous; there have been reports linking large amounts of polyunsaturates to cancer, liver diseases, intestinal disorders, and even arteriosclerosis.

To be sure, the issue of cholesterol and fat is explosively controversial. No one can yet say with absolute certainty that any one factor is a direct cause of cardiovascular illness. One expert says:

> . . . cholesterol is not a major risk factor in heart-related diseases, at least not dietary cholesterol. There are some people with faulty metabolism who oversynthesize and end up with excesses of cholesterol in the plasma. It is seldom good policy however to change the dietary habits of a total population to take care of the one or two percent with faulty metabolism.[16]

On the other hand, a recent poll of 214 scientists in 23 countries showed almost total agreement on the importance of diet's role in the development of coronary heart disease. Those polled were researchers "actively engaging in arteriosclerosis problems in recent years."

Ninety-nine percent of the scientists agreed that there is a link between diet and heart disease, between diet and plasma lipoprotein concentration, and between serum cholesterol levels and the development of coronary heart disease.

Ninety-two percent of those polled said that our present knowledge of diet and heart disease is sufficient for recommending a moderate change in national dietary patterns—that is, toward less calories, less saturated fat and fat in general, and less dietary cholesterol.[17]

Most Americans are caught in the middle of the cholesterol controversy because, as meat eaters, they generally have a difficult time adjusting to a low-calorie, low-cholesterol, low-saturated-fat diet—the so-called Prudent Diet. Middle- and upper-class U.S. consumers are used to eating with abandon. They don't like the idea of being sentenced to a life of forbidden foods, smaller portions of meat, and a limited choice of animal-origin foods. The Prudent Diet strikes many people as contrived and negative—a constant reminder of what they can't eat.

But while a sensible vegetarian diet is by its nature a prudent diet, it carries none of the negative overtones. Vegetarians have not only given up meat, they've abandoned the attitude that says flesh foods are preeminent, the essential mealtime ingredient. Meat eaters on a prudent diet often feel deprived, as though something were missing. (Something *is* missing, of course, or it wouldn't be a prudent diet.) You never miss what you don't desire, however, so experienced vegetarians feel no such tension or loss. While the cholesterol-conscious flesh eater may suffer because he wants to have his meat and eat it too, the vegetarian simply eats everything *but* meat. This subtle change of emphasis means that vegetarians can enjoy the health benefits of a prudent diet without feeling impoverished in the bargain. Many meat eaters are now wondering whether they should actively work to reduce their cholesterol intake. Become a vegetarian, however, and the question becomes irrelevant: a sensible vegetarian diet *is* a low-cholesterol, low-saturated-fat diet.

What about the lacto-ovo-vegetarian? Don't eggs and milk

products contain significant amounts of cholesterol and saturated fat? They do, but because the primary components of a vegetarian regimen—fruits, vegetables, grains, seeds, and nuts—contain *no* cholesterol, a vegetarian could use a quart of whole milk and a few ounces of any cheese daily without topping a cholesterol intake of 200 mg.

A pound of meat, fowl, or fish (depending on the variety) amounts to roughly 300 mg of cholesterol, a day's total intake on a prudent diet. Six ounces of most flesh foods yield approximately 154 mg of cholesterol, though shrimp, organ meats, and sausage are considerably higher. You'd have to drink three quarts of whole milk to hit 300 mg of cholesterol or one quart to equal the cholesterol found in just six ounces of meat.[18] Cheese is higher in cholesterol and saturated fat on an ounce-for-ounce basis than beef. But while eight ounces of beef is a common meal (two large hamburgers), few people would eat a half-pound of cheese at one sitting. As for saturated fat, even vegetarians using reasonable amounts of whole milk and several ounces of cheese daily would hardly consume ten percent of their total calories as saturated fat. (This assumes, however, that they are not also eating excessive hydrogenated fat or vegetable sources of saturated fat—coconuts, cashews, or palm oil. Beware also of invisible saturated fats in nondairy creams, whips, dips, and toppings; also chips, spreads, baked goods, and candy.)

I've used whole milk as an example to emphasize the point that lacto-vegetarians are in little danger of overconsuming cholesterol or saturated fat. Adults generally need only about a pint of milk or a few ounces of cheese to meet their RDA for calcium and most of their protein need. Skim milk and skim milk cheeses are strikingly lower in cholesterol and saturated fat than whole milk.* A vegetarian could literally wallow in skim milk products without ingesting excessive cholesterol.

Realize, however, that even those medical authorities calling for less cholesterol in the diet aren't suggesting that the public eat diets free of *all* cholesterol and saturated fat—only that these substances be kept to reasonable levels. Have your serum cho-

---

* Skim milk products are also virtually free of pesticide residues.

lesterol checked if you're concerned, but don't struggle to reduce your cholesterol intake to zero without a medical reason. (Even patients with atherosclerotic problems are generally put on cholesterol intakes of about 240 milligrams a day.)

Eggs have gotten a bad name, perhaps unfairly and inaccurately, because of their high cholesterol content, but they remain an inexpensive source of low-calorie, high-quality protein and vitamins. Prudent meat eaters restrict themselves to three egg yolks per week and unlimited egg whites. But vegetarians can use eggs more frequently without exceeding the guidelines for cholesterol. Eggs can also be used in casseroles and similar dishes. You'll get the culinary and protein qualities of the egg while eating only about one-half to one-third of an egg per serving, depending on the recipe.

I'm not suggesting that lacto-ovo-vegetarians gorge on whole milk, eggs, cheese, and butter. The point is that because they eat no flesh foods, vegetarians can enjoy a relaxed and varied use of whole or skim milk products and eggs while still maintaining a daily cholesterol and saturated fat intake *well below* what is currently thought to be a moderate level. Vegans would consume *no* cholesterol and little saturated fat (depending on their food selections), though their total intake of fats might be high if their use of seeds and nuts was extensive.

The relationship of dietary cholesterol and heart disease may never be fully resolved, at least not to the satisfaction of scientists. But there is plenty of evidence that serum cholesterol levels, blood pressure, and rates of heart disease are lower in vegetarian groups and those relying on vegetable proteins than among populations eating Western-style diets.

The results of several representative studies—there are many more similar projects on record—will help to illustrate the effect a vegetarian diet (and perhaps other unknown factors) has had on some individuals:

A 1976 program studied the serum cholesterol levels of

Seventh-Day Adventist children living near Sydney, Australia. Of the 183 children (ages 12 to 17) studied, 105 ate only vegetables and dairy products, while 78 ate flesh foods occasionally or regularly. All the Adventist children were compared to a control group of omnivorous non-Adventist adolescents living nearby. Tests showed that the Adventist children had blood cholesterol levels 19 percent lower than the controls. The lowest levels were found in the 105 children who never ate flesh foods.[19]

A 1975 survey of 116 adult Americans on a macrobiotic diet (they ate fish, but no meat, eggs, or dairy products) showed the plasma lipid (fat) content of their blood to be "strikingly low in all age groups." A similar 1974 study of 210 macrobiotics on the same diet showed their blood pressure levels to be lower than those of omnivorous controls.[20]

In another Australian study, the blood pressure of vegetarians 30 to 79 years old was found to be "significantly less" than the levels found in nonvegetarian controls. The vegetarians in this case were again Seventh Day Adventists, but the researchers found it unlikely "that these differences could be explained by differences in alcohol, tobacco, tea, [or] coffee." The study went on to say that "dietary factors, probably intake of animal protein, animal fat, or another dietary component associated with them, are likely to be responsible" for the differences in blood pressure readings.[21]

Many factors other than diet affect serum cholesterol levels, but a team of scientists working at the University of Milan and Maggiore Hospital has shown that vegetable protein itself may act to keep cholesterol levels low. In a report to the British medical journal *The Lancet,* Dr. C.R. Sirtori described a series of tests using diets composed of a variety of Italian foods mixed with granulated soybean protein. Two diets were created: one was a standard low-fat, low-cholesterol diet composed of 62 percent animal protein; the other contained only seven percent animal protein and 63 percent soy protein. Twenty-two patients with chronic high serum cholesterol levels were split into two groups. Each group followed either the standard low-fat diet or the soy protein diet for three weeks and then switched. In each case the soy protein diet dramatically lowered serum cholesterol levels. And when patients switched from the soy protein back to the standard low-fat, their serum cholesterol levels went back up again. The soy protein diet lowered cholesterol levels by 14 percent in two weeks and by 21 percent in three weeks. (None of the patients lost or gained weight.) Dr. Sirtori and his colleagues termed this decrease "remarkable" considering that the patients had all been following a low-fat, low-cholesterol diet at home for three months previously without success.

Dr. Sirtori concluded that people with the type of high cholesterol associated with heart disease "may benefit from a diet in which protein comes only from vegetables" because the results of the soy protein diet were superior to even several months' treatment with a standard low-fat diet.[22]

(A *Lancet* editorial speculating on why the soy protein worked so well guessed that the relatively low methionine content of vegetable proteins might have a cholesterol-lowering effect. Methionine is an essential amino acid used in the body's protein construction.)

Other studies with fruits and vegetables have demonstrated similar cholesterol-lowering effects: certain indigestible carbohydrates like pectin (found in ripe fruits and some vegetables) and plant sterols (found in vegetables, vegetable oils, and fruits) help cut serum cholesterol. And while vegetarians get teased about their use of beans as a staple, some studies have shown that regular consumption of cooked dried beans and other legumes also tends to lower cholesterol levels. (The fiber in beans apparently reduces cholesterol by increasing the fecal expulsion of bile acids produced by cholesterol metabolism.)[23]

Two British researchers reported in May 1976 that they had successfully treated four cases of severe angina pectoris * with a vegan diet. All four patients were free of angina pain and symptoms by the fifth or sixth month of treatment and "were able to engage in strenuous activities." The patients were still free of symptoms five years after the start of their vegan regimen. The doctors reported:

> We have found subjects consuming a diet devoid of animal products have lower levels of plasma triglycerides, cholesterol, and phospholipids than controls. These findings could well

---

* Severe chest pain due to a restriction of blood supply to the heart.

exert a preventive effect on the development of angina pectoris and ischemic heart disease.[24]

This last point is controversial, of course. *Just because you become a vegetarian doesn't mean you're going to be magically protected against heart disease.* There are many risk factors related to development of coronary troubles: obesity, cigarette smoking, diabetes, stress, high blood pressure, high cholesterol levels, a family history of heart disease, and sedentary living all play a role. The National Heart and Lung Institute says that the presence of *either* smoking, high blood pressure, or high cholesterol levels roughly doubles the chances of coronary heart disease. The presence of all three together may increase one's risk by ten times. (Note that Seventh-Day Adventists—primarily nonsmokers, nondrinkers, and lacto-ovo-vegetarians—have a heart disease rate 50 percent lower than the general population.)[25]

Exercise is another important factor, and perhaps a crucial one. Test subjects often show lower blood lipid profiles after vigorous physical training. Studies have also shown that some groups on high-fat, high-cholesterol diets (like the Samburu and Masai of East Africa who live on camel's and cow's milk, blood, and meat) have low serum cholesterol levels and remain free of heart disease.[26]

But regular physical activity is part of these peoples' lives. A Masai man may walk 60 miles in a day while tending his cattle. Does constant physical exercise also exert a preventive effect on the development of atherosclerosis?

Part of the answer to this question may be found in the activity of blood components called lipoproteins. There are several types of lipoproteins, but research into the behavior of high-density lipoproteins (HDL) may eventually explain why some people with high serum cholesterol levels or those eating large amounts of dietary cholesterol remain free of coronary disease.

Some scientists believe the presence of high HDL levels in the blood keeps cholesterol moving to the liver for excretion, rather than allowing it to build up as artery-clogging deposits. Other researchers believe high HDL levels may actually flush the arterial walls clear of fatty debris, preventing the onset of heart disease.

Several surveys, including one of more than 6,000 people, have already shown that individuals with low levels of HDL are more likely to suffer heart attacks than those with high HDL levels. Can a person's HDL be boosted without drugs? Researchers have noted that HDL is most elevated in nonsmokers, underweight persons, moderate drinkers (as opposed to teetotalers), women, men who engage in regular vigorous exercise (middle-aged male runners had HDL levels much like those of young women), and those on vegetable-rich, low-animal-fat diets.[27] No one can promise you'll be safe from heart disease if you follow such a pattern, but revelations about HDL are surely one more vote for dietary moderation and regular vigorous exercise.

A recent study of the health profiles of 1,000 North Americans found, in fact, that the healthiest were those on a vegetarian diet who ran for exercise. Next healthiest were those on a vegetarian diet who didn't run, followed by nonvegetarians who ran. The *least* healthy were nonvegetarians who were also nonrunners.[28] Confusing? Perhaps the best life insurance risk of all is a nonsmoking, relaxed vegetarian marathon runner from a long-lived family who enjoys a glass or two of wine with dinner.

You've probably read newspaper accounts of the Vilcabambans of Ecuador, the Abkhasians of the Soviet Union, and the Hunzans of Northern Pakistan. These people live in agricultural communities, are technologically about 50 years behind the West, and all share a common characteristic: a surprising percentage of them live well past their seventies, but none languishes in nursing homes or retirement villages. They live as vibrant, physically strong, mentally alert citizens who just happen to be 80, 90, and possibly older.

All of these groups lead similar lives. Men and women work hard as farmers, tending their crops, walking long distances, living a life more vigorous than most modern youths in the United States. None of these people can be called vegetarians, but their diets resemble the regimen a health-conscious lacto-ovo-vegetarian might follow.

None of the groups eats meat in significant amounts. The Abkhasians eat boiled chicken once or twice a week; the Hunzans have a weekly feast that includes meat; the Vilcabambans are the poorest of all and eat virtually no meat. All three groups live on diets of homegrown vegetables and fruits, milk, yogurt-type foods, cheese, and grains.

The Abkhasians eat grapes, apples, pickled vegetables, garlic, tomatoes, and other vegetables. They also eat boiled or fried eggs once or twice a week. Hunzans thrive on barley, wheat, buckwheat, legumes, greens, squash, and apricots. They believe their good health is linked to their water, a mineral-rich milky liquid that flows from melting glaciers. The Vilcabambans eat yucca and cassava roots, maize, beans, potatoes, cottage cheese, a variety of fruits, and raw eggs infrequently. All of the groups live on food grown without pesticides or chemical fertilizers. None uses table sugar or refined products.

Whether it's the diet, the relative lack of stress, or the altitude, those scourges of civilized life—heart disease, cancer, diabetes, obesity, and "old age"—are unknown among all three groups. Men and women remain sexually active well past their seventies. Healthy sperm has been taken from a 119-year-old Abkhasian man; Vilcabamban women in their fifties commonly bear healthy children. And according to medical observers, 100-year-old Vilcabambans have the muscle tone of a healthy 30-year-old. Once it was believed that genetic factors were the key to this amazing health and longevity. But gerontologists who have lived with and studied these peoples now believe environmental conditions may be of primary importance: diet, geography, climate, and the prevailing psychological, social, and biological conditions are only a few matters begging investigation. All of the centenarians live simple, often monotonous lives of hard work, much exercise, and low stress. Their air, water, and food are relatively free of pollutants and chemicals.

The evidence thus far suggests that these elements, coupled with a crude, nutritious lacto-ovo-vegetarian diet, may provide the foundation for a long and healthy life. Dr. David Davies, a British gerontologist who has lived with the Vilcabambans, says that when these people leave their mountain homes for life in the surrounding villages and change their diets in the process, their health declines. Once they abandon their pure and simple meals for the excessive meat-eating, canned food, and white flour diets of the towns-people, their vigor erodes. They may still reach old age, says Davies, but they become "more decrepit" than those who stay in the mountains.[29]

Even the health picture of the Hunzans has changed in the past few decades. Processed foods, sweets, and canned meat have finally found their way into the Hunzans' once-remote setting. Visitors returning from this mountain land have reported a decline in the general health of the people, including the appearance of digestive ailments and dental caries, once unknown there. "Clearly," says Dr. Davies, "the caloric content of the diet and its composition is a significant factor in health and aging." [30]

Scientists have experimented with rat populations, feeding them diets similar to the frugal but nourishing meals of the Abkhasians, Hunzans, and Vilcabambans. In several classic studies, rats fed on low-calorie, low-animal-fat regimens with nutrients provided mainly by fruits, grains, and vegetables had longer than normal lifetimes while retaining youthful characteristics and disease resistance. One study summed up its findings:

> . . . [E]xperiments demonstrate that a single factor, namely food intake, can affect the onset of the major degenerative diseases in the rat. Though the nature of the metabolic mecha-nism involved in this phenomenon is obscure, it is evident that *ad libitum* feeding accelerates the development of lesions, whereas food restriction at a level that provides for good nutri-tion and prevents the storage of excess body fat has a delaying effect.[31]

In a more recent study, researchers allowed 121 rats to eat as much as they wanted. The rats lived out their normal life spans —a range of 317 to 1,026 days—and died of natural causes. But the scientists noted that the rats who ate the least lived considerably longer than the rats who consistently overate. And those rats who overate between their 100th and 199th days of life had the shortest life spans. Because this time period roughly corresponds to a human's adolescence, the experimenters cautiously suggested that longevity in humans may be linked in part to a moderate diet, specifically a high-protein diet early in life, followed by a low-protein regimen in later years.[32] Rats aren't people, though, so scientists can only speculate about the ultimate value of food restriction for humans; still, the evidence from numerous studies and experiments clearly favors the conservative eater.

A glance at the world's population, however, shows us that a low-calorie, low-protein, nonmeat diet alone is not necessarily a sure way to good health or a vigorous old age. Tens of millions of people struggle to survive on sparse diets; their only reward is premature aging, deficiency diseases, and early death. The secret seems to lie in diets that are simple but adequate—a minimum of food supplying an optimum level of nutrition. One needn't be a vegetarian to follow such a regimen, but it helps. Sensible lacto-ovo-vegetarianism and enlightened veganism are almost by definition moderate diets.

To be sure, none of these sentiments for moderation are new. Ancient thinkers urged restraint in diet and behavior long before Aristotle or Lao-tse ever drew a breath. And vegetarians have maintained for centuries that their lifestyle was a reasonable and prudent one. But only now, with science taking a closer look, has such intuition been justified. The most recent "official" call for changes in the typical U.S. diet can be found in *Dietary Goals for the United States,* a 1977 report issued by the Senate Select Committee on Nutrition and Human Needs. Citing dietary links to "six of the ten leading causes of death," * the Committee asks Americans to drastically reduce their consumption of animal fats, cholesterol, table sugar, and salt, while increasing their use of fruits, vegetables, and whole grains.

Ironic, isn't it, that such dietary suggestions should come from one house of a legislative body whose agricultural and economic policies have helped set the standards for excessive consumption of food and energy? Ironic, too, that the Committee's goals, formulated after receiving testimony from many eminent nutritionists and

---

* Heart disease, cancer, cerebrovascular disease, diabetes, arteriosclerosis, and cirrhosis of the liver.

medical authorities, should end up paralleling the ideas of health reformers like Rodale, Hindhede, Kellogg, and others? While the Committee falls short of calling for a vegetarian revolution, you can see that a sensible, health-conscious vegetarian diet, as outlined in this book, easily meets or exceeds the guidelines for what the report calls "the building of better health . . . through better nutrition."

Can we come to some realistic conclusions about the health benefits of a vegetarian diet? Too many vegetarian activists get hysterical at this point, promising converts everything from disease immunity to whiter teeth, stronger nails, and eternal life. The statistical and epidemiological evidence favoring either a vegetarian or a moderate diet is impressive, but let's be conservative for a change. Without making extravagant promises, let us list only what current data suggests about a well-chosen vegetarian diet.

1. The low-cholesterol, low-saturated-fat, and high-fiber content of such diets may inhibit the formation of certain types of cancer by encouraging more rapid passage of wastes, a lower output of those bile acids that may be converted to carcinogens, and an alteration in the type and activity of those intestinal bacteria capable of changing bile acids into carcinogens. A lowered fat and cholesterol intake may also forestall the development or slow the progress of heart disease (perhaps in some individuals more than others) by reducing serum cholesterol and blood pressure levels. Higher levels of dietary fiber may also encourage an increased excretion of cholesterol and fat.

2. A low-protein, low-calorie diet may beneficially affect one's hormonal profile, leading to a lowered incidence of breast, ovarian, and endometrial cancer.

3. A diet largely composed of crude vegetables and fruits may boost or facilitate the body's production of those enzymes capable of neutralizing certain absorbed chemical carcinogens. Animal experiments also suggest that a lowered intake of protein

and fat may help the body to defend itself against the effect of chemical carcinogens.

4. Health-minded vegetarians may have less exposure to chemical carcinogens, pesticides, drugs, and synthetic hormone residues. The comparatively high vitamin A and C content of their diets may also inhibit the potency of certain agents and carcinogens.

5. Animal experiments suggest that low-calorie, low-protein diets composed of a variety of nourishing crude foods favor increased longevity, better disease resistance, and a slower aging process.

Thus, a well-chosen vegetarian or low-meat diet coupled with regular vigorous exercise and rest—plus the avoidance of highly processed and fabricated foods, excessive sugar and salt, tobacco, and excessive alcohol and drug use—seems to contribute to the optimum functioning of the human body. Can this be proven to the satisfaction of all scientists and health authorities? No. You may wait, if you wish, for uncontestable proof that such changes will work against major ills, but as Harvard nutritionist Dr. D. Mark Hegsted says in *Dietary Goals for the United States:*

> There will undoubtedly be many people who will say we have not proven our point; we have not demonstrated that the dietary modifications we recommend will yield the dividends expected. We would point out to those people that the diet we eat today was not planned or developed for any particular purpose. It is a happenstance related to our affluence, the productivity of our farmers and the activities of our food industry. The risks associated with eating this diet are demonstrably large. The question to be asked, therefore, is not why should we change our diet but why not? What are the risks associated with eating less meat, less fat, less saturated fat, less cholesterol, less sugar, less salt, and more fruits, vegetables, unsaturated fat and cereal products—especially whole grain cereals? There are none that can be identified and important benefits can be expected.[33]

*Chapter Four notes.*

1. Maurice Maeterlinck (1862-1949) *The Buried Temple.*
2. M. Hindhede, "The Effect of Food Restrictions During War on Mortality in Copenhagen," *JAMA,* 74(6):381, 1920.
3. A. Strom and R.A. Jensen, "Mortality from Circulatory Diseases in Norway 1940-45, *Lancet* 260:126, 1951.
4. Harry Benjamin, *Commonsense Vegetarianism* (Surrey, England: Health for All, 1967), p. 22.
5. M. Hardinge, and H. Crooks, "Non Flesh Dietaries: Historical Background," *Journal of the American Dietetic Association,* 43(6):545, 1963.
6. R.L. Phillips, "Role of Lifestyle and Dietary Habits in Risk of Cancer Among Seventh Day Adventists," *Cancer Research* 35:3513, (November 1975).
7. "The Evidence Leavens: We Invite Colon Cancer," *Medical World News,* 13(3):33, (11 August 1972).
   See also: D. Burkitt, "Epidemiology of Cancer of the Colon and Rectum," *Cancer,* 28(1):3-13, (July 1971).
8. Hardinge and Sanchez cited in Phillips.
9. M.J. Hill, "Metabolic Epidemiology of Dietary Factors in Large Bowel Cancer," *Cancer Research,* 35:3398, 1975.
10. G.W. Hepner, "Altered Bile Acid Metabolism in Vegetarians," *American Journal of Digestive Diseases,* 20(10):935, (October 1975).
11. M.J. Hill, "Bacteria and the Aetiology of Cancer of the Large Bowel," *Lancet,* 1:95-100, 1971.
12. W.R. Bruce, et al., "Non-Volatile N-Nitroso Compounds in Human Feces," paper presented to American Chemical Society Convention, September 1977.
13. Takeshi Hirayama, "Epidemiology of Cancer of the Stomach With Special Reference to its Recent Decrease in Japan," *Cancer Research,* 35:3460-3463, (November 1975).
14. Morton Mintz, "Fat Intake Seen Increasing Cancer Risk," *Washington Post,* 10 September 1976.
15. L.W. Wattenberg, "Effects of Dietary Constituents on the Metabolism of Chemical Carcinogens," *Cancer Research,* 35:3326-3331, 1975.
16. W.J. Stadelman, Professor of Food Science, Purdue University; letter to Senate Select Committee on Nutrition and Human Needs, 15 April 1977.

17. Kaare R. Norum, "What is the Experts' Opinion on Diet and Coronary Heart Diseases?" *Journal of the Norwegian Medical Association,* 12 February 1977; Cited by Senator Edward M. Kennedy in testimony to Senate Select Committee on Nutrition and Human Needs, 24 March 1977.

18. USDA Composition of Foods, Handbook 8-1, revised November 1976; see also R.M. Feeley, et al., "Cholesterol Content of Foods," *Journal of the American Dietetic Association,* 61:134, (August 1972).

19. J. Ruys, et al., "Serum Cholesterol and Triglyceride Levels in Australian Adolescent Vegetarians," *British Medical Journal,* 2(6027):87, (10 July 1976).

20. F. Sacks, et al., "Plasma Lipids and Lipoproteins in Vegetarians and Controls," *New England Journal of Medicine,* 292(22):1148, (29 May 1975); also F. Sacks, et al., "Blood Pressure in Vegetarians," *American Journal of Epidemiology,* 100(5):390, 1974.

21. B. Armstrong, et al., "Blood Pressure in Seventh Day Adventists," *American Journal of Epidemiology,* 105(5):444-9, (May 1977).

22. C.R. Sirtori, et al., "Soybean Protein Diet in the Treatment of Type II Hyperlipoproteinaemia," *Lancet* 1(8006):275-7, (5 February 1977).

23. E.W. Hellendoorn, "Beneficial Physiological Action of Beans," *Journal of the American Dietetic Association,* 69(3):248, (September 1976).

24. F.R. Ellis and T. Sanders, "Angina and Vegetarian Diet," letter to editor, *Lancet,* 1(7970):1190, (29 May 1976); for specifics see F.R. Ellis, et al., "Angina and Vegan Diet," *American Heart Journal,* 93(6):803-5, (June 1977).

25. F.R. Lemon and T.T. Walden, "Death from Respiratory System Disease Among SDA Men," *JAMA,* 198:117, 1966. Adventist men suffered their first heart attack a decade later than men in the general population.

26. Dr. George V. Mann, "The Saturated vs. Unsaturated Fat Controversy," testimony to Senate Select Committee on Nutrition and Human Needs, 24 March 1977.

27. Walter Sullivan, "High Levels of a Protein in Blood Linked to Heart Disease Prevention," *New York Times,* 4 September 1977, p. 1.
    " 'Good' v. 'Bad' Cholesterol", *Time,* 21 November 1977, p. 119.

28. Julia Lamb, "The Healthiest Diet?" *Sports Illustrated* 46(10):68, 1977. Interview with Dr. Joan Ullyot, Health Research Institute, San Francisco.
29. David Davies, *Centenarians of the Andes* (New York: Anchor/ Doubleday, 1975).
30. *Ibid.,* p. 68.
31. B.N. Berg and H.S. Simms, "Nutrition and Longevity in the Rat, III, Food Restriction Beyond 800 Days," *Journal of Nutrition,* 74:23, 1961.
32. "Eat Less, Live Longer," *Science Digest,* February 1976. Refers to the work of M.H. Ross (Fox Chase Cancer Center, Philadelphia) and G. Bras (Rijks University, Netherlands).
33. Dr. D.M. Hegsted, *Dietary Goals for the United States,* (Washington, D.C.: Senate Select Committee on Nutrition and Human Needs, February 1977), p. 3. See also, D.M. Hegsted, "Protein Needs and Possible Modifications of the American Diet," *Journal of the American Dietetic Association,* 68(4):317-320, (April 1976); also Dr. Hegsted's comments in *Cancer Research,* 35:3541-3543, (November 1975).

## ❧FIVE❧

# Protein: Enough Is Enough

Protein.

People speak the word with reverence, like primitives invoking the name of a mysterious and powerful god. Protein *is* mysterious. Few who toss the word about have any idea just what the stuff is, what it does, or how much they need. Yet people worry about getting enough protein. And they assume vegetarians can't get enough. This deep-seated fear of ending up on a CARE poster, plus the cultural importance of flesh foods, has helped make the high-protein meat-centered diet a North American cult, complete with its own ritual and dogma.

The protein worshiper attends the supermarket each week and stands before the sacrificial sirloin. The worshiper heeds the pronouncements of the meat industry and USDA priests, and believes the simple meat/protein litany memorized in childhood:

You need lots of protein or you'll get sick.

Meat has lots of protein.

Eat lots of meat and you'll get lots of protein.

The last line is true, but unfortunately, the reverse is also assumed. That is, if you don't eat meat you won't get enough protein. So let's put it succinctly, briefly enough to fit on a bumper sticker:

HUMANS NEED PROTEIN, NOT MEAT.

But what *is* protein, and why is it so important?

The chemical foundations of life for both plants and animals are carbon, hydrogen, oxygen, and nitrogen. The first three of these elements are found in carbohydrates and fats, but only protein contains nitrogen. Although gaseous nitrogen was discovered and isolated in 1722, it wasn't until 1816 that its importance to animal life was demonstrated. Francois Magendie, a French physician and physiology teacher, experimented on dogs, feeding them compounds he knew to be lacking in nitrogen. When the dogs died, Magendie concluded that the missing nitrogen was somehow basic to animal survival. A little more than 20 years later, a Dutch chemist, Gerrit Jan Mulder, named these nitrogen-bearing substances protein, from the Latin *proteios,* meaning "first," or "holding first place." In 1838, Mulder described protein as:

> unquestionably the most important of all known substances in the organic kingdom. Without it, no life appears possible on our planet. Through its means, the chief phenomena of life are produced.[1]

These "chief phenomena" are, of course, the growth and development of living organisms. New tissue can be created to replace the old only when the necessary construction materials—oxygen, carbon, hydrogen, and nitrogen—are available. Although the atmosphere contains nitrogen in abundance, animals cannot make direct use of it as plants can. Some leguminous plants, such as beans, peas, and alfalfa, can extract atmospheric nitrogen and fix it in their root nodes. Other plants use the sun and photosynthesis to combine soilborne nitrogen with carbon dioxide and water, thereby creating tissue protein. But for animals, nitrogen is available only through food. And the only nitrogen-bearing component in food is protein. So we are left with two choices: we can eat plant protein, or we can eat the animals that eat plants.

Is there a fundamental difference between plant and animal protein? Yes and no. Protein molecules are composed of about 20 amino acids. These are joined together in chains or peptide linkages of various lengths. Biochemist Roger J. Williams suggests we think of proteins as composed of "beads of 20 slightly differing shapes strung together in a definite order and . . . coiled . . . into a ball. . . . Each bead is an amino acid."[2] Although the strands or linkages may vary in length from 50 to several hundred thousand beads, the actual *types* of amino acids involved are limited to about 20. The specific nature of each protein is determined by how these 20 different amino acids are strung together.

Fewer than two dozen different amino acids may not seem like much when you consider the infinite variety of life's forms, but these few amino acids can be linked into roughly 2,400 trillion different combinations. And here is where plant and animal proteins are similar: *the structure of individual amino acids is identical, whatever their source.* Let's use the amino acid lysine as an example. If you extracted the lysine from a bean and placed it under a microscope next to the lysine from a side of beef, you would find no difference between the samples. Lysine is lysine, no matter its origin.

What makes the bean protein different from the beef protein is the number and arrangement of the individual amino acids. Thus, there are differences between plant and animal proteins, but there are no molecular differences. An amino acid is an amino acid whether it comes from you or your philodendron.

This is common knowledge in nutrition texts. But nutritional science, like all expanding studies, has a built-in information lag. It's not surprising to find laymen and medical doctors espousing dietary theories dating from the 1800s: they traditionally receive little training in nutrition. Many still unknowingly subscribe to Justus Liebig's nineteenth century dictum that humans should eat protein that most closely resembles the structure of human protein. Because the distribution of amino acids in flesh foods more nearly resembles that in human tissue than in plant protein, Liebig's suggestion—and popular belief—favors meat as the best protein source. But Liebig (1803-1873) didn't know that all proteins are broken down into individual amino acids by the digestive process. Once digestion and absorption have taken place, ingested amino acids give no hint of their origin. This is why scientists talk about specific amino acids rather than the proteins that yield them.

Liebig, whose early investigations into the chemistry of life processes wielded great influence, also believed that those doing hard muscular work should eat muscle meats to renew tissue and energy. Nutritionists have proved over and over again that muscle power and energy depend on fats and carbohydrates—not protein. Yet many people, particularly coaches, still believe in this old sympathetic magic of eating muscles to produce muscles. You might as well eat brains and eyeballs to be smart and sharp-eyed.

Nutritionists call amino acids the building blocks of life. It helps to visualize them as bricks. Now—imagine you were to build an apartment house with used bricks. Should you use only those bricks salvaged from another apartment house? Must apartment houses be built only with bricks taken from structures that most closely resemble them? This is the house that Liebig built. But the source of the salvaged bricks obviously matters less than the amount and quality of the bricks available to complete the job.

Apply this to human nutrition—you've just finished eating a sandwich. It doesn't matter what kind of sandwich—ham or peanut butter. The protein in the sandwich will be converted into human protein through a process almost identical to tearing down a building and creating a new structure with the salvaged parts. And, like any good builder, the body will even use a blueprint.

Once chewed, partially digested by the saliva, and swallowed, the sandwich material will be broken down in the small intestine into its basic components. (We'll discuss only amino acids.) Digestion reduces the different amino acid chains to either shorter chains or individual "free" acids. At this point, the source of these amino acids is no longer apparent. Once absorbed into the bloodstream, the amino acids are circulated throughout the body to the billions of cells. Each cell is a miniature construction site that will select from the blood only those specific "used bricks" it needs to create its particular protein structure.

The DNA/RNA code within each cell—the blueprint—determines what kind of protein structure each cell will synthesize. So in a real sense we can say, as one nutritionist titled her book, food becomes you. The protein you eat is literally torn down and reassembled cell by cell into that unique collection of cellular architecture you lovingly think of as yourself.

Although the analogy of building construction helps us understand the workings of protein synthesis, there are other factors that affect the process. For instance, not all of the 20 amino acids are of equal importance in human nutrition. W.C. Rose, one of the pioneers in nutrition research, discovered this when he fed a mixture of pure amino acids to a population of young white rats. Rose experimented by withholding specific acids one at a time. He noticed that the absence of certain acids led to various effects: illness, a retardation in growth, and sometimes death. Other acids could be withheld indefinitely with no harm to the test animal.

Rose concluded that certain amino acids were essential to growth and health because their absence caused an upset in bodily functions. Other studies supported Rose's research, and nutritionists have long since agreed that of the 20 or so amino acids, 8 or 9 are essential (9 or 10 in growing children) because the body cannot manufacture them in sufficient amounts. The other amino acids are vital but nonessential in the diet because they can be synthesized by the body in adequate quantities.

The essential amino acids (EAAs) are normally available to our bodies only by taking them in through food. So we can rewrite our bumper sticker to read:

HUMANS NEED THE ESSENTIAL
AMINO ACIDS, NOT MEAT.

The essential amino acids are isoleucine, leucine, lysine, methionine, phenylalanine, threonine, tryptophan, valine, and perhaps histidine. (Histidine was thought to be essential only for growth. Relatively new data now suggest it may also be essential in the adult diet.)

But not only must the EAAs be present in the diet, they must also be present in the right amounts and patterns. Imagine a cell's

DNA/RNA code calls for the construction of a protein whose amino acid chain is composed of three of the acids in a specific order:

glycine      tryptophan      methionine

Both tryptophan and methionine are essential amino acids. Glycine is a nonessential amino acid. Now assume you eat a food that contains no tryptophan. If supplied *only* with this food, our sample cell will never be able to build its particular protein. A missing EAA or one low in the proportions needed for protein building is called the limiting amino acid. Its absence or deficiency effectively limits the entire process of synthesis.

If you ate a food whose tryptophan content was low, such as cornmeal, protein synthesis would continue in our sample cell only for as long as the level of tryptophan lasted. When this limiting acid ran out, the individual cell's protein construction would shut down no matter what the levels of the other amino acids.

This is why animal-origin foods (flesh, dairy products, and eggs) have long been called complete protein. Such foods not only contain all the EAAs, but they also contain them in a pattern most like what our cellular blueprints require. Plant proteins have been called incomplete because they generally lack some of the EAAs in various amounts. But the terms complete and incomplete are inaccurate and misleading when applied to the protein question.

Imagine that someone offers to sell you a truckload of bricks. Describing the shipment as a ton of bricks or a complete load is less accurate than saying 94 percent of the bricks are usable. Similarly, to say a certain food, such as meat, is loaded or high in protein is deceptive. What we need to know is how much of that protein makes it past the digestive process and is actually usable by the body.

Were a food's amino acid distribution to match *exactly* the body's needs, the level of protein usability would be 100 percent. The term used to describe the potential percentage of any food's protein usability is biological value. The egg, for example, is of high biological value because more of its amino acids are able to be used by the body than any other food except human milk.

But before amino acids can be utilized, the food bearing them must be digested. (The amino acids must get into the bloodstream before they can be used by the cells.) The blanket term used to describe both a food's biological value and its relative digestibility is net protein utilization, or NPU. The egg, with its ease of digestibility and high biological value, has an NPU of 94 percent. That is, almost all of the egg's protein will be available to the body when the egg is digested. Other foods with either less digestibility or a less-ideal amino acid pattern will have correspondingly lower NPU ratings.

Meat and poultry, considering their traditional reputations as superior protein sources, don't rate as wonder foods on the NPU scale. (Only fish, with an NPU of 80, comes close to eggs.) Most meat and fowl contain about 30 percent protein. Their overall NPU is only about 67 percent. I say "only" because meat propaganda has led many to believe that flesh is somehow "pure" protein. But there are numerous nonflesh foods supplying adequate protein at less cost to one's pocketbook, body, and soul.

Milk seems low in protein (3½ to 5 percent) if you consider only quantity, but its NPU is an efficient 82 percent; skim, whole, buttermilk, and yogurt all have the same rating. Most cheeses have an NPU range of 70 to 75 percent. You could stop eating flesh foods today and easily get plenty of protein from milk products and eggs. But what about plant proteins? Are they inferior, as we've been led to believe?

Foods of animal origin *are* generally higher in biological value and NPU than plant foods. Animals eat plants or plant-eating animals and their bodies act (as do ours) as storehouses of protein. You can get more protein from less food when eating an animal-source food. Yet this doesn't mean plant proteins are inferior, only that they're less concentrated than animal foods and lacking some of the EAAs.

Must you eat concentrated proteins? Is *more* always better than *enough*?

People have been frightened away from vegetarianism by those charts listing the equivalent amounts of protein in various foods. To get as much protein from beans as you do from a steak, according to these charts, you'd have to eat beans to the point of becoming a threat to society, if not the structural strength of your house. Yet we've seen that a protein's *quality* generally means more than its rough *quantity*. Just because plant foods differ from animal foods in the amounts and patterns of their essential amino acids doesn't mean a vegetarian must eat with a shoehorn to get an adequate amount of protein. An amino acid is an amino acid regardless of its source. If a given food is low in one or more EAAs why can't we boost the quantity of the limiting amino acid, thus increasing the food's overall protein efficiency? We can. The process is called protein complementation.

Let's go back to our cell whose DNA/RNA code called for a protein structure of:

glycine       tryptophan       methionine

Recall that the missing tryptophan in the sample food meant no protein could be constructed. But suppose that, in addition to the deficient food, you ate some sunflower seeds or cashews or collard greens or drank a glass of milk at this same meal. All these foods contain relatively high amounts of tryptophan. Any of them would act to complement the lack of tryptophan in the other food, and the cell, having all its raw materials, could then create its protein.

This same complementary effect is possible with *all* foods. A poor pattern of EAAs in one food can be boosted by corresponding EAAs present in another food when both are eaten at the same meal. A mixture of rice and beans, for instance, is a staple in many cultures. If eaten at separate meals, both rice and beans remain deficient in several essential amino acids. But when the rice and beans are eaten together, the low isoleucine and lysine levels in the rice are complemented by the higher levels in the beans.

|  | Rice | Beans |
|---|---|---|
| isoleucine | low | high |
| lysine | low | high |
| tryptophan | high | high |

And while the NPU of most beans (except for soybeans) is comparatively low, combining the two foods effectively raises the total NPU. Thus, even two so-called incomplete foods can be combined to yield a protein source complete in the essential amino acids. Meat myths and traditions so prejudice the public's thinking, however, that some may find it difficult to believe that mixing vegetable matter can be as good as eating foods of animal origin. The nagging doubt persists that plant proteins are second-class foods. Nutritionists have no such doubts. As two scientists researching the use of plant proteins in the prevention of malnutrition pointed out:

> By combining different proteins in appropriate ways, *vegetable proteins cannot be distinguished nutritionally from those of animal origin.** The amino acids and not the proteins should be considered as the nutritional units.[3]

Even the conservative Food and Nutrition Board has this to say in its report on vegetarian diets:

> If this mixing of plant proteins is done judiciously, combinations of lower-quality protein foods can give mixtures of about the same nutritional value as high-quality animal protein foods. . . . [D]iets of properly selected plant foods can be nutritionally adequate.[4]

Misinformation has kept many from adopting a fleshless diet, even when their sensitivities and ethics actually favored it. The preceding data and arguments should help to ease their fears and convince them that a vegetarian regimen doesn't mean protein deprivation or, at the least, eating an inconvenient and unwieldy diet. And here's another factor to consider.

Several studies have shown that a constant pool of amino acids is always present in the gut and bloodstream, serving to maintain a uniform internal protein balance. These amino acids are endogenous—coming from the continual breakdown of intestinal wall cells, tissue proteins, and digestive secretions. When *food* amino acids are ingested, they mix with this reserve of internal amino acids. The process thus acts to even out any temporary EAA imbalances, such as might occur in a single meal.[5]

This mechanism does *not* mean that humans can either syn-

---

* Emphasis added

thesize the EAAs or subsist indefinitely on proteins deficient in the EAAs. Nor does the process give one license to eat willy-nilly, wrongly assuming that severe EAA deficiencies will automatically be compensated for in the gut. But the body's store of internal amino acids does suggest that vegetarians—particularly vegans— may be better protected against amino acid imbalances than once thought. Protein complementation appears to be both an internal and external process. If nothing else, these data suggest that our remarkable systems are constantly striving to maintain a state of balance. We needn't eat with a gram scale in one hand and an amino acid chart in the other.

Now that we know humans can get protein and the essential amino acids from nonanimal foods, the next question is obvious: how much protein is enough protein?

Vegetarians are questioned more about getting adequate protein than any other aspect of their diet. "How do you get enough?" people ask, wide-eyed. "You must eat a lot of soybeans." Some vegetarians snap back, "And you must eat a lot of steak," which is the vegetarian version of, "So's yer old man."

Protein is a nonnegotiable item in our diet. Unlike fat, protein cannot be stored in significant amounts, so we have a continuing need for it throughout our lives. Our entire body chemistry (metabolism), along with growth and tissue replacement, is directed by those proteins we call hormones and enzymes. Hemoglobin, the medium that carries oxygen from the lungs to the tissues, is made of protein, as are our hair, teeth, skin, nails, bones, serum blood cells, endocrine glands, muscles, organs, cells, fluids, and antibodies. Without this primary substance, as Mulder said, "No life appears possible."

But as we learned from the NPU ratings, getting enough protein isn't as simple as totaling up the number of grams of protein you're eating. Even the NPU may not be a reliable indication. NPU ratings are still largely theoretical. And how efficient are your individual digestive processes? How can you tell? Even with NPU ratings telling us how much protein is made available to our bodies, there is no simple way to determine how much of that protein is actually being used and at what rate by each individual.

A general answer to the "How much is enough?" question might be, "You need enough protein to make up for the protein your body is constantly using." "Stop waffling," you scream in frustration, grabbing me by the lapels. "How much protein do I need *exactly?*"

"Exactly," as my grandfather would say, "we don't know from nothing."

At the turn of the last century, German physiologists Max Rubner and Carl von Voit came to believe that an adult male's protein need was about 118 grams per day. Von Voit determined this in part by measuring the protein intake of German laborers. He also experimented with his laboratory assistant. One study involved feeding his assistant a daily ration of 100 grams (3½ ounces) of butter, one egg, 250 grams of meat, 450 grams of bread, and a half-liter of milk. The assistant went along with the experiment only on the condition that he could also have a daily liter of beer. Von Voit agreed, saw his employee remain healthy, and pronounced 118 grams of protein man's daily requirement.

Von Voit's disciple in the United States was W.O. Atwater. Atwater believed that an American laborer's protein need was 145 grams daily, while a sedentary worker might get by on 125 grams per day. (These amounts are more than twice the current Recommended Daily Allowance for protein set by the Food and Nutrition Board.) But Atwater, Rubner, and von Voit—like Liebig before them—had wrongly assumed that hard physical labor demanded a high protein intake. Modern nutritional science tells us, however, that protein needs remain relatively the same whether one is digging ditches or pushing a pencil. (The exceptions are for individuals doing hard physical work under arctic or tropical conditions, or for those purposely trying to build muscular bulk, such as body-building enthusiasts.) * Only the need for energy (calories) goes up as physical activity increases. Calories come principally from carbohydrates and fats, the best sources being grains, legumes, and fruits. Protein-rich foods do contain calories, but eating them in quantity is an expensive way to meet your energy needs.

Von Voit's estimates were also based on what he noted people were eating, and not on their actual needs. Using this logic, we might conclude that the average North American needs 100 pounds of sugar and 200 pounds of meat annually. Still, the high-protein advocates in Europe and the United States dominated nutritional thinking for decades. A high-protein diet heavy in flesh foods was almost universally considered the ideal. No wonder vegetarians seemed so radical, living on what appeared to be a starvation regimen. R.H. Chittenden, a Yale professor of physiological chemistry working in the early 1900s, was a maverick when he suggested that the high-protein supporters were far off the mark.

The professor spoke from personal experience. At 44, Chittenden was in poor health. He suffered from gall bladder trouble, headaches, and stiff knee joints. But he experimented on himself, purposely eating a low-calorie diet supplying only 40 grams of protein daily. In time, this diet produced positive results. All his physical complaints vanished; he dropped 20 excess pounds and reported an increase in his mental and physical vigor.[6] While never becoming a vegetarian, Chittenden ate little meat and remained on his low-protein diet until his death at 87. He maintained, throughout his career, that 35 to 50 grams of protein daily was probably an optimum intake for humans.

He conducted hundreds of experiments with Yale athletes and Army personnel, and his data convinced him that protein beyond the 35 to 50 gram limit was not conducive to health. Chittenden attracted supporters, and for most of this century the question of protein need has been split between the philosophic descendants of von Voit and Chittenden. But time has been on Chittenden's

* Those convalescing, especially after surgery, and those recovering from trauma or burns will have increased protein needs.

and vegetarianism's side. While there are still no simple answers to the protein question—that is, scientists have yet to arrive at a universally accepted minimum daily protein requirement—contemporary nutrition researchers now believe our protein needs are closer to Chittenden's estimate than von Voit's or Atwater's.

Determining protein needs is no easy matter, though it appears deceptively simple on paper. We know protein is composed of 16 percent nitrogen. We know also that nitrogen is constantly exiting the body—extensively through the feces and urine, less significantly through the skin, nails, hair, and perspiration. The body also uses nitrogen to create the protein of tissue, blood, and regulatory fluids. The minimum amount of protein necessary in the diet, then, would be just enough to offset these losses. This state of equilibrium is called nitrogen balance; it is the normal state for a healthy adult.

Nitrogen balance studies are used to determine protein needs by carefully measuring the minimum amount of nitrogen needed by a human subject in order to achieve a balance between loss and intake. Test results may vary because of testing conditions, variability among subjects, and the human body's remarkable ability to adjust to low levels of protein. But, says the most recent (1974) Recommended Daily Allowances report by the Food and Nutrition Board, the data from nitrogen balance studies and other research (adjusted for margins of error) show that an average human's minimum daily need for protein is about .213 grams of protein per pound of body weight per day (.47 grams per kilogram * of body weight per day.) That is, a 154-pound (70kg) man would require a minimum of roughly 33 grams of usable protein daily to maintain nitrogen equilibrium.

Don't take that as a hard-and-fast minimum, however. There are several factors to be considered: fear, anxiety, pain, and anger

* A kilogram is 2.2 pounds.

can increase your loss of nitrogen by as much as one-third.[7] Exposure to extremes of heat or cold, heavy perspiration, nondisabling infections, and what the Food and Nutrition Board calls "the cumulative minor stresses of life in a competitive society" [8] can all boost your need for protein. Stress can actually impede the absorption of amino acids into the bloodstream; you may ingest sufficient protein, but its usefulness may be reduced by the effects of emotional pressure. Caloric intake also affects protein utilization. The body puts energy needs above all else. If enough calories aren't available to fuel the system, the body will metabolize protein for energy; hence, less protein will be available for tissue construction and maintenance. The reverse is also true. An adequate supply of dietary carbohydrates will allow more protein to be used by the body for tissue synthesis. This is what nutritionists call the protein-sparing action of carbohydrates.

These factors mean nutritionists can't set a *fixed* protein requirement for the general population. Even your own personal protein needs may vary from day to day. To cover these variables, the Food and Nutrition Board has added a 30 percent safety margin designed to meet the needs of 98 percent of the U.S. population. This margin boosts the theoretical minimum to .28 grams of protein per pound of body weight per day (.6 grams per kilogram per day.)

These figures are based on a *total* absorption of protein, however—something that never actually happens, even in the laboratory. The figures must be further adjusted by estimating the biological quality of the total diet. Since the typical diet in the United States is a mixture of animal and plant proteins on at least a 50-50 basis, though often heavier on the animal side, we can assume a general NPU of 75 percent efficiency. (A lacto-ovo regimen has the same NPU.)

Now we can adjust our protein minimums by figuring in the NPU of the overall diet. A simple formula is used:

$$.28 \text{ grams/lbs/day }{}^{*} \times \frac{100}{75} = .37 \quad \text{or} \quad .6 \text{ grams/kg/day} \times \frac{100}{75} = .8$$

* grams per pound of body weight per day

Whether you're now eating a standard U.S. diet of mixed flesh and plant proteins or a lacto-ovo diet, you can figure your daily *range* of protein need by multiplying your weight in pounds by .37 or by .8 for kilograms. Thus, for healthy adults: a 128-pound (58 kg) nonpregnant female would need 47 grams of protein per day; a 154-pound (70 kg) male would need 57 grams of protein daily.

What about vegans and the rest of the world who rely by choice or circumstance on plant proteins? The NPU for a plant-based dietary is roughly 55 percent.

$$.28 \text{ grams/lbs/day} \times \frac{100}{55} = .51 \quad \text{or} \quad .6 \text{ grams/kg/day} \times \frac{100}{55} = 1.09$$

Vegans can easily determine their approximate daily range of protein need by dividing their body weight in half, since .51 is roughly one-half gram per pound.

The pregnant vegan, whose gross protein needs differ from her lactovarian and omnivorous sisters, can roughly figure the range of her increased protein need by dividing her body weight in half and adding on 66 percent of the total. For example:

$$128 \text{ lbs.} \div 2 = 64 + 66\% = 106 \text{ grams daily}$$

The lactating vegan also has an increased protein need of roughly 45 percent over the normal. The same formula may be used to compute this:

$$128 \text{ lbs.} \div 2 = 64 + 45\% = 93 \text{ grams daily}$$

These RDAs are suggestions—recommendations based on

statistical data and the overall needs of a diverse population. The RDAs are neither requirements nor minimums. As most nutritionists emphasize, diets that contain less protein than the allowances cannot be equated with protein deficiency.

Nutritional studies have repeatedly demonstrated that only relatively small amounts of good-quality protein are necessary for body maintenance.* Yet a kind of hysteria over getting enough protein is part of North American culture. Snippets of outdated data and nutritional nonsense, coupled with meat and dairy industry propaganda, cause Americans to regularly eat *twice* the RDA for protein, shoveling in meat, fish, and milk as though kwashiorkor were just around the corner.

The USDA estimates that the average U.S. consumer eats about 100 grams of protein daily, with about 70 percent derived from beef, pork, and dairy products. Aside from the potentially unhealthy high fat and cholesterol in this fare, the body burns excess protein for energy. If the additional calories from protein (or any source) aren't burned off, they will be stored as fatty tissue—another step toward obesity.

Some nutritionists believe a reasonable margin of protein over the minimum is good insurance, favoring efficient disease resistance and tissue health. But a superabundance of protein has no special benefits. Be concerned about getting adequate protein, but don't get carried away. Use your head before you open your mouth.

Vegetarians who regularly eat a balanced diet composed of a variety of whole foods, and who get adequate exercise, needn't fear getting too little or too much protein. Virtually every modern nutrition textbook says the same thing of a nonflesh diet:

> A vegetarian diet can be made entirely adequate in quality of proteins by the liberal use of legumes and cereal products, and by supplementing vegetable proteins with milk and milk products or with eggs.[9]

---

* Protein needs are increased considerably, however, for those suffering severe emotional or physical stress and those recuperating from an illness, surgery, burns, or other trauma.

What about the vegan? Many nutritionists are not enthusiastic about veganism. They believe a diet built solely on plant foods is more likely to be deficient in some key vitamins and trace minerals, if not protein. (A vegan—or anyone—not eating enough calories will cause the body to burn protein for energy. This reduces the amount of protein available for tissue construction and other bodily functions.)

The problem isn't necessarily with plant proteins, however. Plant sources, you'll recall, can be combined to yield good-quality protein—as useful as that from a mixed animal-plant diet. Even the Food and Nutrition Board cautiously admits that "individual pure vegetarians from many populations of the world have maintained seemingly excellent health." [10] Problems with veganism stem more from nutritional carelessness and cultism than from inherent defects in an all-plant dietary.

Numerous studies have shown that well-chosen vegan diets meet the RDAs for all nutrients, even slightly exceeding the RDA for protein.[11] A team of Harvard researchers investigating the effect of an all-plant diet found, as have similar studies, that

it is difficult to obtain a mixed vegetable diet which will produce an appreciable loss of body protein without resorting to high levels of sugar, jams, and jellies, and other essentially protein-free foods.[12]

Obviously, vegans *can* be well nourished. That some are not is due to the regimen's demand for considerably more sophistication and care than a lacto-ovo diet. Avoiding milk products and eggs means the vegan must be far more knowledgeable about nutrition than the average person—even the average lacto-ovo-vegetarian. This is why many nutritionists warn against attempting to raise infants or children as vegans.

The vegan must also be doubly sure to eat a variety of foods rather than relying on a small circle of vegetables and fruits. Vegan diets will be inadequate:

(1) when vitamin $B_{12}$ isn't provided.

(2) when the diet is composed of very low protein starchy foods.

(3) when the diet relies heavily on refined or over-processed carbohydrates.

(4) when not enough calories are ingested to maintain adequate protein utilization.[13]

The majority of nutritional problems among all humans, whether vegans or meat eaters, arises from eating a limited selection of foods. No food is perfect, supplying all our essential nutrients. The best nutritional insurance is to diversify your choice of foods. This task is made easier once you break away from the meat-makes-the-meal tradition.

Thus, the *careful* vegan needn't worry about suffering a protein deficiency. Well-chosen combinations of legumes, whole grains, seeds, soy milk, and other soy products will yield protein of good biological value.

"Okay," some people say, "meat may not be superior after all, but it's a lot more convenient than mixing and matching proteins. Who wants to spend all that time memorizing lists of amino acids, concocting meals like an alchemist?"

Another fallacy. Learning to mix plant proteins is no great mystery, nor is it as time-consuming as some critics make it out to be. The main elements of protein complementation are so simple they can be reduced to a few brief guidelines as easy to remember as your phone number.

Realize first that mixing proteins is a little like assembling a jigsaw puzzle: certain pieces fit together better than other pieces. When all the parts are correctly matched, the resulting picture is of more value than any of the single parts of which it's made. But fortunately, there's nothing puzzling about protein complementation. The essential amino acid strengths and weaknesses of most foods fall into consistent patterns. Matching them up involves no guesswork. You need only remember which *groups* of foods should be combined to match EAA strengths and weaknesses:

1. Mix grains with legumes.
2. Mix legumes with seeds.

3. Mix milk, milk products, or eggs with any or all plant proteins. (Milk and grains are an especially good complement.)

Here's a list of the major nonflesh protein foods.

GRAINS
barley
brown rice (short, long, or medium grain)
buckwheat
bulghur (partially pressure-cooked wheat)
corn (yellow and white)
millet
oats
rye
triticale (high-protein wheat)
wheat (hard or winter for bread; soft for pastry)
wheat germ

LEGUMES
beans:
black
broad (fava)
kidney
lima
mung
navy
pea
soy
cowpeas (black-eyed peas)
garbanzos (chick peas)
lentils
peas

SEEDS
pumpkin or squash
sesame
sunflower

## NUTS

| | |
|---|---|
| almonds | macadamia |
| brazil | pecans |
| cashews | peanuts |
| coconuts | pine nuts |
| hazel or filberts | pistachios |
| | walnuts (black or English) |

## AMINO ACID STRENGTHS AND WEAKNESSES IN FOOD GROUPS

**LEGUMES** (beans, peas, lentils)
*weak:* tryptophan, methionine, and cystine *
*strong:* lysine especially, and isoleucine

**GRAINS** (wheat, oats, rice, barley, millet, corn, etc.)
*weak:* lysine and isoleucine
*strong:* tryptophan, methionine, and cystine

**SEEDS/NUTS** (pumpkin, sunflower, sesame seeds, peanuts, etc.)
*weak:* lysine and isoleucine (except cashews and pumpkin seeds)
*strong:* tryptophan, methionine, and cystine

**MILK PRODUCTS**
*weak:* none
*strong:* lysine

**EGGS**
*weak:* none
*strong:* tryptophan, lysine, methionine, and cystine

**VEGETABLES**
*weak:* isoleucine, methionine, and cystine
*strong:* tryptophan and lysine

* Cystine is not an EAA, but its presence spares methionine.

Mixing these foods is hardly an arcane process. Many of the combinations will be familiar, and the possibilities are virtually endless, as a glance at vegetarian cookbooks will demonstrate. Here are a few examples.

## Grains and milk
milk and granola or whole-grain cereal
pasta and cheese
sandwich and milk
bread, rice pudding, pancakes, etc., made with milk
bread and cheese

## Grains and legumes
wheat bread enriched with soy flour
rice and beans
pea or bean soup and a sandwich or toast
tortillas and beans

## Legumes and seeds
sunflower or sesame meal in legume soup
nut loaf: ground seeds, nuts, and soy grits
hummus: sesame and garbanzos, a mid-Eastern dish

If you want more specific information, NPU ratings for various foods, charts, and recipes tailored to protein complementation, read *Diet for a Small Planet,* by Frances Moore Lappé. But be more concerned with food combinations—as Ms. Lappé suggests—than worried about rigid proportioning or trying to achieve a laboratory-perfect balance of amino acids. Ms. Lappé says of her own recipes, "Even if you do not follow the proportions exactly, you are probably still much better off for having combined the two foods than if you did not." [14]

Don't assume that you must increase your use of milk products or eggs to replace flesh foods. Milk (with its NPU of 82) and eggs (94) deliver more usable protein than do meat, fowl, or fish. Cheese is right behind with an NPU range of 70 to 75. When milk or eggs are mixed with plant protein, the meal's total NPU goes up significantly. And a little goes a long way.

A single egg supplies roughly 15 percent of your protein RDA. Milk is one of the least expensive sources of protein, and only two tablespoons of powdered milk mixed with a cup of wheat or rye flour boost the overall protein usability by almost 50 percent. Even when you mix plant proteins alone—in the right combinations—the NPU may increase by as much as 40 percent.[15]

If you still think it's difficult to get adequate protein without flesh foods, consider this list:

|  | *grams of protein* |
|---|---|
| yogurt (pint) | 16 |
| sunflower seeds (6 tbsp) | 14 |
| peanut butter (2 tbsp) | 8 |
| whole wheat or rye bread (2 slices) | 5 |
| wheat germ (2 tbsp) | 3 |

Just for the sake of this example, assume that during one day you ate *only* these foods in the small amounts listed. This minimal fare would still provide just over 46 grams of protein. That's more than three-quarters the RDA for a 154-pound male and virtually the total RDA for a 128-pound female adult.

A cube of cheese, two inches on each side, yields about 30 percent of the protein RDA for adults. Three cups of milk *or* seven ounces of beans would supply about 50 percent or more of their protein RDA.

A vegan's RDA for protein is higher, you'll recall, because an all-plant diet has a lower overall NPU. Vegans can drop the yogurt from the list above and add:

|  | *grams of protein* |
|---|---|
| tofu (soybean curds) (7 oz.) | 16 |
| peas (¾ cup) | 12 |

The list now yields 58 grams of protein—almost three-quarters the RDA for adult vegans.

I'm not suggesting you eat so limited a diet—just the opposite. But, assuming one has access to wholesome foods, these examples show that protein is hardly a problem for lacto-ovo-vegetarians. Vegans won't have a problem either, as long as they're willing to be diligent about their food choices.

If only a few small portions of nonflesh foods are enough to meet most or all of your daily protein need, then what can be wrong with a varied, well-chosen vegetarian diet? Nothing is wrong with it. Custom and meat market propaganda have only made it seem that way. Stop believing the old myths about vegetarians living on bland or inadequate fare. As Anna Thomas says in *The Vegetarian Epicure:*

> Vegetarian cookery . . . is a rich and various cuisine, full of many marvelous dishes with definite characteristics not in imitation of anything else—certainly not in imitation of meat. . . . [T]he only rules about arranging meals which need to be taken seriously are the rudimentary ones of pleasing the palate and maintaining good health.[16]

*Chapter Five notes.*

1. Mulder cited by Corinne H. Robinson, *Fundamentals of Normal Nutrition* (New York: Macmillan Co., 1971), p. 42.
2. Roger J. Williams, *Nutrition in a Nutshell* (New York: Dolphin Books, 1971), p. 29.
3. R. Bressani and M. Behar cited by U.D. Register and L.M. Sonnenberg, "The Vegetarian Diet," *Journal of the American Dietetic Association,* 62(3) (March 1973), p. 255.
4. Food and Nutrition Board, "Vegetarian Diets," (Washington, D.C.: National Academy of Sciences, 1974), p. 2.
5. E.S. Nasset, "Role of the Digestive Tract in the Utilization of Protein and Amino Acids," *JAMA* 164(2):172-177. See also: E.S. Nasset, "Amino Acid Homeostasis in the Gut Lumen and its Nutritional Significance," *World Review of Nutrition and Dietetics,* 14:134-53 (1972.)
6. Albert Von Haller, *The Vitamin Hunters* (Philadelphia: Chilton Co., 1962), pp. 130-133.
7. Henrietta Fleck, *Introduction to Nutrition,* 2nd ed., (New York: Macmillan Co., 1971), p. 63.
8. Food and Nutrition Board, *Recommended Daily Allowances* (Washington, D.C.: National Academy of Sciences, 1974), p. 43.
9. L. Jean Bogert, et al., *Nutrition and Physical Fitness* (Philadelphia: W.B. Saunders Co., 1973), p. 96.
10. Food and Nutrition Board, "Vegetarian Diets," p. 2.
11. M.G. Hardinge, et al., "Nutritional Studies of Vegetarians: Part V, Proteins and Essential Amino Acids," *Journal of the American Dietetic Association,* 48:28 (January 1966).
12. D.M. Hegsted cited in Register, et al., p. 254.
13. M.G. Hardinge and H. Crooks, "Nonflesh Dietaries III, Adequate and Inadequate," *Journal of the American Dietetic Association,* 45:537 (1964.)
14. Francis Moore Lappé, *Diet for a Small Planet* (New York: Ballantine Books, 1975), p. 158.
15. NPU data from Lappé.
16. Anna Thomas, *The Vegetarian Epicure* (New York: Vintage Books, 1972), p. 4.

# ❦ SIX ❧

# Vitamins, Minerals, and Energy

So far we've discussed protein as though it were the single most important substance in the diet. North Americans may eat as though it were, but there are about 50 different nutrients necessary to good human nutrition. No single food bears all these essentials. More importantly, these nutrients work together in complex patterns. Worrying about getting enough protein without considering the other essentials is poor nutrition and expensive.

The Recommended Daily Allowances (RDA) as set by the Food and Nutrition Board (FNB) have been used as a standard in the following discussion. The RDAs are reviewed and reissued every five years; recommendations are set or changed according to a combination of laboratory findings, statistical samplings, arbitrary judgments, and the personal biases of the Food and Nutrition Board members. Not all nutritionists, vegetarians, and health food advocates agree with the RDAs, believing them to be either too low or too high.

The primary value of the RDAs is as a reference point. RDAs are a nutritional index designed to provide a margin of safety well above what are believed to be minimal needs. The dietary allowances are set high enough, according to the FNB, to allow for individual variability and for some loss of nutrients in cooking and storing foods. The FNB is the first to caution against consulting the charts as Holy Writ. Failure to meet the RDAs for various nutrients is neither a sign of malnutrition nor dietary inadequacy. Your best nutritional insurance is to relax and eat a variety of foods. (The question of supplemental vitamins and minerals will be discussed later.)

This chapter is meant to provide a broad view of nutritional principles, while emphasizing those nutrients that may be of special interest to vegetarians. This section, like the preceding one on protein, should also help to inform those wondering whether a nonflesh or non-animal-food dietary can really provide optimum nutrition.

*Carbohydrates.* No matter what dieters may think, carbohydrates are essential in the diet. Protein may get the publicity, but the body's first requirement is for energy. Carbohydrates are needed for their protein-sparing effect, for normal metabolism, and for those processes that supply energy to our bodies. Carbohydrates are a group of substances that includes simple sugars (fructose, galactose, and glucose), disaccharides (lactose, maltose, and sucrose), and polysaccharides (cellulose, glycogen, and starch). Starches and sugars are used as energy, either immediately as glucose or stored in the liver and muscles as glycogen. Cellulose is indigestible but provides the bulk and fiber necessary for efficient waste elimination.

The trick is not to avoid carbohydrates, but to avoid those *refined* carbohydrates bearing nothing but calories. Refined sugar —whether white, brown, or raw—contains virtually no vitamins, minerals, or bulk, and is almost pure calories. Brown and raw sugar offer no additional advantages. Raw or turbinado sugar is simply that which hasn't gone through the final purification and whitening process. Brown sugar is white sugar that's been colored with a small amount of molasses. (Some ethical vegetarians avoid white sugar because a final step in its purification process may involve filtration through layers of charred beef bones.)

Many people prefer honey, pointing to its traces of vitamins and long history as a food and folk medicine. Conservative nutritionists believe the nutrients in honey are too infinitesimal to rank it of more value than table sugar. However you regard the controversy, honey does have more appeal than white sugar. There are dozens of honey varieties—everything from dark and dusky-tasting buckwheat to mild and light clover or orange blossom. And because honey is sweeter than table sugar, less can be used.

Blackstrap molasses is an end product of sugar refining. It is the dark syrup left after all crystalline sugar has been extracted from the sugar cane. Unlike refined sugar, blackstrap molasses has real food value, supplying calcium, magnesium, iron, and potassium. A few tablespoonfuls can make a worthy addition to the diet.

But added sweeteners of *any* kind are a matter of taste and habit, not necessity. Using molasses or honey instead of sugar is sensible only if every effort is made to use them sparingly, while also avoiding all the hidden sugar in prepared foods, canned fruits, bakery items, and beverages. It's better to get your sugar from an orange rather than a cupcake.

Eating foods high in refined sugar causes your blood sugar level to rise rapidly, giving a rush of energy. This burst is short-lived. The blood sugar soon drops precipitously, often causing fatigue and a craving for more sugar. (Whole foods rich in unrefined or complex carbohydrates do not cause this phenomenon.) People who eat a lot of refined sugar tend to eat less-nutritious foods. The body needs certain essential nutrients but none of these are found in sugar's empty calories. Eat too much sugar and you may wind up with a vitamin or trace mineral deficiency. Nutritionist Dr. Jean Mayer says sugar calories boost one's need for thiamin (vitamin $B_1$, needed to metabolize carbohydrates), and may also increase the need for chromium, a trace mineral.[1] The more sugar you eat, the fewer nutrients you take in. This creates a vitamin-mineral debt that can hardly be made up by the rest of your diet.

North Americans of all ages overdose daily on refined carbohydrates, eating about 102 pounds of sugar per capita annually.

(About 70 pounds of this comes from processed foods and soft drinks.) Excessive sugar consumption leads to obesity, tooth decay, and possibly heart disease and diabetes.

Nutritionists and health food advocates agree on this point: get your carbohydrates from foods providing nutrients and fiber. Stick with whole grains and products made from them, plus vegetables and fruits. (Eggs, dairy products, and flesh foods are poor carbohydrate sources. Vegetable and animal fats contain no carbohydrates.)

*Fat.* This is an ugly word in the weight-conscious United States. But let's distinguish between the roles of body fat and dietary fat. Fatty tissue—which may become excessive when more calories are ingested than can be burned as energy—acts as an insulation layer under the skin, conserving body heat. Fat cushions the vital organs, working like a shock absorber. Fat is also a component of every cell membrane, acts as a body regulator, and can be used as a supply of reserve energy.

Dietary fats are important for their palatability and satiety value, as a source of concentrated energy, as a carrier of the fat-soluble vitamins, and as a source of essential fatty acids. Of the latter, only one—linoleic acid—cannot be synthesized and must be derived from food. The richest sources are vegetable oils: safflower has the most, followed by sunflower, corn, cottonseed, soybean, sesame, and peanut oil. A tablespoon or two of any of these in salad dressing will supply a considerable ration of linoleic acid.

There are three types of fats to be aware of.

• *Saturated.* Hard at room temperature; primarily from animal sources—lard, butterfat, and the yellowish white fat of muscle meats. Saturated fat from coconut oil and palm oil may also be found in imitation dairy products.

- *Unsaturated or polyunsaturated.* Liquid at room temperature; found primarily in vegetable and seed oils. Vegetarian diets centered around grains, vegetables, and fruits generally contain more polyunsaturated fats than saturated fats.

- *Hydrogenated.* Polyunsaturated fats that have been changed to solids or semisolids by the addition of hydrogen. This process essentially converts polyunsaturates to saturated fats. Hydrogenated fats are found in various processed foods, including shortening, margarine, some peanut butter, chip-type snack foods, and some candies.

No RDA has been set for fat but many nutritionists believe we should derive no more than 35 percent of our total daily calories from fats. Americans not only exceed this limit, but they also eat far more saturated fat than is healthy for them. Many health authorities are now advising Americans to sharply reduce the amount of fat in their diets, particularly saturated and hydrogenated fats.

*Vitamins.* While all foods contain some vitamins, no vitamins contain protein, carbohydrates, or fats. You can't skip a meal and make up for it by taking vitamin pills instead. Vitamins are organic substances that help regulate bodily functions. Acting as coenzymes, vitamins aid the action of enzymes during the metabolism of food nutrients. About a dozen major vitamins have been identified, though more may yet be discovered. A deficiency in any one essential vitamin will produce a corresponding deficiency disease, generally (though not always), reversible when the missing vitamin is supplied again. Though present in small amounts, vitamins are crucial to the body's digestive, reproductive, nervous, and muscle systems. Vitamins also affect tissue growth and antibody production.

Whether you derive adequate vitamins from your diet or not will depend on environmental factors, your individual needs, the amount of food you eat, and the composition of your diet. Whole, unfabricated foods are the best source of all known and unknown nutrients. Junk foods fill you up with more shadow than substance. As Michael Jacobson points out in *Nutrition Scoreboard,* "Persons whose diet is one-fifth soda pop, chewing gum, and candy must obtain 100 percent of their nutrients from only 80 percent of their food." [2]

• *Vitamin A* is important to eye health, biochemical functions, and the condition of the skin and mucous membranes. You've probably heard that carrots and dandelion greens are high in vitamin A, but this is misleading. No plant food contains true (preformed) vitamin A. Plants contain carotene, which is converted to vitamin A within a person's body.

Preformed vitamin A is thus found only in animal-origin foods, especially liver, milk fat, and egg yolks. Preformed vitamin A is more efficiently utilized by the body because there is no conversion process. But efficiency isn't everything, thank goodness, or we'd all be eating some animal's liver. Vitamin A is a fat-soluble vitamin and is stored by the body. Eating regular rations of carotene-rich foods should not only supply adequate vitamin A reserves, but should also provide a wide range of additional nutrients and cellulose.

Note that the RDA for vitamin A is based on the assumption that most U.S. residents eat equal amounts of both preformed vitamin A from animal sources and carotene from plant foods. A vegan or one using little milk, milk products, or eggs, should at least *double* the RDA to allow for the conversion factor. [3]

Some people taking large amounts (50,000 international units or more daily) of preformed vitamin A in pill form over several months have developed symptoms of vitamin A overdose. You won't get a vitamin A overdose from eating too much carotene in vegetables or fruits, however. Toxicity doesn't occur because the carotene-to-vitamin-A conversion process is relatively slow.

Sources include whole milk (the amount depends on the

animal's diet, though synthetic A is generally added to containerized skim milk); egg yolks, butter, margarine; and yellow, yellowish red, and green fruits and vegetables (carrots, sweet potatoes, kale, tomatoes, apricots, spinach, and dandelion greens). Little vitamin A is found in muscle meats, vegetable oils, nuts, or grains.

• *Vitamin C* is probably the most controversial vitamin of the day, having attracted followers with the ardor of religious zealots. Its most avid boosters believe vitamin C cures or alleviates everything from runny noses and tennis elbow to cancer. More conservative souls acknowledge only that the vitamin is essential, that it prevents scurvy, that its presence helps maintain and form the protein of connective tissues, and that it influences wound healing and metabolic functions.

Emotional stress, shock, the trauma of burns and surgery, cigarette smoking, and possibly air pollution all increase one's vitamin C needs. The RDA is 45 mg daily, an amount vitamin C enthusiasts consider laughable. They suggest a daily intake of from one-half to one gram daily (1,000 mg)—more if an infection is present. Excess vitamin C is excreted in the urine. Whether long-term megadoses of the substance are healthful or harmful is still being debated by both laymen and scientists. A vegetarian diet generally provides more dietary vitamin C than a flesh-based regimen. Readers should do some research before making a decision on supplementary vitamin C.

Vitamin C is water soluble, easily lost in cooking water or by oxidation after harvest.

Sources include fruits and vegetables, especially citrus, tomatoes, green peppers, leafy greens, broccoli, cabbage, kale, rose hips, melons, mangos, Brussels sprouts, cauliflower, and potatoes. Animal-origin foods have little or no C.

• *Vitamin D* is fat soluble, stored by the body, and is crucial to the absorption and utilization of calcium and phosphorus. Adequate vitamin D is as important to pregnant women as it is to children, whose growing bones and teeth need plenty of stored calcium and phosphorus. A deficiency will cause rickets (soft bones) in children, producing deformed bone structure.

Vitamin D is called the "sunshine vitamin." Exposing the skin to sunlight causes a chemical reaction in the skin oils, creating vitamin D that is eventually absorbed into the system. Research has yet to establish how much vitamin D is produced by this process. (Summer sunlight is apparently more effective in vitamin D production than winter sunlight.)

A prolonged excess of vitamin D, again from pill popping rather than natural sources, is dangerous and perhaps deadly. Most nutritionists warn that total daily intake should not greatly exceed 400 international units. Vegans especially, if not everyone, should consider supplemental vitamin D, however, since some authorities estimate that even diets made up of the best (unfortified) food sources of vitamin D would yield only about 100 to 150 IU daily.[4]

Good sources are liver, butter, egg yolks, and milk. Fortified milk has 400 IU of synthetic vitamin D added per quart. Non-animal-origin vitamin D tablets of 400 IU potency are also available.

• *Vitamin E's* specific importance to human physiology is not yet fully understood. Arguments have been made that vitamin E, as alpha tocopherol, may be a cure for and prophylactic against heart disease. Others say high doses can restore impaired sexual function, protect against the effects of air pollution, and slow down the aging process. Vitamin E is known to be an antioxidant that acts to protect the body's store of vitamins A and C and unsaturated fatty acids. The most active boosters of vitamin E suggest a daily intake of 100 to 800 IU. The RDA is 12 to 15 IU.

Little vitamin E is found in animal foods; the best natural sources are wheat germ, wheat germ oil, cottonseed and corn oil, whole grains, and green vegetables.

• *Vitamin K* is the fat-soluble coagulation vitamin. An

antihemorrhagic, it influences the body's production of blood-clotting proteins. While deficiencies are rare and no RDA has been set, vitamin K is considered essential in the diet.

This vitamin is synthesized by bacterial action in the intestines and is found in plant foods: green and yellow vegetables, and leafy greens, especially cabbage, kale, and spinach. Animal foods and cereals contain little vitamin K.

*The B complex vitamins* are water soluble; excesses are excreted in the urine. The entire complex should be regularly derived from the diet. All the B vitamins play an essential role in metabolizing energy from carbohydrates, fats, and proteins. The B complex also helps to maintain the proper functioning of the nervous system.

• *Thiamine, $B_1$*, is a regulator in carbohydrate metabolism. Its other functions—aiding the nervous system, mental functions, and maintenance of a good appetite—are related to this primary role. Few foods contain abundant thiamine; we generally meet our needs through small amounts from a variety of foods.

The richest nonflesh source is brewer's yeast. Others are wheat germ, legumes (especially peas and soybeans), oranges, whole grains, and enriched cereals. Thiamine is easily destroyed by heat.

• *Riboflavin, $B_2$*, functions as a coenzyme in energy release; it also helps to activate $B_6$, folic acid, and $B_{12}$.

Brewer's yeast and beef liver contain the most; milk is the major source of riboflavin in the United States. Those not drinking milk may have difficulty getting adequate riboflavin unless they use brewer's yeast or other food sources: enriched cereals, whole grains, almonds, Brazil nuts, leafy greens, eggs, and cheese. Riboflavin in solution, as in milk, is damaged by exposure to light.

• *Niacin, B₃*, is important as a coenzyme in energy release; it aids in the maintenance of healthy skin, gastrointestinal tissue, and the nervous system. Getting enough protein influences one's niacin intake. The amino acid tryptophan is converted in the body to niacin; the process requires the presence of thiamine, riboflavin, and pyridoxine. Sixty milligrams of tryptophan may produce roughly one milligram of niacin. A diet with adequate protein may boost one's niacin intake by one-third.

The best nonflesh source is brewer's yeast. Niacin is also found in legumes, peanut butter, and whole-grain and enriched breads and cereals.

• *Pyridoxine, B₆*, plays a major role as part of the enzyme systems that affect protein metabolism; the vitamin also functions in the release of energy from glycogen and in the synthesis of hemoglobin and antibodies. Women taking oral contraceptives have a higher need for pyridoxine and folic acid (and probably vitamin C.)[5]

Sources are muscle meats, liver, egg yolks, brewer's yeast, whole grains, bananas, and vegetables.

• *Vitamin B₁₂* is one vitamin careless vegans may have difficulty obtaining since it is primarily found in animal-origin foods. B₁₂ is a crucial vitamin: interacting with folic acid, B₁₂ governs the production of red blood cells in the bone marrow. A deficiency may result in neurological disturbances and pernicious anemia, though symptoms of depression, stiff limbs, and irritability may not appear for two or three years.

B₁₂ must be acted upon in the intestine by the intrinsic factor, a substance present in gastric secretions. The intrinsic factor binds itself to B₁₂ and facilitates its absorption. Some people, due to a genetic trait rather than diet, may fail to produce the intrinsic factor. Even though they may eat flesh or B₁₂-rich foods, little of the vitamin actually gets into the bloodstream and they suffer deficiency symptoms.

Many vegans dispute the need for animal sources of $B_{12}$, claiming that humans are capable of synthesizing the vitamin in the gut. This is true—with an explanation. Some $B_{12}$ is created naturally in the large intestine when microorganisms interact with cobalt. Not all scientists agree, however, that this synthesis is sufficient to provide $B_{12}$ in adequate amounts throughout one's life. The function, synthesis, and absorption of this vitamin is not yet fully understood.

Some studies of vegans show their serum $B_{12}$ levels to be low but within a normal range after more than a decade without a dietary source of $B_{12}$. Other vegans have developed deficiency symptoms after only several years on an all-plant diet. A potential $B_{12}$ deficiency is nothing to flirt with; undetected or misinterpreted symptoms can become irreversible conditions and can lead to death.

The amount of $B_{12}$ required by most humans is minute. The RDA is three micrograms; * some researchers believe even this is higher than necessary. Milk and eggs provide enough $B_{12}$ to prevent deficiencies in lacto-ovo-vegetarians. Many vegans take a vitamin $B_{12}$ pill daily or weekly as insurance against a deficiency. $B_{12}$ tablets made from nonanimal materials are widely available.

Animal foods, particularly liver, are the richest sources of $B_{12}$. Milk and cheese supply some $B_{12}$; eggs are as $B_{12}$-potent as steak. (Yogurt is *not* a good source; the $B_{12}$ in the milk is depleted by the bacterial action of fermentation.) Soy milk, meat analogs, and brewer's yeast are available with added $B_{12}$. Some varieties of seaweed, some beers, and miso also yield small—probably inadequate—amounts of $B_{12}$.[6]

• *Folic acid* interacts with $B_{12}$ to produce red blood cells, functions with the body's enzyme system, and is especially important when cells are rapidly reproducing or being synthesized. If a person is severely deficient in $B_{12}$ but obtain-

---

* A microgram is one-millionth of a gram.

ing adequate folic acid, the $B_{12}$ deficiency symptoms may be masked by the folic acid. The neurological damage caused by the lack of $B_{12}$—degeneration of the spinal cord and surrounding nerves—may then continue undetected, leading to permanent disability.

Folic acid is widely distributed in plants: leaf lettuce, legumes, spinach, oranges, bananas, mushrooms; it is also found in nuts and grains.

• *Pantothenic acid,* like other members of the B complex, functions as part of the body's enzyme system. It's important in the release of energy and in the synthesis of many body compounds.

Pantothenic comes from the Greek *pantos,* meaning 'everywhere,' and the vitamin is widely distributed in many foods. Liver and kidney are the richest sources, but good nonflesh sources include brewer's yeast, egg yolk, wheat bran, and fresh vegetables—particularly peas, limas, and broccoli.

• *Biotin* plays a role in the utilization of carbohydrate, fat, and protein.

Biotin is found in most foods and is synthesized by bacteria in the human intestines. Nonflesh sources include egg yolks, milk, brewer's yeast, mung bean sprouts, cooked soybeans and some fruits, vegetables, and nuts.

The B complex is just that—a matrix of interacting compounds. Get your B complex from natural food sources rather than dosing yourself with individual B-vitamin pills (excepting $B_{12}$). If you choose to use pills containing the *entire* B complex, take them with your meals so all nutrients are present at the same time.

*Minerals* are necessary to the body as chemical regulators and as construction materials. Calcium, chlorine, magnesium, phosphorus, potassium, sodium, and sulphur are the macrominerals found in large amounts in the human system. Chromium, cobalt, copper, fluorine, iodine, iron, manganese, molybdenum, selenium, and zinc are called micro or trace minerals since they occur in comparatively tiny amounts.

• *Calcium* makes up about two percent of an adult's body weight—more than any other mineral. Ninety-nine percent of body calcium is found in the bones and teeth, but this mineral also affects nerve impulses, enzyme activation, blood clotting, and muscular contraction and relaxation. Calcium also serves as a catalyst for many biological reactions.

The Food and Nutrition Board has set an RDA for calcium, but it carries an important qualification for vegetarians: excessive protein intake tends to limit calcium absorption, thus increasing one's daily calcium needs.[7] Most of the world's people don't eat as much protein as do North Americans. The World Health Organization's RDA is 400 to 500 mg of calcium daily. But the Food and Nutrition Board, recognizing that U.S. residents habitually overeat protein, has set the RDA at 800 mg for adults. Since most vegetarians would be likely to eat close to the protein RDA, they might safely get along on less calcium—about 500 mg daily.

Milk and milk products supply large amounts of calcium. Two cups of milk (skim or whole), or yogurt, or two ounces of most hard cheeses, or two cups of cottage cheese will yield about 500 to 600 mg of calcium. Vegans may rely on soybeans, leafy greens (kale, mustard, collards, and dandelion greens are good sources), and sesame seeds. Spinach, chard, beet greens, rhubarb, and lambsquarters—members of Chenopodiaceae, the goosefoot family—appear to be good sources, but they're not. Their calcium is tied up with oxalic acid, a substance that forms insoluble calcium oxalate and renders the calcium in the vegetable useless to the body. (Don't avoid such greens because of this, however; they're also rich in other vitamins and minerals.)

Other sources include blackstrap molasses, soybeans and other legumes, figs, apricots, and dates. (Fruits supply some calcium; what they yield is well absorbed. Calcium is best absorbed in an acid medium.) Meat, grains, and most nuts contain low levels of calcium.

• *Phosphorus,* like calcium, is widely distributed in the body, influences bone and teeth formation, enables energy to be stored and released, and affects all metabolic processes. Calcium and phosphorus should ideally be ingested on a rough 1:1 ratio for optimum calcium utilization and absorption. Excessive phosphorus intake causes decreased calcium absorption in the body. The body then draws its calcium needs from that stored in the bones. A diet low in calcium and high in phosphorus—soft drinks and flesh foods, for example—may result in a calcium-phosphorus imbalance.

Flesh foods contain large amounts of phosphorus; other sources include milk, eggs, cereal grains (especially wheat germ, whole grains, and oatmeal), cashews, peanuts, dried beans and peas. Brewer's yeast is naturally high in phosphorus; some brands have been fortified with additional calcium to achieve a better ratio. Vegetables and fruits are generally low in phosphorus. Nutritionists assume that a diet with enough protein and calcium will contain adequate phosphorus.

• *Sodium, chloride, and potassium* work together to control the body's fluid balance, acid-alkaline ratio, nerve responses, and muscular contractions. Most North Americans eat far more sodium than their bodies require. Heavy use of table salt, prepared foods, snacks, and sodium compound additives (MSG, sodium nitrate, sodium nitrite, sodium citrate) causes the public to ingest anywhere from two to six times more sodium than needed. While researchers debate whether excessive sodium consumption causes high blood pressure or heart disease, there is evidence that hypertension can be reduced if salt intake is cut back. Excessive salt usage is also known to increase fluid retention—of importance to dieters. Added salt, like table sugar, is an acquired taste and habit. Provided one has access to sodium-bearing foods, no added salt is necessary in the diet.*

---

* Those people doing hard physical labor in extreme heat may need additional sodium to replace losses.

Sodium and chloride are found in meats, milk, eggs, seafood, seaweed, and table salt. Fruits and many vegetables are low in these minerals. Potassium is found in almost all plant and animal foods. Especially rich sources are brewer's yeast, bran, potatoes, molasses, bananas, oranges, and other fruits and vegetables.

• *Magnesium* is found in bones and soft tissues and acts as a catalyst in many biological functions: energy release, synthesis of body compounds, absorption and transportation of nutrients, and transmission of nerve impulses and muscle contractions. Most people in the United States don't obtain the RDA from their diets, especially those eating a lot of refined and junk foods.

Found chiefly in fresh green vegetables, magnesium is part of the chlorophyll molecule. You'll also come by it in seafoods, seaweed, soy flour, nuts, tofu, whole grains, molasses, and sesame seeds.

• *Sulphur* is found in every cell and is related to protein activity. No dietary deficiency symptoms have been noted among humans, nor has an RDA been established.

Sources include the amino acids methionine and cystine, wheat germ, cheese, peanuts, lentils, kidney beans, lean beef, and clams.

• *Iron* combines with protein to form hemoglobin, the substance that carries oxygen from the lungs to the organs and tissues. Getting the RDA for iron appears to be difficult for vegetarians, but it is for meat eaters too. Iron deficiency anemia is a common problem throughout the world, affecting those in developed and underdeveloped countries. U.S. men are relatively free of iron deficiencies, but an iron lack is common in U.S. women (particularly when pregnant), children, and infants. Reasons for this lack include the increasing reliance on iron-poor processed foods and the decline in the use of cast-iron cookware. Those clunky pots discarded for Teflon actually contributed significant amounts of dietary iron. An American Medical Association publication estimates that the available iron in food can be increased by 100 to 400 percent when prepared in iron cookware.[8]

Getting 18 milligrams of iron—the RDA for women 11 to 50—without getting too many calories isn't easy. Some nutritionists suggest that women take iron supplements to help meet the RDA. Pregnant women would need an iron supplement of 30 to 60 mg over the RDA to insure adequate reserves. (Check with your obstetrician or nurse-midwife.)

The iron from animal-source foods (heme iron) is more efficiently absorbed into the bloodstream than iron from plant sources. Many vegetables, such as spinach, contain much iron, but little of it gets through the digestive process. An exception is the soybean and its products. Soybeans have a high iron content, and the mineral is in a form more easily assimilable than from other vegetable sources.

The presence of vitamin C increases iron absorption— an important point, since vegetarian diets tend to be higher in that vitamin than flesh-based diets. Absorption is also governed by one's needs. An adult with adequate iron reserves might absorb only five percent of food iron, while a child eating the same meal might absorb 20 percent or more.[9] Numerous studies of vegetarians and vegans have repeatedly shown their intake of dietary iron to be within the RDA.[10]

Liver is the richest source, but eggs, leafy greens, potatoes, dried fruits, whole-grain breads and cereals, soybeans and soy products (other than oil), pumpkin seeds, and molasses are also good sources. (White bread and other white flour products are usually enriched with iron.)

• *Iodine* is an important component of thyroxine, the thyroid hormone that regulates key metabolic functions. Iodine deficiency conditions—principally goiter—have been reduced in the United States by the use of iodized salt. A teaspoon of iodized salt contains about one milligram of iodine. A pinch or so should supply the RDA. Those who wish to avoid table salt can use powdered kelp or other edible seaweeds as nourishing sources of iodine and other minerals.

Powdered or granular kelp contains one milligram of iodine per teaspoonful.

Small amounts of iodine occur in most foods, varying according to soil and fertilization characteristics of a farming area. Seafood and seaweed are the best natural iodine sources. Little is found in vegetables, legumes, or grains. The iodine content of milk and eggs depends on what the animals have been fed.

• *Zinc* is important in the maintenance of normal taste acuity and growth, particularly sexual maturity, as a component of insulin, as an influence on the healing of wounds and burns, and as part of numerous enzymatic functions. Poor dietary choices and health habits may contribute to a zinc deficiency. Highly refined and fabricated foods are low in zinc and other trace minerals. Excessive alcohol consumption can also cause one to excrete large amounts of zinc.

Getting adequate zinc should be of particular importance to vegetarians and vegans. Some researchers believe the zinc in plants is less available than that in animal-source foods.[11] Careless vegans might not get sufficient zinc from their diets.

Sources are flesh foods, eggs, milk, cheese, seaweed, pumpkin seeds, whole grains, legumes, and some brands of brewer's yeast.

The following *trace minerals* are essential in human nutrition but no RDA has been set for them—with the exception of copper.

• *Chromium* affects the body's ability to metabolize glucose.

Vegetables, brewer's yeast, whole grains, and fruits contain chromium, but the mineral is lost in refined foods.

• *Cobalt* plays an essential role as a component of vitamin $B_{12}$.

Vegans might have difficulty deriving adequate cobalt as its chief sources are foods of animal origin.

Sources are flesh foods, milk, and seaweed. Cobalt is found to a limited extent in land plants, but few data are available on its content or distribution.

• *Copper* influences iron absorption and hemoglobin formation, and acts as a component of various enzymes.

Copper finds its way into the diet through liver, shell-fish, nuts, whole grains, green leafy vegetables, brewer's yeast, and dried legumes.

• *Fluorine* is important in the structure and formation of teeth and bones. Sodium fluoride is added to drinking water in many cities in an attempt to reduce the incidence of tooth decay among children. Some areas have ground water naturally high in fluorine.

Fluoridated water is a controversial source. Fluorine occurs naturally in seafoods, seaweeds, and tea; the content in land plants varies according to soil conditions.

• *Manganese* affects bone formation and is an element in various enzyme systems.

Blueberries and wheat bran have the highest content; nuts, whole grains, tea, legumes, peanut butter, all vegetables, and fruits also contain manganese.

• *Molybdenum* is a component of the enzymes that influence iron reserves.

Organ meats and legumes are the best sources; cereals and brewer's yeast yield it also.

• *Selenium* works with vitamin E, in protecting red blood cells. It is toxic at certain levels, though toxicity from natural foods has only been noted in areas where the selenium content of the soil was quite high.

Seafood, seaweed, brewer's yeast, milk, and cereals (especially wheat) contain selenium.

This brief survey of human nutritional needs should demonstrate that flesh foods are hardly the indispensable foods they're supposed to be. Misconceptions about vegetarianism, the prejudice against a nonflesh diet, and the social importance of meat have long obscured a simple fact: good nutrition is not dependent on eating meat, fowl, or fish. Indeed, plant foods alone supply a majority of key nutrients—vitamins A, C, E, and K; linoleic acid, magnesium and several other trace minerals. The richest source of the B complex is brewer's yeast, a powdery food composed of one-celled plants. Calcium, phosphorus, and the trace minerals are well distributed in milk, milk products, eggs, and a variety of plant foods. Even vitamin $B_{12}$ should present no problem for vegans willing to use fortified foods.

In short, *a well-chosen nonflesh diet can easily supply all the nutrients known to be essential to human growth and maintenance.* Flesh foods have important nutritional values for those who eat them, but nothing in meat, fowl, or fish makes their use compulsory. A vegetarian regimen has long been erroneously classed as a nutritional risk. Yet the facts are clear: dropping a flesh-based diet and switching to greater use of grains, vegetables, fruits, seeds, and nuts can actually *increase* your intake of essential nutrients while reducing your consumption of calories and saturated fats.

Most nutrition texts contain a "Daily Food Guide" as an aid to deriving adequate and balanced nourishment through intelligent food selection. Here's a Daily Food Guide modified to meet the health-minded vegetarian's needs.

(Choose food grown without harmful pesticides or fumigants whenever possible. Food grown in composted, mineralized soil, as in well-managed organic gardens or farms, will generally be higher in trace minerals than food grown under less-ideal conditions.)

• *Grains, nuts, seeds, beans, peas, lentils.* Have two servings or more of protein-complemented combinations daily. Grains and milk for breakfast; sandwich and nut butter, bean spread, or cheese for lunch; legume/grain casserole, quiche, bean soup, vegetable-rice-legume stew, nut loaf, etc. for dinner.

Include several servings of whole grains daily. These may take the form of breakfast cereals, noodles, spaghetti, macaroni (whole wheat pasta is available), brown rice, and several slices of yeast-raised whole-grain bread.

• *Milk products and eggs.* Vegetarian parents concerned about providing their children with adequate calcium, $B_{12}$, and riboflavin may wish to follow the standard nutritional guidelines for daily milk use, below. (Calcium, $B_{12}$, and riboflavin can, of course, be derived from several other sources. Milk is simply the most convenient and concentrated source.)

| Age group | Cups of milk |
|---|---|
| Children under 9 | 2 to 3 |
| Children 9 to 12 | 3 or more |
| Teenagers | 4 or more |
| Adults | 2 or more |

Milk may also be used as cheese:

1-inch cube of cheddar-type cheese $= \frac{1}{2}$ cup milk

$\frac{1}{2}$ cup of cottage cheese $= \frac{1}{3}$ cup milk

Yogurt is more easily digested and its protein better assimilated than regular milk; it has roughly the same nutritional content as the milk it was made from, though some commercial yogurts are higher in protein than an equivalent amount of liquid milk due to added milk solids.

Vegans often use soy milk. While it is higher in iron, thiamine, and niacin than cow's milk, soy milk is lower in calcium, phosphorus, and riboflavin. Soy milk can be made at home, though commercially available mixtures have generally been fortified with various minerals and vitamins, including $B_{12}$.

Eggs can be eaten as such or included in dishes. This latter method makes use of egg protein without causing cholesterol-conscious people to eat too many eggs. Many recipes involving eggs may only deliver the equivalent of one-third of an egg per serving.

• *Vegetables and fruits.* Include at least one serving of a vitamin C-rich fruit or vegetable each day. Oranges, grapefruit, cantaloupes, peppers, broccoli, and strawberries are a few excellent sources.

Include one serving of a good vitamin A source at least every other day. Dandelion greens, kale, collards, winter squash, chard, spinach, and carrots (cooked, shredded, or juiced) are a few good vegetable sources; watermelon, apricots, mangoes, and cantaloupes are good fruit sources of vitamin A.

Vegetables and fruits should play a major role in the health-conscious vegetarian's diet. Regular consumption of these foods provides not only essential nutrients, calories, and fiber, but the foods themselves are also aesthetically appealing. Fruit and vegetable salads should be eaten daily. And all manner of fruit can be eaten out of hand throughout the day, replacing the junk food and coffee break.

What about taking vitamin pills? Some vegetarians, nutritionists, and health food advocates argue that taking vitamin pills is unnatural and expensive, that we should get all our nutrients only from our food. This is certainly the ideal approach. A daily multiple vitamin pill can't make up for a faulty diet.

But, unfortunately, we do not live in an ideal world. U.S. food production and distribution is highly centralized; so-called fresh fruits and vegetables may lose some of their nutrients as they travel long distances to market. And even if you eat only homegrown food, modern environmental factors may inhibit your ability to fully absorb essential nutrients or may increase your need for them. The effects of air pollution, for example, may demand more vitamin E and C than can be obtained from a standard diet. Some research has also demonstrated that relatively large amounts of vitamin A and C may inhibit the formation of certain cancers linked to environmental factors.[12] How are our nutritional needs affected by the sea of untested chemicals, pesticidal residues, pollution, and stress in which we find ourselves? Scientists are only just beginning to study this issue.

Should you take vitamin and mineral supplements? The question isn't restricted to vegetarians. Used sensibly, nutritional supplements are cheap protection against the ill-understood ravages of modern society. Still, the cornerstone of good nutrition is a sensible diet, not a drawer full of pills and powders. The best health insurance of all seems to be a well-chosen vegetarian diet from varied sources and a life free of junk foods, table sugar and salt, chemical additives, tobacco, excessive alcohol consumption, stress, and sedentary living. Supplemental vitamins and minerals might seem superfluous in such an ideal lifestyle; then again, they may be your best investment.

Many people still believe that vegetarians are a pasty-faced, slump-shouldered lot too weak to snap a celery stalk. These beliefs, however popular, don't square with the facts. One of the earliest investigations into the mythical strength-building qualities of flesh foods was conducted in 1907 at Yale University. Professor Irving Fisher formulated a series of tests to "determine the relations of certain dietetic factors to endurance, particularly the factors of proteid [sic] and flesh foods."

Fisher selected 49 men including three groups: flesh-eating athletes, abstaining athletes, and abstaining sedentary subjects. (The word vegetarian was avoided because of its ethical and religious overtones and because some of the abstainers weren't strict vegetarians. A few used small amounts of meat once a week or less. Fisher called the meat eaters "flesh eaters" to emphasize their use of all kinds of meat, fowl, and fish.)

The three groups were subjected to exercises designed to test their endurance: holding their arms outstretched for as long as possible, doing deep knee bends to exhaustion, and repeating leg raises. Fisher purposely weighted the tests against the abstainers to give them a "severe and decisive test." (Fisher wasn't concerned about the philosophical aspects of vegetarianism. His primary concern was to draw some conclusions about the relative merits of high- and low-protein diets.)

Fisher was startled by the test results. "Of the three groups compared," he wrote, "the large flesh eaters showed far less endurance than the abstainers, even when the latter were leading a sedentary life." In the deep knee bending test, for example, only one of the flesh-eating athletes was able to do 1,000 knee bends. Six of the abstainers hit that mark—and one of them was classed as "sedentary." Two abstaining athletes performed more than 2,000 deep knee bends. None of the flesh-eating athletes matched this—only one came within half of that mark. (Fisher was convinced everyone worked to their limit. He watched one of the flesh-eating athletes faint after 502 knee bends.) Overall, the abstainers averaged twice as many knee bends as the flesh eaters. Their achievements in arm holding and leg raises also generally outclassed the flesh eaters.

After discounting various psychological, emotional, and physical factors—which actually favored the flesh eaters—Fisher concluded that

> the difference in endurance between the flesh eaters and the abstainers [was due] entirely to the difference in their diet . . . [and] that, whatever the explanation, there is strong evidence that a low-proteid [sic], nonflesh, or nearly nonflesh dietary is conducive to endurance.[13]

Professor Fisher's educated guess was scientifically established almost 60 years later when a series of experiments in Denmark provided a key to the flesh abstainer's surprising performances.

Danish researchers tested men on a variety of diets, using a stationary bicycle to measure their energy output. Nine male subjects were first put on a mixed diet of meat and vegetables. After three days on this fare, the men were tested on the bicycle. The average time pedaled was one hour and 54 minutes. The men then ate a high-protein diet rich in meat, milk, and eggs. When tested again after three days, they were able to pedal only an average of 57 minutes. The last three-day diet consisted of only cereals, bread, vegetables, and fruits. This time the subjects pedaled an average of two hours and 47 minutes, *with some of the men exceeding four hours.* A Danish doctor reviewing these results made this conclusion:

> The fact that muscles are built of protein makes it tempting to conclude that ingestion of extra protein stimulates muscle growth and improves muscle strength. Such thoughts have influenced the athlete's diet for at least 2,500 years . . . [but] protein is not a special fuel for working muscle cells. Fats and carbohydrates are. . . . [C]onsumption for several days of a carbohydrate-rich diet will improve the capacity for prolonged exercise.[14]

This helps explain how Professor Fisher's flesh-abstaining athletes and sedentary subjects could outdo meat-eating athletes. A vegetarian diet is naturally higher in carbohydrates than one centered around flesh, milk, and eggs. The flesh-eating athletes in the Yale experiments—some of whom ate meat three times a day—may have been literally bogged down by the heavy diet they followed for its supposed endurance-building qualities.

This traditional "meat-makes-might" philosophy still keeps many pro and amateur athletes chained to a training table piled high with animal proteins. The idea of vegetarian athletes has never gone over too well with U.S. sports fans. A "rabbit food" diet may be okay for a cerebral chess player or a crossword puzzle champ, but real athletes need real food—red meat. This ingrained prejudice, however, hardly squares with the reality of vegetarians in athletics.

Paavo Nurmi, the Flying Finn, set 20 world running records between 1920 and 1932 and won nine Olympic medals. Nurmi trained on a vegetarian diet.

In 1956, vegetarian swimmer Bill Pickering of Great Britain swam the English Channel in record-breaking time.

That same year, 17-year-old Australian Murray Rose became the world's youngest Olympic triple gold medal winner, taking honors for swimming the 400- and 1,500-meter freestyle and the 1,500-meter marathon events. Rose returned to the Olympics in 1960 to again win gold and silver medals, retaining his 400-meter title—the first swimmer in Olympic history to do so. He went on in later years to set new records in the 400- and 1,500-meter events. Rose had been a vegetarian since he was two years old.

Endurance? The current world record for continuous sit-ups—17,003—is held by a vegetarian, Marine Captain Alan Jones of Quantico, Virginia. (A vegetarian *Marine?* Yes, and Captain Jones also runs 100 miles a week for exercise.)

Probably the largest number of vegetarian athletes can be found in Great Britain, where vegetarianism has always been relatively popular. The Vegetarian Cycling and Athletic Club, founded in 1887, boasts of holding scores of national and local records in wrestling and long-distance cycling, running, and walking. The club points out that although vegetarian athletes are a minority in Great Britain, they consistently win events far out of proportion to their small numbers.

The most celebrated U.S. vegetarian athlete currently is basketball star Bill Walton of the Portland Trailblazers. When Walton first came into national prominence, his lifestyle was a source of controversy. Sports writers chided him when his performance was weak, ascribing his failures to a kooky diet. When Walton looked good, writers implied it was in spite of his strange eating habits. But times are changing. A recent article in *Sports Illustrated* mentioned Walton's food preferences only in passing, calling him the "world's best all-around basketball player."

Three other vegetarians deserve mention here. While they are not athletes, they might win medals for their vitality. Consider comedian-social activist Dick Gregory, who regularly runs long distances to publicize the issues of world hunger and peace. Gregory, who was once an overweight chain-smoker, has run the 700 miles from Chicago to Washington, D.C., averaging 30 to 40 miles a day, on a diet of only fruits and vegetables.

And one of the best testimonials to the energizing qualities of a sound vegetarian diet can be found in the lives of Helen and Scott Nearing. Their books *Living the Good Life, The Maple Sugar Book,* and others, and their Maine farm have become rallying points for the self-sufficiency and organic gardening movements in this country and Europe. If anyone remains unconvinced that a vegetarian diet can maintain strength and health, let him read the words of Helen Nearing as she describes the vigorous life she and her husband have followed for almost 50 years:

> As vegetarians, we raised our own food, ate it and enjoyed excellent health. We cut our own firewood, cooked and heated with it. We built up the topsoil by adding compost and other organic matter, drained and filled in swamps, dug a pond, thinned and weeded our wood lot, clearing some additional acres from which we could cut hay, and built a sun-heated greenhouse. . . .[15]

One can hardly imagine a more robust life than that pursued by the Nearings. The pond referred to was the result of Scott Nearing's labors with only a pick and shovel. Energy on a vegetarian diet? In his fifties, Nearing hauled out 15,000 wheelbarrow loads of sod and muck to complete the job. Both Nearings are also well known for their construction of natural stone buildings— they've built more than a dozen. They haul and place the heavy rocks and mortar by hand. And when Helen Nearing wrote the words above in 1974, both she (at age 73) and Scott (94) were hard at work building two more large stone structures on their farm.

That a vegetarian diet of simple homegrown food could long sustain the Nearings' physically and intellectually active lives may come as a surprise to those accustomed to thinking of vegetarianism as a sacrifice. Yet this is what vegetarians have been trying to convince people of for centuries—that a sensible nonflesh diet can, in Scott Nearing's words, "maintain a healthy body as an operating base for a sane mind and a purposeful harmless life." [16]

*Chapter Six notes.*

1. Dr. Jean Mayer cited by the U.S. Senate Select Committee on Nutrition and Human Needs, *Dietary Goals for the U.S.* (Washington, D.C.: February 1977), p. 44.

2. Michael Jacobson, *Nutrition Scoreboard* (New York: Avon Books, 1975), pp. 70-71.

3. Eva D. Wilson, et al., *Principles of Nutrition,* 3rd ed., (New York: John Wiley, 1975), p. 223.

4. *Ibid.,* p. 229.

5. Jacobson, p. 92.

6. The herb comfrey is often referred to as a good source of $B_{12}$. A recent analysis of comfrey leaves, however, revealed only traces of the vitamin (about 0.4 of a microgram per kilogram of leaves), hardly enough to meet normal human needs. See "Vitamin $B_{12}$ for Vegans," letter in the *Lancet,* 2(6084):458 (13 August 1977). Some information on $B_{12}$ in miso can be found in William Shurtleff and Akiko Aoyagi, *The Book of Miso* (Brookline, Massachusetts: Autumn Press, 1976).

7. Wilson, p. 156. See also S. Margen, et al., "Studies in Calcium Metabolism: I. The Calciuretic Effect of Dietary Protein," *American Journal of Clinical Nutrition,* 27:584-589 (1974.)

8. Phillip L. White, ed., and Nancy Selvey, *Let's Talk About Food* (Acton, Massachusetts: Publishing Sciences Group, 1974), p. 211.

9. L. Jean Bogert, et al., *Nutrition and Physical Fitness,* 9th ed., (Philadelphia: W.B. Saunders Co., 1973), p. 270.

10. F.R. Ellis, et al., "Veganism, Clinical Findings and Investigations," *American Journal of Clinical Nutrition,* 23(3):253 (March 1970); U.D. Register and L.M. Sonnenberg, "The Vegetarian Diet," *Journal of the American Dietetic Association* 62(3):253-61 (March 1973).

11. Zinc availability from legumes may not be as restricted as previously thought. See K.A. Haeflein and A. Rasmussen, "Zinc Content of Selected Foods," *Journal of the American Dietetic Association,* 70(6):610 (June 1977).

12. T.H. Maugh, "Vitamin A: Potential Protection from Carcinogens," *Science,* 186:1198, 1974; S.S. Mirvish, et al., "Ascorbate Nitrite Reaction: Possible Means of Blocking Formation of Carcinogenic N-Nitroso Compounds," *Science,* 177:65 (1972.)

13. Irving Fisher, "The Influence of Flesh Eating on Endurance," *Yale Medical Journal,* 13(5):205-221 (March 1907). H. Schouteden carried out similar endurance tests with vegetarians and flesh eaters at the University of Belgium in 1904. His results were similar to Fisher's. "Vegetarianism," *Encyclopedia Americana,* 27 (New York: Americana Corp., 1977).

14. Per-Olaf Astrand, "Something Old and Something New . . . Very New," *Nutrition Today* (June 1968), pp. 9-11.

15. Helen Nearing, *The Good Life Album of Helen and Scott Nearing* (New York: E.P. Dutton, 1974), p. 11.

16. Helen and Scott Nearing, *Living the Good Life* (New York: Schocken Books, 1970), p. 141.

## ❧ SEVEN ❧

# My, What Big Teeth We Have

"But humans have *always* eaten meat. Meat is man's *natural* food."

Aside from discouraging would-be vegetarians, this oft-heard argument contains two false assumptions: (1) that *all* humans have *always* eaten meat; and (2) that humans have a natural or innate *need* for flesh foods and *must* include them in their diets. This popular misconception suggests that humans are carnivores and that a vegetarian diet is therefore unnatural and unhealthy— like raising a lion on lettuce.

> One farmer says to me, "You cannot live on vegetable food solely, for it furnishes nothing to make bones with," and so he religiously devotes a part of his day to supplying his system with the raw material of bones; walking all the while he talks behind his oxen, which, with vegetable-made bones, jerk him and his lumbering plow along in spite of every obstacle.[1]

Henry David Thoreau recorded this anecdote in *Walden;* he saw the irony in the "meat-makes-might" reasoning. Critics of a vegetarian diet suppose that flesh foods alone build strength and well-being. Yet, like the farmer's oxen, the biggest, strongest land animals are herbivorous: elephants, rhinos, hippos, and water buffalos. True, humans cannot live on grass the way these animals do. But while we prefer to think of ourselves as kin to tiger, panther, wolf, and bear, especially the more macho men among us, humans are actually more closely related to plant and fruit eaters than beasts of prey. Humans can be fearsome predators, but it is our big brain plus our ability to make and use tools and weapons that allows this—not our relatively puny anatomy.

> "Man is a carnivorous animal. Why—just look at our big canine teeth. We were *designed* to eat meat."

Not true. Very little in our anatomy links us to carnivorous animals. Anyone who thinks our stubby canine teeth mark us as carnivores has seen too many Dracula movies.

Strictly speaking, a carnivore is a mammal belonging to the order Carnivora, which includes cats (both domestic and wild), dogs, wolves, bears, weasels, seals, foxes, skunks, and otters. Carnivores are characterized by their canine teeth, the fangs, which sit next to the upper and lower incisors. Behind the canine teeth are the molars, which vary in shape according to the species. Generally, a carnivore's upper premolars and lower molars are oversized and hold a cutting edge rather than a grinding surface. These cutting teeth, called the carnassials or flesh teeth, are used to shear through flesh like a pair of scissors.

Carnivores obviously have a ferocious ability to bite and rip, but they cannot effectively chew their food. Their dentition and jaw structure allow only vertical movement, with little or no ability to grind. Add to the formidable teeth the physical power, endurance, and claws, and you have a creature custom-made for life as a predator. A lion could no more survive in a fruit grove—unless it ate the fruit pickers—than a cow in a desert.

Herbivorous animals have an anatomy specialized at the other end of the spectrum. There is no order Herbivora. Creatures who feed primarily on vegetation include animals of various orders: elephants, sea cows, horses, bison, and the entire order Ruminantia —deer, moose, sheep, cows, goats, and giraffes among them. Most ruminants have no upper incisors or canines. Goats and deer, for example, have a tough pad in front of their palates. This pad is used with their sharp lower incisors to pull and crop grass and brush. The horse, however, has incisors on both top and bottom and clips grass with a scissoring action.

Herbivorous animals also have the extensive lateral jaw action and flattened molars needed to chew, grind, and pulverize the tough vegetation on which they live. Ruminants, with their multiple stomachs, must thoroughly chew their food once to send it to their first stomach, and again when it returns as cud. Carnivores do eat vegetation, as anyone knows who's seen a cat or dog eating grass. Carnivores also eat their prey's intestines, including partially digested green matter. And grazing ruminants do eat flesh, in a way, by routinely swallowing insects along with grass and browse—though this may not play a significant role in their nutrition. But overall, we can say that most carnivores and the various herbivorous animals are locked into their respective food choices by a specialized dentition and physiology.

What about humans? Does our anatomy program us for specific foods? We are generalized animals; it's easy to draw the wrong conclusions about what we are supposed to eat. We have the same kinds of teeth as many other mammals—incisors in front for cutting, with canines on either side, and molars along the jaw lines. But the form and function of our teeth are unique. Our celebrated canines, for instance, are relatively small and inefficient when you match them against the awesome weapons of a tiger or housecat. Carnivores use their fangs to stab and puncture their prey. Human canines are vestigial in comparison.

Man's earliest ape-ancestors may have had large canines for display and defense, but as they learned to use tools and hand-held weapons, their tooth size was probably reduced by natural selection. Our cousins the chimps and gorillas still have formidable canines, although we shall later see that these teeth are rarely if ever relied on as hunting weapons. Human dentition and jaw structure—characterized by our tiny canines, flattened molars, large incisors, and mobile jaw—are more like that of herbivorous animals than the true flesh eaters.

The carnivore has pointed molars and an essentially immobile jaw. Carnivores must swallow their food in chunks, literally wolfing it down. Most carnivores have tiny incisors dwarfed by the large fangs on either side. But human incisors are efficient cutting tools—perfectly suited to shredding the fiber of fruits, vegetables, and nuts. Once prepared by our incisors, food is further ground up by our molars. Our mouth, teeth, jaw structure, and saliva composition require that food be chewed to a semiliquid or paste before swallowing. Humans can't safely rip and gulp down a meal the way a true carnivore does, as many choking deaths prove each year. Humans not only lack the teeth, claws, explosive strength, and speed of fulltime flesh eaters, but their basic physiology is also dramatically different from carnivores.

The carnivore's digestive tract is only three times the length of its torso. Because raw meat is already decomposing and becoming toxic, it's biologically important that a carnivore be able to rapidly digest its food and quickly expel the wastes. The carnivore's digestive system—with its smooth, short alimentary canal secreting enough hydrochloric acid to dissolve bones—is well suited to this task. The unchewed hunks of flesh and gristle are quickly broken down and potentially toxic remains are shortly excreted.

The human digestive system is nothing like that of the carnivores. Our intestinal tract is 12 times longer than our torso—a long series of ribbonlike convolutions, compressed and sacculated. Substances taken into such a system take a relatively long time to be digested and expelled as waste. This is appropriate when the food ingested is largely vegetable matter with its tough components of fiber and indigestible cellulose needing a longer breakdown time, but questionable in the case of meat and other low-residue foods. (Hence the publicity for a high-fiber diet.)

There are other differences. The carnivore's urine and saliva are acidic, while ours are alkaline. Our saliva contains ptyalin, the enzyme that predigests starch in the mouth. Since carnivores don't eat large amounts of starch (found in plant foods), they don't need or produce ptyalin.

Carnivores don't sweat. They regulate their body temperature by breathing or panting, exchanging hot and cool air through their lungs. Herbivorous animals and humans perspire through pores, through which they also pass various wastes. Unable to perspire, carnivores pass impurities out through their urine. And lastly, carnivores drink water by lapping it with the tongue. Herbivorous animals and humans take water in by suction.

| Carnivores | Humans |
|---|---|
| fangs to stab and hold | vestigial canines |
| pointed molars used to shear | flattened molars used to grind |
| small incisors | large incisors |
| little or no ability to chew | mobile jaw |
| short intestinal tract (three times torso length) | long intestinal tract (12 times torso length) |
| smooth alimentary canal | convoluted alimentary canal |
| acidic urine and saliva | alkaline urine and saliva |
| body heat regulated by breathing | body heat regulated by perspiring through pores |
| wastes passed through urine | wastes passed through skin |
| drinks by lapping | drinks by suction |

Since humans can eat flesh, they are—when they're not being typed as carnivores—often called omnivorous. This further confuses the issue, since humans have little in common with so-called omnivores. (There is no order Omnivora.) Bears are a good example of an omnivorous animal. Their mythical ferocity aside, bears live on a diet of fruit, honey, insects, frogs, fish, small mammals, mushrooms, and roots. They will also feed on grass, grazing like cows. Though they are of the order Carnivora, bears are the least carnivorous of the flesh eaters. Other animals with omnivorous tastes are the raccoon, opossum, fox, common rat, and coyote. Although humans are capable of eating omnivorously, they have little physiological resemblance to true omnivores. (Coyotes are order Carnivora, rats belong to the Rodentia, and the opossum is of the Marsupialia.)

We are all mammals, but humans belong to the order Primates, suborder Anthropoidea, family Pongidae. Our immediate relatives are the great apes: chimpanzee, gorilla, orangutang, and gibbon. If we want to consult the animal kingdom for clues to our true nature, we should turn to the apes rather than to carnivores or herbivorous animals.

Humans are not *direct* descendants of apes, of course; ape and hominid branched off at some point within the last twenty million years, each going in its own evolutionary direction. Precisely why and how that branching occurred is still a mystery, but the divergence of man and ape happened late enough—perhaps within the last five million years, according to some theories—to leave definite links between humans and apes (not monkeys).

Humans and African apes, says physical anthropologist S.L. Washburn, "are biologically so close as to be nearly inseparable in many essentials." [2] The DNA structures of human, chimpanzee, and gorilla are almost the same; the amino acid structures of hemoglobin (the blood's oxygen-bearing protein) are identical in man and chimpanzee; immunological studies show man, chimp, and gorilla alike, with correspondingly wider differences between humans and other primates; the alimentary system, skeletal structure, and central nervous system in humans, chimpanzees, and gorillas are virtually identical. Almost every one of our organs correspond; we all share the characteristically mobile face and grasping hands. Humans differ chiefly in their greater cerebral development and advanced bipedalism.

For a long time, vegetarian theorists used the startling similarities in man and ape as prima facie evidence that humans were vegetarians by design. Since our nearest relatives didn't eat flesh in their natural state, went the logic, neither should humans. The argument suffered a bit when Dr. Jane Goodall conducted her famous field studies of wild chimpanzees in Tanzania. Dr. Goodall saw that chimps ate a diet of fruits, buds, leaves, seeds, and tree bark, often supplemented by insect larvae, termites, ants, honey, bird's eggs, and fledgling birds.

Her observation that chimpanzees ate flesh startled primatologists and vegetarians alike. Wild chimps had never before been seen eating flesh. Yet Dr. Goodall watched chimps kill and eat monkeys, infant bushbucks, bushpigs, and small baboons. Chimpanzees have also been known to kill and eat human babies. "Horrible," says Dr. Goodall, "but understandable. Baby humans are no less appealing than baby baboons." Besides, "It should be equally horrifying to reflect on the fact that in a great many places throughout their range, chimpanzees are considered a delicacy by humans." [3]

But chimps are hardly as rapacious meat eaters as the average North American. Dr. Goodall reported that the chimps she observed seemed to eat flesh only in cycles or crazes that were stimulated by an accidental or chance capture of prey. This incident then triggered a period of deliberate hunting and flesh eating. After a month or two, the craze seemed to wear off, the result of a "satisfaction of [their] craving" or a loss of interest due to the difficulties of hunting. The chimps then returned to their staple diet of vegetation, insects, and fruit. [4]

Such meat-eating crazes are infrequent, according to Dr. Goodall. The chimpanzees she studied only made about 12 kills a year. Nor do the Goodall observations prove that all chimps regularly eat flesh. Vernon Reynolds, who carried out a similar study of wild chimps in Uganda's Budongo Forest, never saw them eating meat or using tools.

The other of our close relatives, the gorilla, has an undeserved reputation for being a ferocious beast with a murderous temper. While a few gorillas may learn to eat meat in captivity, in their wild state they are shy, peaceful eaters of plants and fruit. George Schaller, whose two-year study of mountain gorillas in East and

Central Africa is described in *The Year of the Gorilla,* says, "I never saw gorillas eat animal matter in the wild . . . no bird's eggs, insects, mice, or other creatures . . . even though they had the opportunity to do so on occasion." But before we use chimpanzee or gorilla behavior to justify human flesh eating or vegetarianism, consider Schaller's warning that we cannot make "sweeping generalizations about the behavior of apes. . . . [S]triking differences may even occur within the same species in different parts of its range." [5]

What can we conclude about human food selections? We see that while humans lack the fangs and digestive equipment of carnivores, they have eaten flesh for millenia by fabricating weapons and using cooking and other methods to render flesh more digestible. We know that humans lack the multiple stomachs of the ruminant, yet they do well eating vegetables, grains, and fruits. Humans lack the huge self-sharpening incisors of the rodent, yet they can gnaw, crack nuts, and live on almost as varied a diet as the common rat.

Thus, humans are not generically carnivores, frugivores, herbivores, or omnivores. Humans are, like the great apes, a unique, anatomically generalized, widely adaptable species exhibiting various individual tastes and behavioral patterns. Humans and chimpanzees are capable of flesh eating, but nothing in their anatomy or physiology compels them to do so. That some humans eat flesh while others don't proves only that "striking differences . . . may occur within the same species." We Pongidae may safely adopt any number of eating habits so long as we derive adequate nutrition from our food choices.

Why waste time debating which diet—flesh or vegetarian— is the more natural for humans? Dr. Alfred Kinsey once confronted a similar question about sex. Asked to define an unnatural sex act, Kinsey replied, "It's one you can't do." Since humans can survive with or without animal foods, both meat eating and vegetarianism are obviously natural. A more appropriate question is which of the two—meat eating or vegetarianism —is the most beneficial?

Another popular argument used against vegetarianism is the idea that humanity owes its survival and development solely to our ancestors who killed with clubs and spears. Robert Ardrey capsulizes this theory in *The Hunting Hypothesis*.

> If among all the members of our primate family the human being is unique, even in our noblest aspirations, it is because we alone through untold millions of years were continuously dependent on killing to survive.

Many students of our ancestry agree with this concept. They believe that our earliest ancestors had to "hunt and eat meat or perish." [7] Some theories even suggest that substances in meat—elongated chains of essential fatty acids, for example—were directly responsible for the human's advanced brain development. The implication is that this history somehow obliges us to continue the meat-eating tradition.

An alternate anthropological view also has its supporters. This theory suggests that early primitive men were anatomically ill equipped to be full-time predators, that plant foods were the basis of their diet, and that meat was obtained only infrequently. Hunting with primitive weapons—bones, sticks, rudimentary spears—was far more difficult than modern humans realize. Even the ability to throw a rock with accuracy demands practice and innate skill. Gathering and foraging for plant foods, says this theory, had to occupy more of the primitive human's time than the arduous and fickle consequences of hunting.

True humans have inhabited the earth for at least 3 million years. Yet well-organized hunting with efficient weapons may have only occurred during the past 500,000 to 1 million years. By this reckoning, the human race has been relying on hunting and meat eating for less of its total time on earth than it has been relying on plant foods. The man-as-hunter theorists counter by saying that tool (weapon) making and using, bipedalism, and increased cerebral development were all linked in a positive feedback relationship. Only the selective pressures of the hunt could have worked to transform a limited ape-creature into *Homo sapiens.*

But we err to speak of the human race as though it were a single, homogeneous unit. Our forebears (those we know of) fell into different groups with a variety of behavioral patterns acted out in different parts of the planet. Hunting may have been necessary for one group and rare for another, depending on the distribution of food and prey. The Ice Age, for instance, is supposed to have been a time when humans were forced into eating a primarily flesh diet. Yet the ice never covered the entire planet, and scientists aren't even sure what the climate was around the edges of the advancing ice. There may have been significant variations in temperature and physical conditions within relatively short distances. Some humans may have been forced to live on wooly mammoth and cave bear, while others continued to rely on their mainly nonanimal fare. To assume that our ancestors exhibited identical behavior is to forget the striking differences primates display.

The idea that our ancestors lived by their wits and weapons has an undeniably romantic appeal, however. How much more exciting to think of our antecedents as Pleistocenic Nimrods, rather than as grubbers of roots. And which tales are more worthy of recounting around the sputtering camp fire? Would our kin glorify the monotony of berry picking and the gathering of fallen fruit and nuts? Or would they regale each other with thrilling tales of stalking prey, danger, breathless moments, bravery, the savage power of beasts, and the magic forces governing a hunt's success or failure? Oral tradition may have contributed to an overemphasis of hunting's significance, while minimizing the coequal or predominant importance of foraging.

The full story of human evolution remains clouded. Anthropologists and paleontologists are constantly sorting through old and new evidence, discarding theories almost as fast as they devise them. They admit that speculation and hypothesis about our past far outweigh hard facts. How can we speak authoritatively about what we ate, when who we were is still largely unknown? Reams of material have been written about the habits of our ancestors, the Australopithecines, who roamed the African plains 14 million years ago. Yet Australopithecine remains amount to only about a dozen bone fragments. *Ramapithecus,* an earlier hominid, is represented by only half a palate bone.

"Twenty years from now there will be more evidence," says Dr. Lucille St. Hoyme, Associate Curator of Physical Anthropology at the Smithsonian Institution, "and the situation will be even more confusing. Talk to a dozen anthropologists and you'll get 16 different opinions." [8] So, to suggest that humans are primarily hunters *or* gatherers is to impose speculative limits on an enigmatic and virtually unlimited animal.

"Man is a hunter, gatherer, forager—whatever he has to be, for whatever reason," says anthropologist Dr. Charles McNett of American University, teacher of a course in the history of human food procurement. "Humans will eat anything that won't kill them in order to satisfy their dietary needs." [9] They can do this because they've never specialized physically. Human cultures, rather than their bodies, have specialized. And cultures can change rapidly in response to environmental changes. Should a food source dwindle or vanish, humans can turn to other foodstuffs. Anatomically specialized creatures unable to adapt may die of starvation. Humanity's remarkable generalization—not flesh eating alone— ensured the species' survival.

Anthropologists refer to the way humans gather food as procurement systems. The East Coast Indians who greeted John Smith, for example, had several procurement systems that followed a regular seasonal schedule: corn growing in summer, deer hunting in fall and winter, fishing and foraging in spring. Depending on which time of the year you observed these tribes, you might mistakenly dub them primarily farmers, hunters, or foragers. But, like humans in general, they were all three. Thus there is no point in trying to establish which diet, meat or plants, most conforms to an historical dietary baseline. According to Dr. St. Hoyme and other experts, we can say very little for certain about the diet of early humans.

"We can't say for sure what they ate, how much of it, how their bodies utilized it, or what their nutritional needs were," says Dr. St. Hoyme. "And nobody has lived like early man for the past 20,000 years. There are no human groups today living under the approximate conditions of our primate ancestors. What was the dietary baseline? We don't know."

We can say that the proper diet for humans is the one that works. Eskimos living in the traditional way cannot be vegetarians, any more than shipwrecked sailors can choose to abstain from eating fish—not if they wish to survive. Cultural responses to food must be consistent with the food supply and its distribution. So even if we could somehow determine humanity's original diet, what good would it do us as modern humans?

Think of all the variables. What was the state of our ancestors' metabolism? In what ways might their digestive, enzymatic, and hormonal systems have differed from ours? What external forces influenced their food selection, its preparation, its biological absorption? What were the differences in climate, radiation levels, the composition of water, air, and soil? What kinds of now-extinct plants or animals might they have relied on for food?

The important question—knowing what we do of our own nutritional, cultural, and environmental needs—is which dietary pattern is best for modern humans? That Australopithecines may have eaten the brains and sucked the marrow of their kills on the arid savannahs eons ago needn't influence your tastes any more than the fact that your father drove a Ford, while you prefer a Chevrolet. Knowledge of the past has great scientific and cultural value, but the behavior of our ancestors hardly compels us as individuals to act similarly.

Consider the theory that humans are innately—genetically—predisposed to violence and aggression. Such a concept would, if true, explain why human history is one long war dotted with infrequent lapses of peace. But does the fact that humans have an inborn mean streak compel us to beat our children and kick the dog? Or are we free as individuals to channel our aggressions into art, music, crafts, and our professions? We are the progeny of Da Vinci as well as Attila the Hun. Why should the predatory behavior of *Australopithecus africanus* or contemporary *Homo sapiens* in any way diminish the value of a personal philosophy based on vegetarianism or nonviolence? The brutality and atrocities of the past have never stopped humans from reaching for the best within them: compassion, love, and creativity.

We need not launder history. If Ardrey and others are right and the hunting experience created the human animal, then we have a delicious piece of irony: the predator is the parent of vegetarianism. Had the ages of hunting not contributed to the formation of abstract thinking, visualization, language, and symbolization, humans might never have developed the ability to make moral or aesthetic distinctions in the first place. Rather than deny the duality of our nature, let us celebrate it as Thoreau did.

> I found in myself, and still find, an instinct toward a higher, or, as it is named, spiritual life, as do most men, and another toward a primitive rank and savage one, and I reverence them both. I love the wild not less than the good.[10]

Millions of people have turned to vegetarianism because they know it can be both beneficial and culturally consistent. Hardly a radical idea or fad, abstinence from flesh foods is thousands of years old, stretching back to the beginnings of philosophic thought. Were a freely adopted vegetarian diet not totally appropriate for humans, the last vegetarian would have died off ages ago. Instead, the system perpetuates itself, never fully revolutionizing the world, perhaps, but never dying out, and often flourishing.

We may, in fact, be entering a vegetarian renaissance as more and more people are beginning to realize that a meat-based dietary is long overdue for abandonment. There are three fundamental reasons why vegetarianism is an ideal food procurement system for the modern world.

1. The world is incredibly smaller than in humanity's nomadic days. Our planet's ecosystem is strained to the breaking point. Cultural and national distinctions aside, we are one race, one tribe.

A culture's food procurement systems were once relatively limited in their long-range effect on other groups. But now such systems—their styles, emphases, and changeability—can rock the entire world. That a few rich nations are addicted to intensive meat production and consumption, with developing nations tending to ape them as their own economies improve, causes the poor to be literally robbed to overfeed the wealthy. Adequate food, water, air, energy, and land are all at a premium. Large-scale meat production not only uses too many precious resources, but it also fouls and abuses them in the process.

2. Habitual overconsumption of meat appears to be damaging the health of industrialized peoples. The modern North American sits, drives, dozes, and watches. Largely sedentary, he gobbles up animal fat and protein as though it were still the Pleistocene. Heart disease, cancer, and digestive diseases have now been linked to various dietary factors, with meat consumption high on the list. An efficient food procurement system should not kill its participants. Many vegetarians, on the other hand, appear to have a better-than-average health record.

3. Is it right to kill other creatures when that slaughter is unnecessary? Wholesome, nourishing alternatives to flesh foods exist and abound in the United States. No matter what our bloody past, most people find the idea of killing animals repulsive; they go out of their way to rationalize the dilemma raised by slaughter. Yet the killing goes on year after year. Billions of creatures are slaughtered, hunted, and trapped only to satisfy an ingrained taste, a custom. Is unnecessary slaughter ethical and proper? Is it consistent with the needs and sensitivities of most modern people? Does such killing mesh with our personal notions of spiritual evolution?

The world has changed. Ecologically, socially, politically, and emotionally, the planet and many of its inhabitants have clearly entered a new phase. And because every environmental change demands a corresponding cultural change, we are faced with many questions about our future. One of those questions is: which food procurement systems will serve us best as individuals and group members in this transformed world?

Vegetarians think they have some of the answers.

## Chapter Seven notes.

1. Henry David Thoreau, *Walden,* from "Higher Laws."
2. S.L. Washburn and Ruth Moore, *Ape into Man* (Boston: Little, Brown & Co., 1974), p. 21.
3. Jane Goodall, *In the Shadow of Man* (Boston: Houghton Mifflin, 1971), p. 199.
4. *Ibid.,* p. 207.
5. George Schaller, *The Year of the Gorilla* (Chicago: University of Chicago Press, 1964), p. 198.
6. Robert Ardrey, *The Hunting Hypothesis* (New York: Atheneum, 1976), p. 11.
7. *Ibid.,* p. 58.
8. Dr. Lucille St. Hoyme, Smithsonian Institution, Washington, D.C.: interviewed by author, August 1976.
9. Dr. Charles McNett, American University, Washington, D.C.: interviewed by author, October 1976.
10. Thoreau, *Walden.*

# Meanwhile, Back in the Jungle

Do vegetarians deprive themselves of wholesome nutritious foods by refusing to eat meat, fowl, and fish? Or has the wholesomeness of flesh foods always been debatable? While opposition to killing animals has been the traditional reason for adopting a nonflesh dietary, an increasing number of people are now turning to vegetarianism because of various hygienic concerns.

Either they question the healthfulness of a diet heavy in animal fats, or they believe, as do the Natural Hygienists, that the human organism operates best on a simple diet of plant foods; and/ or they're worried about the presence of harmful chemicals or disease agents in flesh foods—the subject of this chapter.

When an animal's heart and brain stop working, we say the creature is dead, but the body's cellular life is much slower to die. Whatever blood remains in contact with the cells contains enough oxygen and nutrients to keep the tissues temporarily alive. Nourished so, the cells continue to produce waste materials that would normally be carried off by the circulating blood. But in a dead body all such poisons are trapped in the blood and decaying tissues.

One of the earliest lessons learned about meat was that a slain animal had to be drained of blood as quickly as possible to rid the body of waste matter that might taint the flesh. Some of these substances, however, are beneficial to the meat lover. Nitrogenous extracts trapped in the animal's muscles are partly responsible for meat's flavor. Released by cooking and ingested, these water-soluble chemicals tend to stimulate the appetite by acting in the digestive tract. Other materials locked in the animal's tissues are less appealing. Those involved in meat production know this and warn:

> Meat animals should never be slaughtered when they are over-heated, excited, or fatigued, but should be perfectly quiet and rested.[1]

Such tenderness springs from chemistry, not compassion. An animal slain when frightened is subject to pain poisoning, a phenomenon that affects the taste and quality of its flesh. When an animal is excited or angered, its body naturally produces those chemical changes necessary for its survival. Various psychophysical processes are intensified, readying the animal for fight or flight. But when an about-to-be-slaughtered creature can neither fight nor run, the discharged hormones and fluids build up in its body rather than being used in the playing out of a defense mechanism.

In humans under stress, these trapped secretions may be linked to the development of heart disease, cancer, and other ailments. Anyone suffering from an ulcer knows how easily gastric juices can become corrosive, literally burning holes in the intestinal walls. Similarly, creatures about to be slaughtered by traditional methods are not always perfectly quiet and rested. Indeed, depending on the design of the disassembly line, the animals may be terrified and confused. Packed together and herded along with electric prods, they bellow and squeal in fear as their heightened senses pick up the smells of blood and death. When they reach the killing floor they are struck down or knifed or electrically stunned.

Fear causes their hearts to pump rapidly, forcing blood and anxiety-produced chemicals into the tiniest capillaries of their tissues. The creatures will be bled out, but some of the fluids, hormones, and other chemicals will remain in their flesh.

What effect do such extracts have on those who eat this flesh? Maybe nothing more than a stimulating boost to the appetite. Yet only in the last few decades have a majority of humans had the means to eat large amounts of flesh foods on a daily basis throughout their lives.

More research will have to be done on the effect of stress-produced matter in meat. Scientists do know, of course, that hormones are powerful agents capable of causing drastic changes in animals. Is it possible that the long, complex human intestinal tract may act as a mixing bowl, distributing meat's secondhand hormones and toxins throughout a consumer's body?

Flesh eaters also wind up eating whatever bacteria are trapped in the animal's tissues. Decaying flesh is a bacterium's heaven; a better medium for infestation and multiplication can hardly be imagined. And not only does meat harbor those bacteria infecting the living animal, but it may also carry molds, spores, yeasts, and bacilli picked up during postmortem handling.

This is true of almost all foods, but the problems are more numerous in flesh foods with potentially more hazardous results. (Would you rather risk eating an old banana or an old hamburger?) The longer flesh foods sit around—refrigerated or not— the more time agents of decay and disease have to increase their numbers and potency. Supermarkets and butchers are quick to tell the public that they are dedicated to providing only the freshest meat. Store advertising makes it sound as though cattle are being poleaxed right in the back room, their flanks and chops wrapped and stacked in the bins before the blood has had time to congeal. But few butchers would sell truly fresh meat. Nor would many meat eaters enjoy the flesh of most just-killed creatures. Anyone who's read mystery novels knows that rigor mortis sets in soon after death, stiffening the muscles and flesh. Most fresh meat is therefore tough and tasteless. As a book on meat processing explains:

> Beef, mutton, venison, and game birds become more tender and palatable by the process of ripening, hanging, aging, or maturing.[2]

Sides of beef are commonly hung for 10 to 14 days at 34 to 36°F. The stiffened carcass is naturally tenderized by enzymes and bacteria that break down the fibrous connective tissues. The difference between carrion and the steak in a showcase is one of control: the aging of the beef has been supervised, while the rotting of a roadside carcass has gone on apace. Few meat eaters, however, would like to hear the words putrefaction, rigor mortis, and rotting applied to their sirloin and pot roast. But flesh is flesh, though the euphemisms ripening, toughening, and enzymatic action are kinder to the ear.

Obtaining wholesome meat has been a problem for meat eaters ever since our ancestors stopped killing and eating their prey on the spot.

Concerned government officials and consumer groups wage a constant battle to protect meat eaters from intentional and accidental abuses. But the regulation of flesh food is enormously difficult. Not only is a staggering volume of meat sold and distributed in this country (tens of billions of tons annually, not counting poultry and fish), but also the victims of meat-related crimes generally eat the evidence before transgressions have even been detected. The auto industry can sometimes recall its mistakes before the public is endangered. But the meat industry and USDA—and the consumer—rarely have such luck.

Modern packinghouses no longer remotely resemble Upton Sinclair's lurid descriptions of Packingtown in *The Jungle* (1906), but enough old and new dangers still exist to leave many vegetarians, consumer advocates, and scientists convinced that meat eaters are threatened.

Read the words of a USDA official who spoke with me off the record.

> We do a good job, but the public can only get the kind of protection it's willing to pay for. It's unrealistic to expect every single piece of meat passed to be 100 percent pure. The price of meat would go out of sight if we had to make a complete analysis of every carcass. Some questionable carcasses do get past the inspection process. It's unavoidable.

Read his comments another way: other than vegetarians, the only people reasonably safe from "questionable carcasses" are those who raise their own animals and those who buy their meat from organic or natural sources.

Consider the complexity of the modern packinghouse: a large

poultry plant may slaughter and process as many as 500,000 chickens a day. (A small plant by USDA standards may kill 45,000 birds daily.) Assuming a large plant is properly staffed, about 26 full-time meat inspectors (graduate veterinarians and civil service laymen) would be assigned to check carcasses moving on the line. Each inspector is responsible for checking the condition of 20 to 22 birds per minute—over 10,000 birds a day. That allows roughly *three seconds* to check each bird passing by. (About the same amount of time is allowed to cattle and hog inspectors.)

Birds are inspected both before and after slaughter. An inspector must be able to spot in seconds any of the numerous ills poultry are prone to: ornithosis, fowl pox, fowl typhoid, fowl cholera, infectious bronchitis, New Castle disease, psittacosis, coccidiosis, coryza, air sacculitis (avian pneumonia), and avian leukosis (cancer) are only a few.

The USDA's Food Safety and Quality Service says a three-second check is sufficient time for trained personnel to spot each carcass for prevalent conditions. The inspectors use sight, smell, and touch, though suspicious conditions may require tissue samples and microscopic analysis. But even the most conscientious inspectors are forced by circumstances and the pressure of time to let suspect carcasses leave the plant. No records are kept on how many tainted or diseased birds get through to market every day, but meat eaters end up eating these grisly statistics. This is a particularly unappetizing fact, considering that at least 26 avian diseases are transmittable from bird to human. And approximately the same inspection procedures and policies prevail in plants handling cattle and hogs.

Cattle and hog inspectors also make an antemortem and postmortem examination, searching live animals in motion and at rest for evidence of rabies, listeriosis, anthrax, tetanus, epithelioma, mastitis, swine erysipelas,* vesicular exanthema, vesicular stomatitis,* actinomycosis,* actinobacillosis,* shipping fever, infectious bovine rhinotracheitis, selenium or fluorine poisoning, hyperkera-

---

* Diseases transmittable to humans.

tosis, salt poisoning, fescue foot, ergotism, cutaneous streptothricosis—and so on, amounting to more than 30 possible diseases and conditions.

Live animals obviously unfit for human consumption are culled before slaughter. Some of the animals are condemned because they drop dead right in the holding pen. But not all of the sick or contaminated cattle and swine can be spotted in the antemortem survey. The rest are supposedly caught on postmortem inspection. Yet even when inspectors do isolate a diseased carcass, there is still no guarantee that the meat will be discarded. *A standard USDA-approved practice is for inspectors to condemn only the diseased or contaminated portion of the carcass, letting the rest of the flesh go on to market.* In 1976, about 13 million cattle, calves, sheep, lambs, and swine were, in USDA's words, "retained for various diseases and conditions, but passed for food after removal of affected parts." [3] All of us are used to cutting a bad spot out of an apple or banana, but in these cases the carcasses retained showed evidence of any of 45 conditions. These included everything from pneumonia, parasites, abscesses, and tuberculosis, to drug and pesticide residues.

Even animals suffering from certain kinds of cancer are routinely dismembered, the cancerous portions being discarded while the presumably wholesome remainder goes on to the consumer. In 1976, about 117,000 animals with various neoplasms,* were "passed for food after removal of affected parts." [4] The USDA says such surgical practices are safe, however unaesthetic. There is no evidence, says the government, that humans eating meat from the south end of a carcass are endangered by cancerous tissue removed from the north end. Not all cancer researchers agree with USDA's position. Many scientists simply say they really don't know if the removal of tumors alone is enough to make the rest of the carcass safe for human food. More research needs to be done. The USDA is saying, in effect, that consumers are safe eating such meat until further notice.

The fact that animals are being condemned at all, or at least

* The majority were cattle suffering from a malignancy ranchers call cancer eye.

that some of their parts are being retained, may be cheering to some meat eaters. "Well," they say, "if nothing else it shows that Uncle Sam is on the job inspecting my meat." But in 1976, as in the year before, less than 290,000 animals were condemned out of the almost 119 million that were sold for human consumption (not counting poultry). When less than one-half of one percent of all animals converted to food are condemned, it means one of two things: either most animals going to slaughter are in good health or the inspection program isn't catching all the sick ones.

*Item:* A USDA investigation by its own Office of Inspector General (OIG) found substandard conditions in almost half of 38 plants randomly selected. OIG reported that both federal and plant inspectors failed to do their jobs "in a forceful and effective manner." The investigation found confusion, low morale, and misconduct among plant workers, poorly trained personnel, instances of falsified records, and limited effectiveness in laboratories testing meat for wholesomeness.[5]

*Item:* A report by the Government Accounting Office charged that the 1967 Wholesome Meat Act was being improperly administered. The study found that while 17 percent of the nation's 15,000 intrastate packinghouses *failed* to meet federal sanitation and inspection standards, they still managed to win an acceptable rating from USDA.[6]

The USDA claims that the majority of animals presented for slaughter are in good health. "Most of them are young animals who have been pampered and cared for in a feedlot," a USDA veterinarian told me. But Beatrice Trum Hunter writes in *Consumer Beware:*

Radical changes in livestock rearing have resulted in a dramatic deterioration in animal health. . . . [T]he control of infectious diseases has only been possible by continuously resorting to a vast aggregate of drugs.[7]

Says *Cooperative Farmer* magazine, "Despite many advances in swine husbandry, U.S. pork producers continue to lose 25 percent of all pigs . . . before weaning." The article admits that such losses are due to the "trend to more and more automation and mechanization," and suggests that farmers use a variety of antibiotics, antitoxins, and vermicides to combat these pig-breeding problems.[8]

That laconic Old MacDonald in a straw hat has been replaced by an agribusinessman in a hard hat who injects, feeds, dips, and sprays his livestock with a variety of chemicals. And just as his animals are routinely medicated, so too is the American meat eater. Contrary to the assurances of the USDA—which must police the industry it promotes—and the Food and Drug Administration, meat eaters are regularly eating residues of suspected and known carcinogens and antibiotics.

In *Eating May Be Hazardous to Your Health,* FDA biochemist Jacqueline Verrett emphasizes that half of all the antibiotics produced in the United States go into "feedstuff for animals intended for human consumption, to make them gain weight faster and keep them disease-free." [9]

Who administers these chemicals—oxytetracycline, penicillin, progesterone, testosterone, zeranol, tetracycline, sulfachlorpyridazine, and dozens of other antibiotics and hormones that may remain as residues in meat? Not necessarily a veterinarian, but a stockman who laces his feeds and injects his animals, sometimes figuring that if a little is good, more might be better.

Both the FDA and USDA admit that the cause of residues in the majority of cases results from on-the-farm mixing and handling of medicated feeds and the failure of livestock producers to withdraw drugs far enough ahead of slaughter. The medications used are so potent that when a producer switches from medicated to nonmedicated feed—but fails to thoroughly clean out his feed bins during the transition—drug residues are likely to show up in the meat.[10]

The FDA has finally started moving toward restricting the use of certain antibiotics in animal feed that are also used to combat human diseases. Both penicillin and tetracycline, for example, are routinely used in the feed of all the turkeys, 80 percent of the swine and veal calves, half of all the cattle, and a third of all the chickens raised in the United States for human consumption.[11] The FDA's present administration would prefer to have these drugs used only for therapeutic purposes—to treat specific livestock illnesses. The meat industry is outraged at this suggestion. We can therefore expect a long series of hearings and court actions. Antibiotics, meanwhile, will continue to be used in animal feeds on a routine basis.

When antibiotics are used carefully to treat diseases of bacterial origin, the lifesaving results may be spectacular. But when antibiotics are applied lavishly and indiscriminately, the negative consequences may be just as staggering. An overuse of antibiotics—whether prescribed willy-nilly for every runny nose among humans or routinely fed to livestock—can encourage the growth of antibiotic-resistant bacteria.

Diseases easily controlled with drugs thus become untreatable. Bacteria can not only rapidly transfer this resistance among themselves, but they can also become resistant to seven or eight different drugs at once. Twelve thousand people died of dysentery in Guatemala in 1974 because the bacillus responsible had grown resistant to normal antibiotic treatment. Similar cases of bacterial resistance are accumulating in medical literature.

Dr. Bernard Dixon, microbiologist and author of *Magnificent Microbes,* says, "Transferable resistance is a natural phenomenon. We have forced it into a serious problem. The use of antibiotics in factory farming has provided virtually ideal conditions for resistance to flourish and spread."

The consumer who regularly eats foods with antibiotic residues may suffer allergic reactions and stomach upsets (which may not even be attributed to the food eaten) and may unknowingly encourage the growth of resistant bacteria within his or her own body.[12]

And how do you like your hormones—barbecued or basted?

Synthetic hormones used in feeds have revolutionized livestock production by producing faster growth and weight gains on less feed. The most infamous of these hormones—DES (diethylstilbestrol)—bulks cattle up 15 percent faster on 10 percent less feed, saving producers about a pound of grain for every pound gained by the animal.* One small problem: DES has caused cancer in laboratory animals and humans.

The Food and Drug Administration took eight years to finally ban DES in animal feed, even though many FDA scientists had long warned that the hormone might cause cancer in humans eating DES-tainted meat.† (At this writing, however, DES is still being used. The FDA's ban was overturned on a technicality by a federal court.) The FDA hierarchy defended DES with the zeal of an industrial lobbyist, maintaining that any infinitesimal residues that might slip past inspectors were harmless even if ingested over a period of years. But, as Dr. Verrett reports:

> Researchers from the National Cancer Institute assured Congressmen that it might be possible for only one molecule of DES in the 340 trillion present in a quarter pound of beef liver to trigger human cancer, as far as they know.[13]

The supermarket meat eater seems to be playing a no-win game. Get rid of DES? So what. There are plenty of similar chemicals in the agribusinessman's arsenal. Some of them are known carcinogens.

*Item:* The FDA warns doctors not to administer dienestrol diacetate to pregnant women; the hormone may cause vaginal cancer. The same substance is widely used in poultry feed. The

---

* This is according to beef industry studies. Other studies have shown that DES doesn't stimulate weight gain.

† Since 1959, more than 20 countries have banned DES and other growth hormones used in livestock production. Italy and Sweden banned importation of U.S. DES-fed beef.

government admits that residues are likely, but says it has no reliable tests for determining them.[14]

*Item:* Melangesterol acetate (MGA) is a synthetic hormone used as a growth stimulant. Its originator admits that it produces tumors in female mice. MGA is still being used.[15]

*Item:* Arsenic (as arsanilic or arsonic acid) is routinely fed to broiler chickens to stimulate growth and kill parasites. The law requires that such feeds be withdrawn prior to slaughter so arsenic residues will not appear in meat. A 1973 investigation by ABC News found arsenic in four out of five samples of final feed used by major chicken producers. Arsenic is known to be a carcinogen.[16]

Many other pesticides, heavy metals, and toxic materials find their way into our food indirectly from the general environment rather than from animal feed or livestock management alone. But while pesticide residues are a problem for all—vegetarians included—contamination of meat, fish, and poultry is worse than in all other food classes. Pesticides and similar agents are not only retained longer in animal fat than in plant tissues, but the food chain effect may actually serve to concentrate and multiply these levels in animals—particularly fish. Yearly surveys made by the *Pesticides Monitoring Journal* (published by the U.S. Environmental Protection Agency) show that animal-origin foods continue to have comparatively higher levels of pesticide residues than plant foods. Meat, fish, and poultry have the highest levels—about twice those of dairy products. While all plant foods tested showed at least some pesticidal or other chemical residues, *the levels detected in vegetables and fruits were generally one-tenth of the residues in flesh foods.*

The Food and Drug Administration sets so-called tolerance levels for toxic substances, of course, but the limits often have more political than scientific logic. Tolerances are set with little or no evidence that contaminants are actually safe at their assigned levels. Some limits are simply set at the highest level found in a given sample. And the FDA has been known to arbitrarily *increase* tolerances, as it did with mercury, claiming that previously assigned lower tolerance levels were unrealistic or unenforceable.

State officials don't have any better record in dealing with toxic substances in food. In 1973, a poisonous chemical known as PBB (polybrominated biphenyl) was accidentally mixed with livestock feed in Michigan. By the time the error was discovered, as many as nine million Michigan residents may have eaten PBB-tainted meat and milk.

PBB is highly toxic, causing nervous disorders, potential damage to the body's immunological system, and birth defects. As of early 1977, however, cattle with PBB residues were still being sold for human consumption in Michigan. The state set a safe PBB residue level for cattle, though health and veterinary experts maintained they had no idea what PBB's ultimate effects would be on humans and unborn children.[17]

Is there a possibility for a similar mishap on a national scale? A single feedlot harboring 40,000 cattle—not an unusual number—may produce 20 million pounds of edible meat when all the animals are killed and packed. Assuming the average meat eater consumes one-half pound of meat per day, the misuse of a drug, pesticide, or other toxic substance at even one feedlot may ultimately affect 20 to 25 percent of the meat-buying public—perhaps 40 million people.[18]

Inspection for drug residues involves a computerized, statistical, random sampling method designed to "represent a cross section of the [animals] slaughtered throughout the nation."[19] This means that only several thousand carcasses are analyzed while hundreds of millions more go on to the consumer. By the time a drug residue is discovered, the contaminated carcasses may have already been served for dinner.

The widely used herbicide 2,4,5-T is annually sprayed on millions of acres in the United States. The agent is used to kill vegetation along railroad, power company, and pipeline rights-of-way and to control weed growth in forests, pastures, and rangelands. But 2,4,5-T and other chlorinated phenols are known to contain dibenzo-dioxins—the most poisonous chemicals known to science, capable of causing birth defects in humans.

Knowing this, reporter Thomas Whiteside wonders in a lengthy *New Yorker* magazine article, "The Pendulum and the Toxic Cloud":

> . . . how to account for the results of an analysis of samples taken in 1975 of the fatty tissues of cattle that grazed on Western rangeland that had been sprayed with 2,4,5-T during the previous year, for the samples showed significant levels of dioxin—levels of up to 60 parts per trillion. How is it that from grazing land sprayed with this . . . herbicide the government permits the distribution to the American dinner table of meat that has been contaminated with measurable amounts of one of the most toxic substances known to man? [20]

A USDA report to Congress admits:

> . . . it is not possible to detect toxic drug, antibiotic, and chemical residues during slaughter inspection of livestock and poultry. Definite evidence of the presence of a residue depends upon laboratory analysis of the proper tissue, collected by the inspector, and sent to the laboratory for analysis. . . . [A] one-by-one sorting of animals or birds to remove those containing residues is impossible because each animal could contain multiple residues . . . and a separate analysis is necessary for each residue or group of residues. [21]

In 1976, less than 150 animals were condemned for drug residues, 57 for pesticidal residues, and 29 for miscellaneous residues. That's less than 300 animals out of 119 million—not counting poultry. [22]

*Item:* In the summer of 1975, USDA found residues of the drug ipronidazole, a suspected carcinogen, in a consignment of several thousand turkeys. A mix-up occurred and somehow a shipment of healthy birds was impounded while the contaminated meat was converted into turkey rolls and sent to market. An FDA inspector discovered the error and alerted his superiors. The FDA chose neither to recall the tainted meat nor to prosecute the turkey producer because, as an FDA memo revealed, "those actions might embarrass the agriculture department." [23]

What about fish—once the safest of flesh foods? Evidence is now mounting that eating fish or shellfish taken from polluted waters may pose a greater hazard than merely drinking contaminated water. U.S. waterways are awash with literally thousands of toxic chemicals. Not only do industries and sewage treatment plants spew thousands of tons of wastes into our rivers and streams every year, but accidental chemical spills, illegal dumping, industrial accidents near water, and widespread spraying of pesticides also add to the deadly insult.

Several studies have demonstrated that people whose drinking water is contaminated by organic carcinogens and other toxic agents have an increased risk of cancer of five to 25 percent.[24] But if it's dangerous to drink the water in many communities, it's potentially more hazardous to eat the fish taken from those and surrounding waters.[25]

Many of the compounds damaging to humans can "accumulate in fish to concentrations thousands or millions of times greater than in the water from which they were caught," says Dr. Robert Harris of the Environmental Defense Fund.[26]

Pentachlorophenol (PCP), a widely distributed industrial waste whose genetic effect on humans is unknown, can accumulate in the fatty tissue of fish in amounts ten thousand times over that of the water. And what's worse, PCP may contain traces of dioxin.[27]

Hexachlorobenzene (HCB) is a suspected carcinogen in humans that has been found in the drinking water of several cities. Bass taken from contaminated waters have shown an HCB concentration 44,000 times greater than the water. The EPA has already found HCB in 95 percent of samples of human breast milk taken for study.[28]

Polychlorinated biphenyls (PCBs), industrial wastes linked

to cancer and birth defects, are found in most U.S. waterways. Fish can concentrate PCB contamination by a million fold. And this, says Dr. Harris, is only "the tip of the iceberg." [29]

*Item:* The National Water Quality Laboratory in Duluth, Minnesota isolated the chlorinated organic compounds in a single Lake Ontario fish. They found in *one* herring:

Trichlorobenzene
Tetrachlorobenzene
Pentachlorobenzene
Hexachlorobenzene
Hexachlorobutadiene
Tetrachlorotoluene
Pentachlorotoluene
Hexachlorostyrene
Heptachlorostyrene
Octachlorostyrene
Pentachloroanaline
Tetrachloroanthracene
DDT, DDD, DDE, DDMu
Chlordane
Nonachlor
Octachloronaphthalene

—plus the pesticide mirex and 11 metabolites of PCBs. All of these compounds can accumulate in body fat. All are known or suspected carcinogens.[30]

Like fish, shellfish can concentrate toxic chemicals in their tissues. But bivalves—oysters, clams, and mussels—present another problem. As filter feeders, they flush water through their systems, winnowing out minute particles of food. If the water in which they're located is polluted, contaminants will be trapped in the animals' feces. Because bivalves are usually eaten whole and raw or lightly steamed, the consumer also eats the fecal matter left in the creatures' intestinal tracts—up to half a teaspoon of contaminated sediment per bivalve.[31]

Common sense suggests that those who eat fish should obtain them from unpolluted waters. Good luck. Other than small lakes or your own pond or tank, few U.S. waters are free of pollution of one sort or another. In October, 1976, the National Oceanic and Atmospheric Administration reported an increase in the incidence of cancerlike growths on shellfish taken from polluted coastal bays and rivers. Six independent studies of shellfish in Washington, Oregon, Virginia, Delaware, Maryland, Connecticut, Rhode Island, Massachusetts, and Maine found the occurrence of neoplasms in shellfish to be epizootic (the equivalent of an epidemic among humans) in some areas.[32]

"As dead canaries warn of potential mining disasters," says the Environmental Defense Fund's Dr. Harris, "diseased fish should warn of the potential hazards to fishermen and to the general public who must depend on polluted waters for drinking water supplies and sport fishing areas." [33]

*Item:* A Michigan water quality report says it's no longer safe to eat any species of fish found in Michigan's Great Lakes. Some fish of every species are banned or limited everywhere in the state.[34]

*Item:* Medical and public health personnel in several parts of the United States have advised women of child-bearing age "either not to consume sport fish or consider bottle feeding their infants" due to the prevalence of PCBs in fish.[35]

Don't assume from the foregoing that salt water fish are a safe alternative. "We can't say much about salt water fish yet," Dr. Harris told me, "because not enough research has been done on ocean fish contamination."

What happens to flesh foods *after* they leave the packinghouse is anybody's guess. Federal meat inspection doesn't apply to wholesale or retail outlets. State or local inspection of retail meat is generally little more than a casual glance—if inspection exists at all. Jon A. McClure describes a modern day *Jungle* in *Meat Eaters Are Threatened,* an account of his decade of experience as a meatcutter. McClure saw rotten meat being converted into delicatessen barbecue; old ground beef having its color renewed by a bath of industrial floor cleaner; and floors, equipment, and hand tools filthy with dirty water, blood, decayed meat, and sawdust. Over a ten-year period in five states and more than 60 supermarkets, McClure found ground beef tubs containing:

> gum, cigarettes, plastic combs, boning knives, trash, hair, detergent, floor cleaner, nitrates, cardboard, plastic and glass buttons, pieces of food trays, beer can tops, sunglasses, metal staples, employee name tags, and one prophylactic device.[36]

McClure's revelations, like the errors and excesses in federal meat and poultry inspection, would have less significance were they not part of a larger historical pattern of abuses.

*Item: Consumer Reports* found samples of supermarket hamburger "on the way to putrefaction." The testing revealed high counts of coliform bacteria (indicating fecal contamination), insect parts, and rodent hairs.

An earlier study found "appalling" bacteria counts in nationwide samples of frankfurters. A count of ten million bacteria per gram indicates the beginnings of putrefaction. Forty percent of all the samples were at or over that level. One brand had a count of 140 million. Only one-quarter of the samples had bacteria counts under one million. (A count of one to four million bacteria per gram can cause stomach distress.) [37]

*Item:* A New Hampshire butcher told National Public Radio in 1976 that he had yet to see anything thrown away in a supermarket meat department. He told of out-of-date cold cuts regularly being rescued from trash barrels, ground into sausage, and sold under the store's brand name. Meat grinders alternately used to grind beef and raw pork were usually left uncleaned "for several weeks" at a time. He described filthy and illegal procedures as being the norm.[38]

Foodborne illnesses are the most common nonfatal diseases in the United States, according to the U.S. Public Health Service. Food poisoning—with symptoms like those of a 24-hour flu— often goes unreported or undetected. (A mild case for a healthy adult, however, can be fatal in an infant, elderly person, or one already ill.) While foodborne illnesses aren't restricted to meat products, flesh foods are especially prone to trouble.

Bacteria are easily transferred from raw meat to other foods. Unwashed utensils or cutting surfaces, sloppy meat market, restaurant, or home kitchen practices may spread salmonella, staphylococcal entertoxin, shigella, and clostridium perfringens. Pork scraps mixed in with ground beef can infect the eater with trichinosis. People foolish enough to eat raw meat—as in steak tartare— may ingest beef tapeworms or contract toxoplasmosis, a disease causing birth defects and blindness in newborns. Raw fish and shellfish are subject to comparable dangers, including fish tapeworms, infectious hepatitis, and paralytic shellfish poisoning.

What further dangers can possibly await meat eaters bringing home the bacon? Well, even that hallowed North American institution—the backyard barbecue—has been found questionable. Those drops of fat dripping off the sizzling steak onto the glowing chunks of charcoal become superheated, change their chemical properties, and form benzo(a)pyrene—a carcinogen. Benzo(a)pyrene is, in fact, one of the cancer-inducing agents found in cigarette smoke. A well-grilled steak coated with greasy smoke can contain as much benzo(a)pyrene as the smoke in 30 packs of cigarettes.[39]

And as for the bacon—don't bring it home, says Dr. Michael Jacobson, codirector of the Center for Science in the Public Interest. Jacobson calls bacon "the most dangerous food in the supermarket."[40] Almost every brand of bacon, sausage, and luncheon meat in the supermarket is cured with sodium nitrite and sodium nitrate *—primarily to preserve the meat's color and eye appeal. When nitrite hits the human gut, however, it sometimes mixes with amines to form nitrosamines—the deadliest family of carcinogens.

Amines are found in cereals, prescription drugs, patent medicines, beer, wine, tea, and cigarette smoke. Fried bacon is especially dangerous, according to some researchers, because it contains its own amines. Researchers are also concerned about all the other meat products containing nitrites: smoked fish, corned beef, ham, frankfurters, salami, bologna, liver sausage, and others.

*Item:* The American Meat Institute reports that in 1977, Americans ate 1.4 billion pounds of bacon and 900 million pounds of bologna.

*Item:* The National Hot Dog and Sausage Council estimates that Americans ate 229 million hot dogs over the 1977 Memorial Day weekend. The 1977 consumption of hot dogs was a record 20 billion—or 90 frankfurters for every person in the United States. The Hot Dog Council calls the frankfurter a "very great American delicacy."

*Item:* Dr. William Lijinsky of the Frederick Cancer Research Center (National Cancer Institute)—a recognized authority on nitrosamines—says taking in nitrosamines in regular small doses as in foods laced with tiny amounts "is the most conducive means to producing cancer in animals." [41]

*Item:* In late 1977, the FDA and USDA finally moved to review their policies on nitrites in meat processing. The agencies asked the meat industry to supply data demonstrating the safety of nitrites and nitrates. USDA assured the public, however, that there was no danger in consuming nitrite-treated meats "at the present time."

---

* Nitrate breaks down in food to form nitrite.

The problems outlined in this chapter—plus the evidence against heavy consumption of cholesterol and saturated fats—have led many health-conscious people to become vegetarians or to at least cut back on the amount and type of flesh foods they eat. Still, no one, vegetarian or not, can be 100 percent safe from man-made contamination. Air and water pollution and the insidious threat of industrial wastes affect us all. We are also subject to naturally occurring toxins, molds, and diseases in nonanimal foods. Some substances in plant foods, such as oxalates and phytates, have a natural tendency to combine with specific minerals, inhibiting their absorption by the body. Pesticides, heavy metals, and air-borne contaminants may all be found in nonanimal as well as animal-origin foods.

But animals, as we've discussed, tend to accumulate and concentrate poisons in their tissues and organs. While vegetarians won't be immune to food dangers, they will have at least eliminated their exposure to flesh foods—the most meddled-with, potentially troublesome foods available.

Yet perhaps you're not ready or willing to break completely with meat eating. Perhaps you prefer to remain a "partial vegetarian" or occasional meat eater. Then you should at least pay close attention to the source of your food. Rural people have traditionally raised their own animals for meat, milk, and eggs without the help of chemical companies, drug salesmen, and federal and state bureaucracies.

Now a whole new generation of organically minded suburban and semirural homesteaders has turned to small-scale farming in search of untampered-with food. Should you choose to continue eating flesh foods—albeit less frequently and more selectively—

then buy food directly from those homesteaders, farmers, and cooperatives who put public health ahead of profit and image.

Reducing your reliance on flesh foods and turning away from the supermarket will help to limit your intake of adulterated or contaminated animal foods, but it will leave unanswered the ethical questions raised by slaughter. If you're troubled both by the ethical issues and the potential contamination of flesh foods, then why not consider becoming a lacto- or lacto-ovo-vegetarian? *

Which path you choose—vegetarianism, veganism, or occasional meat eating—is your personal decision. The important point, however, is to develop a greater sense of food awareness, and to become more knowledgeable about the production and origins of your food supply.

* Lactovarians should be concerned about residues in milk and eggs. Your exposure to contaminants can be sharply reduced by using these products prudently, by using nonfat or low-fat milk products (pesticidal residues are discarded in the fat), and by obtaining milk and eggs from organic producers and distributors.

## Chapter Eight notes.

1. Frank G. Ashbrook, *Butchering, Processing, and Preservation of Meat* (New York: Van Nostrand Reinhold Co., 1955), p. 66.
2. *Ibid.,* p. 10.
3. USDA, *Statistical Summary:* Federal Meat and Poultry Inspection for 1976 (Washington, D.C.: January 1977).
4. *Ibid.*
5. *Consumers' Research,* October 1974, p. 61.
6. Government Accounting Office Report B-163450 (Washington, D.C.: 21 November 1973).
7. Beatrice Trum Hunter, *Consumer Beware* (New York: Bantam Books, 1972), p. 117.
8. *Cooperative Farmer* (Southern States Cooperatives: Richmond, Virginia, June/July 1976).
9. Jacqueline Verrett and Jean Carper, *Eating May Be Hazardous to Your Health* (New York: Simon and Schuster, 1974), p. 176.
10. USDA, *National Food Situation,* "Sulfa Drug Residue Violations Continue in Hogs: USDA Intensifies Monitoring" (Washington, D.C.: September 1977), p. 33.
11. "No More Antibiotics in Feed?" *Cooperative Farmer* (Southern States Cooperatives: Richmond, Virginia, August 1977), p. 20.
12. Verrett, p. 177.
13. *Ibid.,* p. 170.
14. *Ibid.,* p. 176.
15. *Ibid.,* p. 175.
16. "Food: Green Grow the Profits," ABC News Closeup, telecast 21 December 1973; script pp. 25-26.
17. Edwin Chen, "Michigan: If Something Odd Happens . . ." *The Atlantic,* 240(2):12-20 (August 1977).
18. Ron M. Linton, *Terracide* (Boston: Little, Brown and Co., 1970), p. 130.
19. *National Food Situation,* p. 33.
20. Thomas Whiteside, "A Reporter at Large: The Pendulum and the Toxic Cloud," *The New Yorker* (25 July 1977), p. 55.
21. USDA, "Report of the Secretary of Agriculture to the Committee on Agriculture, House of Representatives; Committee on Agriculture and Forestry, U.S. Senate" (Washington, D.C.: 1972).
22. *Statistical Summary,* p. 3.
23. John Stowell (AP), "FDA Rejected Recall of Bad Turkey Meat," *Washington Post,* 21 March 1976, p. A3.

24. Interview with Dr. Robert H. Harris, Associate Director of the Toxic Chemicals Program, Environmental Defense Fund, Washington, D.C., 11 October 1977.

25. *Ibid.*

26. Testimony of Dr. Robert H. Harris before the Subcommittee on Investigations and Review of the House Committee on Public Works and Transportation: Washington, D.C., 27 July 1977.

27. *Ibid.*

28. *Ibid.*

29. *Ibid.*

30. *Ibid.*

31. Jill Klein, "Shellfish Are Dirty and Dangerous" *Prevention,* September 1972, p. 139.
See also: Harold Bengsch, "The Nature of Shellfish and Ecological Factors Which Contribute to their Role in Food-Borne Human Disease," *Journal of Environmental Health,* January/February 1972.

32. National Oceanic and Atmospheric Administration, National Marine Fisheries Service, *Marine Fisheries Review,* 38 (10) (October 1976).

33. Harris testimony.

34. William K. Stevens, "Contaminated Trout Being Sold: U.S. Puts Pressure on Dealers," *New York Times,* 21 June 1977, p. 1.

35. *Op. cit.* Harris.
See also: Lawrence Wright, "Troubled Waters," *New Times,* 13 May 1977, pp. 27-43.

36. Jon A. McClure, *Meat Eaters Are Threatened* (New York: Pyramid Books, 1973), p. 109.

37. "A Close Look at Hamburger," *Consumer Reports,* August 1971, pp. 478-483.
"Frankfurters," *Consumer Reports,* February 1972, pp. 73-79.
See also: "The High-Filth Diet, Compliments of FDA," *Consumer Reports,* March 1973, pp. 152-154.

38. Reported on "All Things Considered," National Public Radio Network, 27 May 1976.

39. W. Lijinsky and P. Shubick, "Benzo(a)pyrene in Charcoal Broiled Meat," *Science,* no. 145 (3 July 1964), p. 53. Benzo(a)pyrene, taken by mouth, does not have the carcinogenic potency of benzo-(a)pyrene inhaled in cigarette smoke. "But *any* exposure to carcinogens, even in tiny amounts," says Dr. Lijinsky, "represents a hazard." (Conversation with the author, 10 February 1978.)

40. Jean Carper, "Bacon: The Fat is in the Fire," *New Times,* 6 April 1976, p. 48.
41. Interview with Dr. Lijinsky on WAMU-FM (Washington, D.C.) 10 June 1977.
    See also: M. Jacobson, *"How Sodium Nitrite Can Affect Your Health,"* (Washington, D.C.: Center for Science in the Public Interest, 1973); W. Lijinsky, and S.S. Epstein, "Nitrosamines as Environmental Carcinogens," *Nature,* no. 225 (1970), pp. 21-23; and *The Lancet,* "Nitrate and Human Cancer," 2(8032):281, 6 August 1977.

# ❦ NINE ❦

# Bleeding Like a Stuck Pig

Killing animals is a grisly business. Some readers may find the revelations in this chapter repulsive, too graphic in macabre detail to be read all the way through. But if the telling is gruesome, what is the actual exploitation and slaughter of animals?

Those people who eventually become uncomfortable about the raising and killing of animals for food generally have one of three reactions: (1) they become vegetarians; (2) they raise and slaughter their own animals, believing that direct participation is less hypocritical than pretending that meat originates in the supermarket; or (3) they rationalize slaughter as inescapable ("I can't do anything about it, anyway") and essential to human nutrition.

This last group—perhaps a majority of U.S. meat eaters—is directed by habit and tradition. They've been conditioned to accept without question the notion that farm animals are carefully reared, led off to the packinghouse with the bovine, porcine, or avian equivalent of beatific smiles, and finally converted to cutlets and chops with nary a whimper. This hand-me-down fable is neatly expressed in the code phrase, "They're raised for that."

But few meat eaters other than homesteaders and farmers realize that a revolution has occurred in the way farm animals are raised for market. And let's stop using the word farm when discussing modern agricultural practices. A farm calls up images of red barns and silos silhouetted against azure skies, strong-bodied children playing in meadows, and cattle grazing on hillsides.

The new farming—factory farming (called intensive livestock husbandry by its advocates)—finds these traditional scenes of farm life good for calendars and bad for business. Agribusiness has only one goal—the most profit for the least expense. Aesthetics, harmony with nature, ecological balance, and a love of the land don't count for much. They're not cost-effective.

Farmers have always used animals in one way or another and they always will. But the small or family farm generally operated symbiotically. Farmers gave their animals and land personal, sometimes loving care, knowing that their diligence would be rewarded by healthier, more productive land and livestock. The factory farm, however, is devoted to feed conversion ratios and computerized livestock management techniques. The giant corporations controlling factory farms are committed to getting the most out of any animal or piece of land for the least cost in the shortest possible time.[1]

Beef cattle were once left to graze on pasture until they gained enough weight to be sent to market. This was a slow, natural process yielding a relatively lean, tough animal. But factory farming demands more efficiency, bulkier animals, lower feed cost per head of cattle, and bigger profits. (Agribusinessmen often refer to animals as units.) The modern practice is to ship five- to seven-month-old calves to feedlots holding 10,000 to 50,000 animals. (A few lots are capable of holding 100,000 cattle.) The shipping itself may be a brutal or fatal experience.

The only federal law governing the shipment of livestock dates from 1906. This law relates only to railroad shipment. Hardly overflowing with compassion, the law requires that cattle be fed, watered, and rested at least every 28 to 36 hours. But railroad cattle cars are little used today. And no federal humane treatment laws regulate the interstate shipment of livestock by truck—now a common means of transport.

Have you ever driven down a highway and found yourself pulling out to pass a big rig hauling cattle? As you passed by, did you glance at the cows and steers jammed against the slatted sides of the trailer? You probably had no idea that a trucker hauling livestock may legally drive two or three days nonstop, leaving the creatures he carries without feed or water. Truckers who do stop to rest or water their cargo do so because they choose to, not because the law makes it mandatory.

But to the trucker, time is money. It's not surprising that much livestock is trucked nonstop through days of suffocating heat or below-zero nights, uncared for, crowded, and literally frightened to death. Animals contract shipping fever, a type of pneumonia that kills one percent of all livestock in transit. Some of those arriving alive have broken limbs or other injuries caused by crowding and piling. Injuries reduce profits, so producers try to keep such disabilities to a minimum. Others, like the chicken industry, find it more profitable to crowd and mistreat animals, absorbing the dead and maimed livestock as a normal loss.

New stresses await at journey's end. Cattle already confused and frightened at their treatment and strange surroundings must now trot through a dipping trough of insecticides and then run a gauntlet of castration, dehorning, branding, and injections of various chemicals. The trauma of shipping and handling causes some animals to lose 10 percent of their original weight—but no matter. They will be forced to regain that and put much more weight on in a very short time.

As ruminants, cattle are best suited to feeding on grass and other roughage. A total grain diet is abnormal, causing them to gain weight much faster than they might on grass. This is just what the stock owners want, of course. Feedlot cattle are routinely overfed, getting—as one observer described it—the equivalent of a Christmas dinner three times a day for months. Grain is expensive, however, so the search for a cheaper feed or chemicals like DES that might reduce feed intake goes on endlessly. That DES-fed animals produce watery, fatty meat or that consumers may be ultimately harmed by eating it hardly seems to matter. Profit is what matters. The meat sells. People eat it.

Agribusiness will feed cattle literally *anything* that might be converted into marketable flesh. Because the design of the cow's multiple stomachs allows it to convert cellulose and other fibrous matter into calories, stockmen know that cows don't need food —as we normally think of it—to gain weight. Cattle have been fed molasses-laced sawdust, shredded newspaper and feathers, plastic pellets, processed sewage, tallow, grease, poultry manure, feedlot bedding, cotton trash, and processed slaughterhouse wastes.

Through the months feedlot cattle are thus exploited, they remain penned in yards, jammed together by the tens of thousands. Their sense of territory is disregarded, as are all their normal needs and inclinations. Even the floors in some feedlots may be slatted rather than solid. A slatted floor eases manure removal but is cruel to hooves and legs. Animals have that much more difficulty in moving about the 50 square feet of floor space allotted each one.[2] In the end, feedlot cattle are reduced to a single activity: growing fat.

Fat is what hog producers are after, and they apply the same general intensive farming practices to pigs. Though hogs may still be reared in relatively open surroundings, some U.S. producers are already moving toward indoor, rigidly confined housing. Some authorities estimate that 70 percent of all hogs raised in the United States may be confined to buildings by 1985; confinement means less hog movement with fewer calories burned and more weight gained per pound of feed. The practice benefits the farmer, however, not the pigs.

European factory farms are already using the Protecta system on breeding sows. An iron framework of pipes and clamps is used to hold the sow pinned to the ground so that she can neither turn nor stand. Designed to keep the sow from killing her piglets by lying on them, the Protecta keeps the mother clamped to the floor for four to seven weeks. Nursing piglets can be rough when they fight for teats. A sow normally protects herself by pushing the babies aside or moving about to find relief from their nagging. But the imprisoned sow is defenseless. By the time her litter is weaned, her teats and nerves are a mess.

The Protecta and similar systems have yet to catch on widely in the United States, though some producers are already confining sows to narrow stalls, keeping them strapped or tied to the floor. Piglets are removed relatively quickly (within two or three weeks, though they'd normally nurse for upwards of two months) and placed in cages to be fed by mechanical teats. Once weaned, the young pigs are moved on to finishing pens where they will either be sold to another farm or fattened for market.

"In either event," says a pamphlet of Friends of Animals, Inc.:

> . . . the pigs' normal life span of about 10 to 12 years is reduced to four to six months spent hobbling on concrete, metal or plastic slats slippery with excrement with nothing to do but eat, drink and gain weight.[3]

Their reputations aside, pigs are intelligent and sensitive animals, reacting sharply to stress and boredom. Being jammed together makes them restless and combative. They may fight and bite at their neighbors' tails. (One expert recommended an antidote for boredom. He suggested stockmen hang a chain from the ceiling to give the pigs something to look at.) Factory farmers have an ingenious solution for tail biting, however. They routinely amputate the pigs' tails, thus solving the problem.

Both pigs and cattle are also subjected to an Orwellian array of intensive breeding practices. But even the preliminary selection of those animals most likely to produce meaty offspring involves some cruelty if the stockman chooses to use a backfat probe. This is essentially a sharp-pointed rule that is stabbed into the hog's back, through the fat to the muscle. Three such measurements of backfat thickness are commonly taken and averaged.

Hogs with good breeding characteristics may be manipulated with artificial insemination, hormone treatments, and surgical manipulation of eggs and embryos. A sow on a factory farm may have her ova surgically removed a half-dozen or more times in a year. The eggs are then implanted in other sows, producing more "quality" pigs than a single sow might yield in her lifetime.

And as if castration of boars weren't enough, another practice used is surgical penis deviation. The boar's penis is rerouted through the side of the animal's body. While the pig can urinate, it is unable to mate and is used solely to help the artificial inseminator by locating females in heat.

Ruth Harrison, a British writer who reviewed factory farming techniques a decade ago, realized that when animals are so treated, they soon cease to be regarded as flesh and blood creatures.

They become "animal machines"—the title of Ms. Harrison's book. As badly as cattle and swine may be handled, the metaphor is no more apt than when applied to the rearing of chickens and veal calves.

The chicken house, a small clapboard building with a tin roof and enclosed yard, is still an essential part of small farms and homesteads. Chickens are free to run loose, scratch for worms and bugs, take dust baths, and establish their pecking order. But to the few giant corporations controlling the U.S. poultry industry, such liberties are wasteful and unproductive. And to the chicken industry, production is everything.

Chickens are normally sensitive to noise, excitement, and unfamiliar birds. Each flock of 90 birds or less soon develops a hierarchy or pecking order. Birds are thus able to develop a sense of territory and rank. When chickens are upset, either by stress or nutritional deficiencies, they respond with aggressive pecking and cannibalism. They also get sick and die more easily. The small farmer realizes this and tries for a well-managed henhouse.

But the factory farm deals in huge numbers. As long as the overhead stays within bounds, the condition of individual birds doesn't matter. Modern chicken houses are block-long windowless buildings that house 10,000 to 25,000 broilers with about one-half square foot of floor space per bird. Living in this controlled environment, the birds are unable to establish their instinctive social order, nor do they ever see daylight or bare ground—much less a worm. Broiler chickens, like feedlot cattle and hogs, have one function during their brief unnatural lives: eating heavily chemicalized feeds in order to gain weight rapidly.

But intensively reared birds subjected to noise, crowding, and confusion soon develop stress symptoms bordering on hysteria. Because they sicken frequently, they're fed antibiotics. Because they violently peck at each other—sometimes killing and eating weaker birds—they're routinely debeaked. (The end of the beak is cut off with an electrically heated knife—not a painless process).

Because their stress can be partially reduced by darkness,

many mature chickens are raised in perpetually dimmed houses. Younger birds may be kept in 24-hour artificial daylight, the better to stimulate their growth.

These huge chicken houses are heated in winter by the birds' body heat. But in summer, with only large fans used to keep air circulating, a sharp change in the climate can mean disaster. The record hot temperatures and humidity of the summer of 1977 proved too much for these overcrowded chickens. In Maryland alone, chickens died by the tens of thousands in July. The situation was even worse farther south.

Unnatural breeding methods make intensively reared birds especially vulnerable to even minor changes in their environment. Forced to grow fat quickly, the young birds have difficulty adjusting to their abnormally excess weight. Unsteady on their legs and on the edge of panic, the birds just "plop over and die" when the houses get too hot.[4]

And if the heat doesn't get them, intensively housed birds may kill themselves. A sudden shock or disturbance in the house can spark panic, causing the birds to run towards the corners of the building. Squawking in terror, falling all over themselves in a futile attempt to escape, the birds pile up in a heap. The birds caught underneath die of suffocation.

The world of the laying hen is equally unreal. The majority of the almost 300 million laying hens in the United States are confined to wire cages for the duration of their short, egg-producing lives. Several debeaked birds are crowded into one cage. To maximize space, the cages are stacked in tiers. (A major egg producer in California keeps five birds in each 16-by-18-inch cage, housing 90,000 birds in each building.) Because the cage floors are set on a slight downward tilt so eggs will roll forward for collection, the hens have a hard time standing comfortably. Birds may only be able to sit or stand, with no room to even stretch their wings.

Their claws grow unchecked in the cages, sometimes getting caught in the wire flooring. Because one man may handle 50,000 birds at the same time, hens who get entangled may stay trapped;

the flesh on their toes may eventually grow around the wire bars, ensnaring them until death. No creature is suited to life in a cage. Metal soon rubs away feathers and skin, leaving raw flesh open to pain and infection. But no one cares about the sick and injured until their numbers cut into profits. It's cheaper to shovel out the dead birds.

When the hens' egg production wanes, producers may resort to stimulating a forced molt. This shock treatment involves a sharp restriction in food and a drastic cut in light exposure. The rapidity of the change kills some birds outright. Those who survive yield a few more months of increased production.

Overcrowded, subjected to all the conditions that terrify a bird, fed the cheapest feed, stimulated by drugs and chemicals, manipulated by an artificial environment, the tormented battery birds (as they are called in Britain) are the ultimate animal machines. When their productive lives end after a year to 18 months (birds less intensively housed normally go on laying eggs far longer), they will be shipped to the slaughterhouse. They will not even be fed in the last days of their lives. Why waste feed on unproductive units bound for the packinghouse?

Knowing this, how can lacto-ovo-vegetarians justify their use of eggs? They can't, really, unless they at least buy eggs from a source that avoids cruelty and intensive methods. Most natural food stores sell eggs from hens free of chemicalized feed and intensive conditions. Family farms and homesteads still keep free-running chickens. Most homesteaders are happy to sell their surplus eggs—usually at lower than supermarket prices. Buying eggs directly also means, in most cases, that you'll be able to inspect the premises and ask questions about how the birds are reared and what they're fed.

As the chicken has been made into an egg machine, so has the dairy cow been exploited as a four-legged milk pump. Small farms still keep a family cow pastured in a meadow, but the agribusinessman has no time for bucolic musings about the nobility of brown-eyed Bossy. His search is for Super Cow! The modern dairy cow is bred, fed, medicated, inseminated, and manipulated to a single end: milk production.

While a cow on a small farm may give 6,000 to 10,000 pounds * of milk yearly, and the average commercial herd cow yields 14,000 to 15,000 pounds, dairy scientists are always pushing to increase milk output. One record-breaking cow recently produced 44,000 pounds of milk in a ten-month period—four times the national average. But constantly working to increase milk output doesn't necessarily come cheap to the cow. Confinement is already standard for large herds. Cows are allowed to move about only in a pen, though most of their lives are spent on the concrete or slatted floors of their stalls. Some operations forego the exercise pen and confine their cows to stalls for months at a time. Swollen udders, mastitis, sore legs, infected feet, and stress-related conditions are common among intensively reared cattle.

When a cow's milk production drops—as it must with age—the creature is summarily shipped to the slaughterhouse. Vegans are correct in charging that milk consumption indirectly supports exploitation and slaughter. But again, concerned lactarians can obtain milk produced under less-intensive conditions. Small farms often sell surplus milk, natural food stores offer milk from nonfactory farms, and some homesteaders will sell their surplus goat's milk, the goat being a favorite milk producer on the small farm.

None of this will satisfy vegans and animal liberationists who want total freedom from animal products—and total freedom for animals as well. Vegans will point out that one invariable by-product of dairying is excess calves. Cows must be bred each year in order to freshen and produce milk. What happens to their offspring? The small farm may keep the calf as a herd member, but the dairy industry ships most calves on to the feedlot and slaughterhouse. And some of the calves—brought into the world only to satisfy the needs of the milk industry—end up as veal calves.

Of all the atrocities of intensive farming, and there are many more than space will allow in this book, few are as cruel as those visited on the veal calf. Meat eaters fond of veal may think the pale, tender flesh they enjoy comes from a particular breed of calf. It does not. The so-called veal calf is an ordinary calf removed

* Whole milk weighs approximately 8.6 pounds per gallon.

from its mother only three or four days after birth. The calf, like other mammals, is dependent on its mother for nourishment, affection, and physical contact. But no affection is wasted on the veal calf.

The calf is locked in a slatted stall. No bedding is provided. The stall is just large enough to let the calf stand or lie down. When the animal does lie down, it must do so on its own legs; it cannot stretch out. It cannot even turn around in the stall. This treatment has a specific purpose. Pale, tender veal comes from a malnourished, anemic animal whose feed and movement are severely restricted. Allowed to move or exercise, allowed to feed on grass, grain, or stall bedding, the calf would develop dark and toughened flesh—the last thing the veal producer wants. His goal is to produce the heaviest veal animal in the shortest time. To do this, he will feed the calf an iron-deficient liquid diet based on a formula of dry milk and additives. The calf's water intake will be restricted to increase the appetite and to limit the iron content of the diet.

But because the calf naturally craves iron, it may lick the iron fittings on its stall or attempt to lick its own urine. Veal producers combat this by tethering the calf's head and placing a bar behind its hind legs, further restricting its movement. This solves another problem: since the calf has been so quickly removed from its mother, its urge to suck remains strong. The animal will attempt to suck on its stall or its own body. Immobilizing the calf stops these vices—as the factory farmer calls all habits not conducive to profit making.

Other veal producers prefer to deal with stress symptoms by turning off the lights when the calves aren't feeding. Because feeding amounts to less than an hour a day, and because most veal-rearing buildings may be windowless, veal calves may spend their wretched lives confined in darkness. Unable to suck, ruminate, eat or drink properly, and deprived of contact with other animals, veal calves stand prisoners on the slatted floors of their dark stalls for three or four months. Weak and susceptible to illness, they are dosed with antibiotics and drugs. They will leave their pens only when ready for slaughter.

People who have difficulty relating to the plight of factory farming's victims should visualize the above conditions applied to those animals we call pets. Imagine five dogs stuffed in a cage, unable to move, their teeth pulled to minimize biting, their flesh worn bloody by the metal bars. Imagine 10,000 of them, 50,000 of them imprisoned so for a year or more. Imagine dogs in thousands of cages stacked tier upon tier. Imagine the odor, the noise: tens of thousands of dogs, many of them sick and injured, howling out their agony to unconcerned humans.

Dogs and cats and horses are protected against such brutality by laws, though common decency, mental competence, and compassion alone would prevent most people from sanctioning wanton cruelty. Yet no compassion extends to the animal prisoners of factory farms.\* The barbarities of intensive husbandry are acceptable, even desirable (keeps prices down), only because enough people still believe in the myth of happy barnyard animals—or because they shut their eyes and ears to the truth.

Ironically, the evidence of these billions of tortured lives is eaten each day by people who would rise enraged at the sight of a neighbor's dog tied to a tree too long or a stray cat teased by thoughtless children. But unfortunately, the closest most Americans get to farm animals is when eating them. "Oh well," some people might say, "at least the animals are slaughtered humanely."

The British Vegetarian Society, through its magazine *The Vegetarian*, would have us know differently.

> A split second before the gun was fired, the cow moved its head. And instead of falling, stood with a small fountain of blood several inches high spurting upwards from the small hole in its head made by the captive bolt. It took several long seconds before the gun was reloaded and fired again. . . . [A]fter-

---

\* Animal welfare laws protect circus, zoo, and laboratory animals—*not* farm livestock.

wards, the cow was hoisted in the air, still kicking, before having its throat cut. Its udders began to spurt milk.[5]

The United States does have the Humane Slaughter Act, a federal law meant to ensure that livestock are dispatched with a minimum of suffering. But this statute, as we'll see, is a curious piece of legislation. The fact is that numbers and profits in agribusiness are too big to leave much room for consideration or compassion. Animal welfare becomes an issue on the factory farm and in the packinghouse only when mistreatment cuts into profits.

Doing in animals quickly and cleanly is hardly a new idea, of course. Farmers and homesteaders have traditionally tried to make the best of an unpleasant business by lopping the chicken's head off with a stroke or shooting the hog dead with a single, well-placed bullet. Yet surprisingly, institutionalized humane slaughter techniques didn't come into widespread use in this country until after 1960—rather late, considering the extent of our social consciousness in recent decades.

Only pressure from animal welfare groups and humane associations finally impelled Congress to pass the Humane Slaughter Act in 1958. Prior to July, 1960, when the law went into effect, more than 95 percent of all animals under federal inspection were slaughtered by methods now deemed inhumane. The Act decrees:

> . . . in the case of cattle, calves, horses, mules, sheep, swine, and other livestock, all animals [must be] rendered insensible to pain by a single blow or gunshot or an electrical, chemical or other means that is rapid and effective, before being shackled, hoisted, thrown, cast, or cut.[6]

Although the Humane Slaughter Act says forcefully, "It is therefore declared to be the policy of the United States that the slaughtering of livestock and the handling of livestock in connection with slaughter shall be carried out only by humane methods," the law is all bark and no bite. The Act carries no provision for punishment of those who choose to use inhumane slaughtering techniques. Brutal handling of livestock and cruel slaughtering methods can't even be called illegal since the Humane Slaughter Act requires only *voluntary* compliance.

There is, however, an oblique punishment for those plants

using inhumane killing techniques. Since the Act requires federal agencies to buy meat only from establishments complying with the Act, any plants using inhumane slaughter would be unable to bid for government contracts. They would thus lose out on the lucrative business of supplying meat to the armed forces, USDA school lunch programs, or any of the many agencies and programs purchasing meat. But using this economic inducement rather than the threat of punishment leaves a substantial loophole.

What about those packinghouses with no interest in government contracts? There are many. They may use whatever methods of slaughter they choose, however inhumane or barbaric. You may be surprised to learn that the Federal Meat Inspection Act and the Humane Slaughter Act are two distinct laws unrelated to each other. A packer without a federal contract may kill or handle his livestock in any manner and still have the meat federally inspected and shipped to market. The federal stamp of inspection is no guarantee that the animal was humanely slaughtered.

The four slaughtering methods the government has declared humane are:

1. Captive bolt
2. Carbon dioxide
3. Electrical stunning
4. Gunshot

The captive bolt gun or mechanical stunner is powered by compressed air or blank cartridges. The device fires a pencil-thick sliding bolt into the animal's forehead. Similar bolts may be mushroom shaped, designed to stun by concussion rather than penetration of the skull.

Carbon dioxide is used on swine (sometimes sheep and calves) who ride a conveyor belt down to a pit filled with a 65 to 75 percent concentration of $CO_2$. The gas causes unconsciousness, though how fast this occurs depends on the animal's size.

The electrical stunner usually consists of two electrodes wielded by a packinghouse worker. The stunners are shoved against the animal as it is driven by, shocking it into insensibility.

Small operations and most farmers still favor gunshot, using a pistol or rifle to fire a .22 or .38 caliber bullet into the animal's brain.

Notice that none of these methods is designed to kill the animal outright. The object is to stun the creature while keeping its heart beating long enough to pump out as much blood as possible. The animals are alive, but presumably insensible to pain. Once unconscious, the animal is shackled and hoisted up by one hind leg and quickly stabbed through the breast or neck with a six-inch double-edged sticking knife, severing the major arteries. If done correctly, as an eyewitness described the sticking of a hog, the blood "gushes out, at about a 45-degree angle downward, thick as a ship's hawser." [7]

But slaughter techniques are only as effective as the people using them. The slaughterer using a captive bolt gun on cattle, horses, mules, sheep, calves, or goats is supposed to down them with one shot. Yet animals—whatever their supposed lack of intelligence—do not merely stand passively on the killing room floor, chewing their cud, serenely awaiting the moment of death.

USDA regulations warn that:

> Delivery of calm animals to the stunning areas is essential since accurate placement of stunning equipment is difficult on nervous or injured animals. . . . [T]his requires that, in driving animals to the stunning area, electrical equipment be used as little as possible and with the lowest effective voltage.[8]

(The electrical equipment referred to is the infamous electric cattle prod, standard equipment in packinghouses.)

USDA guidelines also warn that:

> The stunning operation is an exacting procedure and requires a well-trained and experienced operator. He must be able to accurately place the stunning instrument to produce immediate unconsciousness. He must use the correct detonating charge with regard to kind, breed, size, age, and sex of the animal to produce the desired results.[9]

Some small British slaughterhouses adopted a follow-up to the captive bolt to further disable animals. If nothing else, it shows how far some people will go in developing various efficient methods of dispatching animals. Called a pithing wire, this foot-long piece of stiff wire is poked sharply into the quarter-inch hole left in the cow's skull and reamed about to traumatize the brain and spinal cord. The pithing wire—not used in the United States, according to USDA experts on slaughter techniques—is supposed to scramble the cow's nerve centers, preventing it from getting to its feet. But as one witness found, pithing

> . . . caused the animal to kick even more violently . . . and although a surgeon may tell you that the kicking is merely a nervous reaction, you can sense the desperation, that awful fight within. It grips you like an electric current. The pitiful little sigh as the fight is lost may also be a nervous reaction as the deflating lungs activate the voice box—we have heard the same pathetic little sound from human friends.[10]

Carbon dioxide gas is used for swine, sometimes for sheep and calves, but not for beef cattle. It is probably a blessing compared to other slaughter techniques. But $CO_2$ pits, expensive to build and maintain, are only used by large packinghouses. And even big companies may prefer alternate slower methods: gas relaxes the animals' bowels, creating a considerable mess.

Electrical stunning is preferred by many packinghouses, particularly those killing swine. Electricity is relatively quick if the equipment and employees are functioning properly. But several factors can limit the effectiveness of electrical stunning: corroded electrodes may decrease the amount of current delivered; a worker may fail to apply the electrodes with enough pressure to make good contact; or a too-wet, mud-caked, or excessively hairy area on the animal's body may reduce the transmitted shock. If either the operator or the equipment fails, the shock may only paralyze the creature, leaving it alert to the agony of hoisting and sticking.[11]

The USDA also calls the use of gunshot "an exacting procedure," requiring not only an experienced slaughterer, but also the proper firearm loaded with hollow point or "frangible iron composition bullets." And although you might think a single gunshot would be quick and deadly, it doesn't always work out that way. Says Richard Rhodes, writing in *Harper's Magazine:*

> I never saw our farm manager more upset than the day we were getting ready to butcher five pigs. He shot one through the nose rather than through the brain. It ran screaming around the pen, and he almost cried. It took two more bullets to finish the animal off, and this good man was shaking when he had finished. "I hate that," he said to me. "I hate to have them in pain. Pigs are so damned hard to kill clean." [12]

Humane slaughter methods have been adopted by many packinghouses for several reasons, none particularly based on compassion. Humane slaughtering techniques allow bidding on federal contracts, minimize danger to workers, and reduce the incidence of bruised or damaged carcasses. At this writing, 98 percent of all cattle, 95 percent of all hogs, and 85 percent of all sheep and calves under federal inspection are killed by methods listed in the Humane Slaughter Act. That still leaves at least several million or more animals annually killed by traditional methods in plants not federally inspected or plants without government contracts. Traditional techniques make no provision for stunning animals prior to slaughter.

The traditional method for killing hogs, for example, is to shackle, hoist, and stick a fully conscious animal. Hogs may also be killed by being "thrown" or "cast." This dangerous technique involves several men who must literally wrestle the pig to the ground. Once they manage to turn the animal on its back, someone stabs the screaming hog through the brisket. Sheep, lambs, and calves may be treated similarly. As one text on meat production suggests,

> Since calves struggle for a longer period after sticking than other classes of livestock, it is well to hoist them before sticking.[13]

And although the Humane Slaughter Act also mentions as humane "a single blow" to the animal's head, a USDA committee later classified the traditional poleax or knocking hammer as inhumane. The poleax still is being used in some slaughtering operations, however. Basically a sledgehammer, the poleax is cheap, but hard on man and beast. The slaughterer must face his frightened victim, wind up, and try to slam the heavy hammer between and about one inch above the animal's eyes. Says Peter Singer in *Animal Liberation:*

> If the swing is a fraction astray the hammer can crash through the animal's eye or nose; then, as the animal thrashes around in agony and terror, several more blows may be needed to knock it unconscious.[14]

In calling the poleax inhumane, USDA advisers wisely realized that the poleaxer's blows would become increasingly more inaccurate as the work day continued. Besides, how do expert poleaxers learn their trade if not by making mistakes on live animals?

How many packinghouses still kill with barbaric methods like the poleax? How many small operations still hoist conscious animals before sticking? No USDA figures are kept on intrastate plants. But since half the states have no laws pertaining to slaughtering techniques, the USDA estimates that there are at least 276 plants using inhumane methods to kill millions of animals each year. (This figure is the result of an informal USDA telephone survey. A USDA official admits the actual figure may be much higher.)[15] Several bills have been submitted to Congress calling for mandatory humane slaughter in all the states. Thus far, none of this legislation has made it out of committee.

The farcical aspects of the Humane Slaughter Act can be seen in its failure to protect poultry. Why are chickens, turkeys, ducks, geese, and other fowl excluded from federal and state humane slaughter laws? "Well," says a USDA poultry specialist, "nobody gets much upset about how chickens are handled. You can identify with a little brown-eyed calf, but a chicken is just a dumb bird." Animal welfare groups say it was hard enough to get humane laws passed regarding mammals; only so many changes in U.S. traditions and customs can be effected at one time. Some of these groups hope to have humane slaughter coverage extended to poultry in the future. (The more-militant animal liberation-vegetarian groups want to see all slaughter discontinued.)

For now, however, chickens continue to be handled like dumb birds. They are, in large poultry packinghouses, attached by their feet to a moving belt or chain. Conscious birds are shuttled along upside down to either a knife-wielding human or a motorized revolving blade that slices their necks through just short of decapitation. (The head is left attached to the body for inspection purposes.) A good worker can kill about 3,000 birds an hour. Small operations may still kill birds either by breaking the neck or by forcing a knife blade into the bird's mouth, piercing the base of the skull and causing a fatal hemorrhage. This method is cruel and unusual by any standards. "If a good bleed does not occur," cautions one textbook, "try again until there is free bleeding." [16]

Then there are fish. Because fish are neither mammals nor likely subjects for anthropomorphizing, few people think of compassion as being remotely applicable to tuna, sardines, bass and the like. Commercial fishing boats hook and net tons of fish, dumping them into holds where they slowly suffocate or are crushed to death under their own weight.

Sport fishing is the most popular outdoor sport in the United States. Few people ever consider that hooking fish and watching them flop about until dead is anything more than a relaxing afternoon. Children are taught to bait their own hooks and put the fish out of its misery as object lessons in self-reliance. Angling is so deeply ingrained in the American experience that a vegetarian attacking what Izaak Walton called a "calm, quiet, innocent recreation" might as well attack Mom and The Flag. Yet what is fishing (and hunting) if not ritualized violence?

Shoppers would complain if a dead cow or pig were to be stretched out full-length in a supermarket showcase. But row upon row of dead, staring fish stacked on chipped ice elicits no more response than, "Are they fresh?" Live lobsters imprisoned in fish counter tanks are objects of scorn and fun. Children tap on the glass and giggle, "Ooh, aren't they ugly?"

Gourmet cooks hardly concerned with the lobster's lack of beauty will plunge the live creature into boiling water and watch approvingly as it turns bright red. That many people claim to be vegetarians while continuing to eat fish, crustaceans, and shellfish shows not only their misunderstanding of the basic meaning of vegetarianism, but also demonstrates the prevalent insensitivity toward nonmammals as living, feeling creatures.

Fish are less like us than a little brown-eyed calf, but does this lack of mammalian characteristics give us license to destroy them wantonly, as a pastime? Henry David Thoreau wrote in *Walden:*

> I have found repeatedly, of late years, that I cannot fish without falling a little in self-respect. I have tried it again and again. I have skill at it, and, like many of my fellows, a certain instinct for it, which revives from time to time, but always when I have done I feel that it would have been better if I had not fished . . . and when I had caught and cleaned and cooked and eaten my fish, they seemed not to have fed me essentially. It was insignificant and unnecessary, and cost more than it came to. A little bread or a few potatoes would have done as well, with less trouble and filth.[17]

We come now to the most controversial part of the humane slaughter issue: the kosher or ritual slaughter practiced by Orthodox Jews and Muslims. Kosher slaughter in the United States—for reasons to be explained—requires that a conscious animal be shackled and hoisted before having its throat cut. Brutal? Yes, say animal welfare groups. No, says the Humane Slaughter Act, which exempts

> . . . the ritual requirements of the Jewish faith or any other religious faith that prescribes a method of slaughter whereby the animal suffers loss of consciousness by anemia of the brain caused by the simultaneous and instantaneous severance of the carotid arteries with a sharp instrument.[18]

Shehitah or kosher slaughter was actually designed to be painless and compassionate. Many early rabbis believed killing animals was inherently cruel but necessary to meet human needs.

Compassion for animals is traditional in Judaism; hunting for sport and the abuse of animals for amusement are specifically forbidden by law. The strict rules and specialized techniques of shehitah were developed to produce a quick death. Animals must be killed by a single, uninterrupted knife slash across the throat; the carotid arteries must be cut with one stroke. The 14-inch blade used by the shohet—a specially trained slaughterer—must be razor sharp, free of any nicks or imperfections that might cause it to bind or drag.

Shehitah, according to most veterinarians, causes almost immediate death. Blood dumps out in such volume that the brain is almost instantly drained, causing unconsciousness. But some animals do kick for a time after the initial bleeding. Critics of shehitah say these thrashings may not be totally reflexive. Enough blood may remain in the brain to maintain life (if not sensibility) for perhaps 15 seconds. Can the animal feel pain during this brief time? Veterinarians disagree.

Shehitah may have originally been designed to provide a merciful death, but a curious combination of federal and religious laws have turned that goal into a mockery. Hebrew law requires only that an animal be conscious before cutting—not that it be hoisted. But the 1906 Meat Inspection Act requires that a slaughtered animal not fall into its own blood. Thus, to satisfy both laws, kosher slaughterhouses must shackle and hoist conscious animals. Jerking a thousand-pound steer up by one leg and letting it hang for agonizing minutes until the shohet makes his "merciful" cut hardly squares with the spirit of the Humane Slaughter Act or with Judaism's ancient principle of *Tsa'ar Ba'ale Chaim* (Do Not Inflict Pain on Animals). This is the abattoir's version of Catch-22.

A few kosher slaughterhouses now use a squeeze cage that immobilizes the animal above the floor without shackling or hoisting. Hydraulic fingers hold the creature's head immobile while the cut is made. The device is expensive, however—ten to twenty thousand dollars each—and few small operators can afford its purchase.

Meat eaters can't avoid the flesh of ritually slaughtered animals by simply avoiding kosher meat. Orthodox Jews and Muslims are permitted to eat only certain cuts of meat. The remainder of the carcass, primarily the hindquarters, is shipped to the open market. This represents a tremendous volume of meat in some eastern states. And because kosher meat is inspected twice—by a rabbi and by a meat inspector—it has developed a reputation among both Jews and non-Jews as a more wholesome product than nonkosher meat. Whether this reputation is deserved or not, the demand for kosher meat has actually increased by about a third during the past five years.[19]

The bitter controversy surrounding the methods used in kosher slaughter involves a complex of issues as diverse as animal welfare, anti-Semitism, and Constitutional guarantees of religious freedom. The debate over the rightness of using ancient slaughter techniques in modern times divides many in the Jewish community. Some rabbis believe Jewish tradition provides ample room for change. They, and some Jewish laity, would like to either abandon kosher slaughter entirely or modify it by making the squeeze cage compulsory in all kosher slaughterhouses. Some have suggested that animals might be rendered unconscious by $CO_2$ without violating Hebrew law. But most Orthodox Jews—like fundamentalists in any religion—consider all but the squeeze cage a travesty, an infringement on their religious freedom and their need to adhere to the letter of ancient law. Other observant Jews have become vegetarians or eat only fish to avoid participating in shehitah. (Nothing in Jewish or Islamic law compels one to eat flesh foods; injunctions govern only the origin and handling of specific foods.) The controversy over the issue of kosher slaughter can never be solved without angering one side or the other. But to ethical vegetarians, there is no issue.

To single out Orthodox Jews as using a cruel method of slaughter to satisfy civil and religious laws implies that more modern methods are less cruel. They are, of course, in a strict comparison; but focusing on this argument misses the larger issue: *any* slaughter method is cruel if it results in the needless death of an animal. Many animal welfare groups find themselves in the peculiar position of attacking one method of slaughter while supporting another, saying—in effect—that killing animals is defensible when the slaughter technique is approved. Like the man who tried to stop a lynching, they compromise by suggesting that the lynch mob at least hang the victim from a lower limb.

As an ethical vegetarian, I've often wondered how the words humane and slaughter can be so easily fitted together. According to *Webster's,* humane means "compassion, sympathy, or consideration for other human beings or animals." Since the most considerate behavior is to avoid inflicting pain or discomfort on another creature altogether, the idea of showing compassion while needlessly killing an animal is somewhat contradictory.

I say "somewhat" because I have no doubt that many small farmers and homesteaders make a sincere effort to be considerate of their livestock right up to and including the moment of slaughter. The family operation raising a few hogs or a steer in no way resembles the monstrous assembly line in a packinghouse.

If you're an occasional meat eater seriously concerned with the way animals are reared and eventually dispatched, then either plan on raising and slaughtering your own animals or buy your meat from someone who shows some regard for his animals' natural needs and comfort.

Animals on the homestead are more likely to be treated as beings rather than units. They often become an integral part of the family's life. Concern and sympathy for the animals sometimes runs so deep, in fact, that killing them becomes a wrenching experience. Did you ever watch the reaction of 4-H youngsters saying farewell to their steers at the county fair?

Many homesteaders send their livestock off to be slaughtered by someone else. Firing the final shot into an animal you've raised from birth is just too awful for some people to contemplate, no matter how quick or humane the death.

If you're at all disturbed by seeing animals killed—much less by the prospect of doing it yourself—then perhaps you're a latent vegetarian. Perhaps you're suppressing your deepest feelings by remaining even an occasional meat eater.

Imagine there were overnight changes in factory farming, that the intensive and brutal practices described in this chapter were suddenly replaced by husbandry that provided for the comfort and natural needs of animals. Imagine that slaughtering advanced to the point that cattle, fowl, pigs, and fish could be dispatched in a truly painless, even gentle manner. Such a revolution would surely make life and death easier for countless animals, and it would please many animal welfare activists. But would it satisfy ethical vegetarians? Not at all. Novelist Brigid Brophy writes:

> I don't myself believe that, even when we fulfill our minimum obligations not to cause pain, we have the right to kill animals. I know I would have no right to kill you, however painlessly, just because I liked your flavour, and I am not in a position to judge that your life is worth more to you than the animal's to it.[19]

Consider the astronomical numbers of animals slaughtered for food just in the United States: almost 38 million cattle, 70 million pigs, four million calves, six million sheep, 300,000 horses, and 50,000 goats are killed annually under federal inspection.[20] Can the presumption of humane slaughter alone justify the extinction of more than 119 million animals every year? If so, how does one justify the killing of poultry who are not accorded humane treatment under the law? In 1977, more than 13 million ducks, 128 million turkeys, and three billion chickens were killed.[21] These figures for mammals and birds are for those slaughtered under federal inspection. The actual number of animals killed is considerably higher when you add in those creatures destroyed in intrastate or kosher plants, those killed in foreign packinghouses for export to the United States, those killed on farms, or those killed by hunters and trappers who shoot, club, spear, and snare millions more for their flesh, feathers, fur, hides, and heads.

Thus, every year in the United States alone, about as many animals as there are humans on earth are slaughtered. Can this slaughter be excused merely by dubbing it humane, painless, or merciful? Ethical vegetarians don't believe that methodology can somehow reduce the moral weight of one's actions.

The best philosophical traditions in our culture say we should feel *something* in the face of violence and cruelty—guilt, remorse, compassion, shock, or outrage. But we are also encouraged to suppress those feelings when violence and cruelty supply us with meat. That twinge in the stomach remains, however, and it is not always easily suppressed. "It is a faint intimation," wrote Thoreau about his growing discomfort with fishing, "yet so are the first streaks of morning."

Perhaps that intimation, that twinge is the tugging of a spiritual gyroscope trying to guide us toward what we already know: that killing animals is a nasty business made all the worse when the slaughter is unnecessary; that many of us wear the mantle of predator lightly and uncomfortably; that *all* life is worthy of mutual consideration and compassion; and that respect for the rights of others doesn't end with the human race. Respect for a fish? Consideration for a chicken? Is this anthropomorphic vegetarian sentimentality, or can a case be made for the rights of animals? "Because the heart beats under a covering of hair, feathers, or wings, is it therefore, to be of no account?" [22]

*Chapter Nine notes.*

1. Factory farming excesses have been well documented. See: Ruth Harrison, *Animal Machines* (London: Vincent Stuart, Ltd., 1964); Beatrice Trum Hunter, *Consumer Beware* (New York: Bantam Books, 1972); Peter Singer, *Animal Liberation* (New York: New York Review of Books, 1975).

2. Singer, p. 136; see also Albert Levie, *The Meat Handbook,* 3rd ed., (Westport, Connecticut: AVI Publishing Co., 1970).

3. "Factory Farming," Friends of Animals, Inc. pamphlet, (New York: May 1976), p. 9.

4. Vernon C. Thompson, "Heat Wave Killing Maryland, Virginia Chickens," *Washington Post,* 17 July 1977.
   See also: Stephen Singular, "Brave New Chickens," *New Times,* 29 April 1977, pp. 40-55; also Singer, p. 105.

5. J.W. Tipton, "What Switched You On?" *The Vegetarian* (Cheshire, England: British Vegetarian Society, June 1973), p. 18.

6. Humane Slaughter Act of 1958, Public Law 85-765.

7. Richard Rhodes, "Watching the Animals," *Harper's Magazine,* March 1970, p. 91.

8. "Animals and Animal Products," Title 9, Chapter 3, (Meat and Poultry Inspection), Subchapter D: Humane Slaughter of Livestock, part 390 (USDA/APHIS).

9. *Ibid.*

10. Geoffrey Rudd, *Why Kill for Food?* (Cheshire, England: The Vegetarian Society, 1956).

11. Paul J. Brandly, et al., *Meat Hygiene,* 3rd ed., (Philadelphia: Lea and Febiger, 1966), p. 96.

12. Rhodes, p. 94.

13. Thomas P. Ziegler, *The Meat We Eat* (Danville, Illinois: The Interstate Printers and Publishers, Inc., 1968), p. 116.

14. Singer, p. 160.

15. Off-the-record conversations with veterinarians and employees of USDA's Food Safety and Quality Service (FSQS) and Animal Plant Health Inspection Service (APHIS) in the summer of 1977, Washington, D.C.

16. Ziegler, p. 214.

17. Henry David Thoreau, *Walden* (from the chapter "Higher Laws").

18. Humane Slaughter Act.

The Vegetarian Alternative

19. Brigid Brophy, "The Rights of Animals" (Cheshire, England: The Vegetarian Society, 1965) pamphlet, p. 6.
20. USDA, "Statistical Summary: Federal Meat and Poultry Inspection for Fiscal Year 1976" (Washington, D.C.).
21. *Ibid.*
22. Jean Paul Richter (1763-1825), "Levana, oder Erzichungsehre," quoted in J. Todd Ferrier, *On Behalf of the Animals* (London: The Order of the Cross, 1968), p. 87.

## ❧ TEN ❧

# Behold, I Have Given You Every Herb

You have just dined, and however scrupulously the slaughter-house is concealed in the graceful distance of miles, there is complicity.
—Ralph Waldo Emerson

Of all the reasons for vegetarianism, none has deeper roots in human history, none so stirs the emotions, and none creates more controversy than the ethical argument—that it's morally wrong to kill and eat animals. When the Greek philosopher Empedokles cried out in the fifth century B.C., "Will you not put an end to this accursed slaughter? Will you not see that you are destroying your-self in blind ignorance of soul?", he wasn't bewailing the high cost of meat. Nor was the Greek essayist and biographer Plutarch (A.D. 46?-c.120) concerned with the hygienic qualities of flesh foods when he asked in an essay:

Can you really ask what reason Pythagoras had for abstaining from flesh? For my part I rather wonder both by what accident and in what state of soul or mind the first man did so, touched his mouth to gore and brought his lips to the flesh of a dead creature, he who set forth tables of dead, stale bodies and ventured to call food and nourishment the parts that had a little before bellowed and cried, moved and lived. How could his eyes endure the slaughter when throats were slit and hides flayed and limbs torn from limb? How could his nose endure the stench? How was it that the pollution did not turn away his

197

taste, which made contact with the sores of others and sucked juices and serums from mortal wounds? [1]

Many of civilization's earliest thinkers—Buddha, Mahavira, Ovid, Plotinus, Porphyry, Pythagoras, and others—were opposed to flesh eating because they believed the slaughter of animals was immoral, cruel, and debasing to the human spirit. Later philosophers, artists, and scientists shared these feelings, either becoming vegetarians or supporting the validity of such views. Their ranks included Da Vinci, Einstein, Emerson, Gandhi, Krishnamurti, Alexander Pope, Rousseau, Schweitzer, Shaw, Shelley, Tagore, Thoreau, Tolstoy, and others.* All of them justified Thoreau's observation that every person

> . . . who has ever been earnest to preserve his higher or poetic faculties in the best condition has been particularly inclined to abstain from animal food, and from much food of any kind. [2]

But unlike the medical, economic, and ecological reasons for a nonflesh diet, ethical arguments cannot be proved with statistics or laboratory data. Although ethical vegetarians believe their arguments against slaughter and flesh consumption are inescapably logical, the morality or immorality of killing animals (or humans) can only be discussed, debated, and finally accepted or denied on faith alone. To debate such issues is, of course, uniquely human. We are the only species—as far as we know—blessed and cursed with the ability to make abstract judgments, to philosophize, to worry and ponder over the intrinsic moral value of our actions. But the question of what is proper human behavior is enormously complicated by our cultural variability.

Human social behavior appears to be as generalized as human feeding habits. Depending on who is making the observations and judgments, *Homo sapiens* may be judged noble or monstrous, peaceful or aggressive. Our notions of good and evil are formed by our individual personalities, our physical surroundings, and by what our group defines as acceptable behavior. Good and evil are thus relative terms, with virtually no forms of behavior universally accepted as good or evil. Murder, cannibalism, war, rape, torture—all are variously condemned or encouraged depending on

---

* Da Vinci, Gandhi, Krishnamurti, Shaw, Tagore, and Tolstoy were vegetarians.

the society. (Mother-son incest is about as close as human societies come to sharing a universal taboo.) In general, however, we can define good as behavior that preserves a culture's values, while evil destroys or disorganizes social order.

Knowing this, can ethical vegetarians properly condemn flesh eating as morally wrong? Yes and no. No—if they're condemning it on a universal scale: there are no universal moral values that apply to killing animals or humans. But yes—if the morality of slaughtering animals is questioned and discussed within the context of a specific group or culture. To keep the discussion manageable, and to save us from the folly of debating the relative morality of Eskimos, Kalahari Bushmen, or Trobriand Islanders, we must restrict ourselves to two basic questions: How does the killing of animals square with the moral values expressed in the United States and other western nations? And, how does slaughtering and eating animals fit in with your personal notions of right and wrong? To discover this, we must first determine not whether humans are innately good or evil, but what our spiritual goals are, as expressed in our cultural institutions.

While specific notions of goodness may be relative, a glance at the world's major religions reveals a common theme. Called the Golden Rule in the West, the idea of mutual consideration is embodied in Buddhism, Christianity, Confucianism, Hinduism, Islamism, Judaism, and dozens of other religious and secular systems. "Do unto others as you would have them do unto you" is a basic, almost universal recognition that self-control and mutual respect are necessary to preserve both individuals and the group. Most human social systems are characterized by precepts and laws designed to move people away from uncontrolled behavior toward mutual consideration. True, humanity's practical record in applying the Golden Rule has been a dismal one. War and cruelty on a mass scale have dominated most of man's tenure on earth. Still, mutual consideration and respect remain the expressed goals for most individuals and social systems in the West— lip service notwithstanding.

Dr. Albert Schweitzer once asked in a sermon if one could isolate a fundamental ethical attitude—the grounding of all of religious teaching. Schweitzer was primarily concerned with the teachings of Jesus, but his answer touches on the bases of almost *all* religions and secular ethical systems.

> What is this recognition, this knowledge within the reach of the most scientific and the most childlike? It is reverence for life, reverence for the unfathomable mystery we confront in our universe, an existence different in its outward appearance and yet inwardly of the same character as our own, terribly similar, awesomely related. The strangeness between us and other creatures is here removed. . . . Nature knows no similar reverence for life. . . . In every stage of life, right up to the level of man, terrible ignorance lies over all creatures. They have the will to live but no capacity for compassion toward other creatures. They can't feel what happens inside others. . . . The world given over to ignorance and egotism is like a valley shrouded in darkness. Only up on the peaks is there light. . . . Only one creature can escape and catch a glimpse of the light: the highest creature, man. He is permitted to achieve the knowledge of reverence for life. His is the privilege of achieving the knowledge of shared experience and compassion, of transcending the ignorance in which the rest of creation pines.[3]

There are exceptions to what Dr. Schweitzer says, but certainly the best in our culture promotes this basic compassion and respect for life. What are the first lessons we teach to our children? Babies are born with no preconceived notions of social order or morality. Their instincts and genetic tendencies aside, children are foreigners to human culture; they must be taught the rules of right and wrong step-by-step. When we find our toddler innocently twisting the cat's tail, we say, "No, no." Gently extricating the cat, we give the child his or her first lesson in ethics: "Be kind to the kitty."

What parent or teacher would encourage a child to be cruel to animals—to kick cats or destroy birds' nests? Children may do these things out of ignorance and primitive aggression, but concerned adults attempt to redirect such behavior, always leading the child toward self-control and compassion. People who teach children to be violent or sadistic are generally regarded as mentally ill or criminal. Normal and constructive behavior is that which teaches children to treat their pets, siblings, schoolmates, and relatives with mutual respect, never inflicting harm when it can be avoided.

As Dr. Schweitzer makes clear, something within us, whether innate or learned, lets us "feel what happens inside others." This is the root of moral behavior—to refrain from causing others pain. Most people would agree with this, yet here is where ethical vegetarians find an obvious contradiction: if compassion and mutual consideration are the orders of the day, why is the maltreatment of certain species condemned while the maltreatment of other species is ignored or encouraged? We are conditioned in this society to be sensitive to the suffering of animals—especially dogs, cats, horses, and endangered wildlife—but we justify the exploitation and destruction of other animals because "they're raised for that." We teach children to love their pets, to be kind to animals and people, and to restrain their primitive aggressiveness. Then we tell them to eat all their chicken. The eighteenth century essayist and poet, Oliver Goldsmith, might have been describing North Americans when he wrote this criticism of his fellow Englishmen.

> The better sort here pretend to the utmost compassion for animals of every kind; to hear them speak, a stranger would be apt to imagine they could hardly hurt the gnat that stung them. They seem so tender, and so full of pity, that one would take them for the harmless friends of the whole creation, the protectors of the meanest insect or reptile that was privileged with existence. And yet (would you believe it?) I have seen the very men who have thus boasted of their tenderness, at the same time devour the flesh of six different animals tossed up in a fricassee. Strange contrariety of conduct. *They pity, and they eat the objects of their compassion!* [4]

How is this variable compassion, this double standard, explained? A variety of arguments are traditionally used—most of them invoked by people who admit an unwillingness or inability to do their own slaughtering.*

"If we didn't eat cows, swine, and fowl they'd overpopulate and crowd us off the planet."

---

* These are actual arguments drawn from several years of research, public lectures, and conversations.

The argument wrongly equates human meat eating and meat production with the built-in controls on overpopulation found in nature. Carry the logic a step further: if humans suddenly stopped eating seafood, would the oceans become overcrowded and choked with fish? How did this planet survive the eons until humans arrived to manage the earth's creatures and resources? The reverse is true, of course. Severe ecological imbalances of numbers or processes are almost always due to human meddling. The question is based on the unlikely possibility that the United States could become a nation of vegetarians overnight.

Yet even a gradual reduction of meat eating wouldn't necessarily leave us with a surplus of billions of livestock and birds. We would not—as the argument hysterically implies—be up to our hip boots in chickens and pigs copulating wildly in the streets. Astronomical numbers of livestock exist in the United States because food and agricultural industries breed them intensively on a supply and demand basis. Were the demand for meat to decline, the numbers of animals reared would also decline. This happens now, with stockmen increasing or reducing their herds according to fluctuations in prices and marketing trends. Your individual decision to become a vegetarian can only result in fewer animals being bred for commercial slaughter.

The argument actually makes a better case for cannibalism. *Homo sapiens* is the species whose numbers are increasing geometrically, threatening to crowd us off the planet. Why not eat people or pet dogs and cats or rats whose numbers are also out of control? Vegetarians like to think there are more creative approaches to problem solving.

"If we didn't breed animals we'd be denying them the right to live. Better for an animal to have a short life than no life at all."

Here we are told that we have an obligation to breed animals, that we may not withhold the gift of life. The fact that these animals will suffer the cruelties of intensive farming or that their lives will be arbitrarily snuffed out to please human desires is presumably the small price they must pay for a brief taste of existence, such as it is. The argument is bizarre. As Peter Singer says in *Animal Liberation:* "This is absurd. There are no such entities as nonexistent beings, waiting around in limbo for someone to bring them into existence." [5]

We can indirectly affect the lives of unborn generations of animals and humans by the way we treat the natural environment, but we cannot directly affect something that doesn't exist. We can't deny the unborn anything because there is no one or nothing there to begin with.* Our obligations are to the living, not the nonexistent. As Singer says: "In this area it is easy to talk nonsense without realizing it."

"Meat eating is part of our culture. It's traditional."

This is the weakest, though one of the most common arguments for meat eating. To argue that a behavior pattern is valuable or unchangeable merely because it's always been done that way is illogical at the least. Slavery, robbery, murder, and other physical and mental cruelties are also part of our culture, yet few people call for their continuation.

Traditions are not, after all, physiological laws. Humans must be bipeds, must breathe air, must derive their nourishment from food. But no innate physical factors force us to eat any particular food—certainly not meat. Only environmental conditions or cultural pressures decide how wide or limited our diets will be. Similarly, while scientists continue to debate whether humans are inherently aggressive, no one has yet suggested that all humans have an inborn bloodlust, that they are biologically

* Ancient Zen koan: "What did your face look like before you were born?"

driven to eat flesh—like lions and vultures. Custom, as much as chemistry, directs a human's food choices.

Ethical vegetarians would agree that meat eating is traditional. But they would suggest that we hold this tradition up to the light, asking whether the mass killing and eating of animals contributes to the common good, to our individual well-being, and to our personal moral expectations. We might ask whether slaughter ultimately ennobles us—whether the tradition of the poleax and sticking knife are really worth preserving when there are reasonable alternatives.

"Man is a predator. Killing and eating animals are his natural behaviors."

This is a variation on the preceding argument and it makes as little sense. As we saw in chapter three, to classify humans as predators is to ignore their basic variability and depth—like calling Beethoven a piano player. Our natural behavior, certainly our individual daily behavior, is whatever we determine it to be—depending on our environment, heredity, and culture. Stripped to its essential thought, the sentence above is really saying something ridiculous: "Our ancestors ate meat; we must do the same." Yet think about it. The majority of people who eat meat in the industrialized world are able to do so precisely because they are not predators or hunters. They are shoppers.

A predator's meat supply is naturally limited by physical conditions and the hunter's skill at stalking prey. Modern shoppers, however, can have a neatly wrapped package of meat delivered to their front door or cooked to order in a restaurant—hardly consistent with our bloody past.

Why choose one fragment of humanity's past as an example of our natural behavior? Why not say man is naturally compassionate, or man is a plant eater, or man is an enigma capable of both destructiveness and creativity. Man, meaning all of humanity, is whatever he happens to be at any particular time in history you confront him. Never mind what Neanderthal or Cro-Magnon did or had to do. You have a choice.

"Animals kill other animals."

This generalization is supposed to justify meat eating because other animals do it—as though animal behavior can be automatically used as a guide for appropriate human behavior. The same logic can also be used to justify women eating their mates, mothers eating their young, and people in general eating their feces, as spiders, fish, and dogs sometimes do.

The statement is also inaccurate. Obviously, not all animals kill other animals. Many creatures (humans included) thrive on a nonflesh diet. Those animals who do kill other beings for food do so out of design, not choice. Animal predators rarely kill wantonly or senselessly. None kill as humans do—for sport. And only man is capable of killing or mistreating his own or other species on a massive scale.

Nonhuman predators feel no aesthetic or ethical misgivings when they kill. Should we dismiss our moral and cultural objections to violence and slaughter merely because no other animals are capable of such feelings? Rather than blindly letting any aspect of natural phenomena dictate behavior, ethical vegetarianism centers on those qualities uniquely human: imagination, empathy, and compassion. The behavior of most animals may be unforgivable. Ours needn't be.

"Humans have dominion over this planet. Animals are here for us to use like coal and oil."

Or as one woman told me, "If God didn't want us to eat meat, he wouldn't have put cattle on earth." This is the sort of traditional selfish thinking that's fouled and ravaged our planet and pushed all creatures toward extinction. What sort of justification for meat eating or anything else is the argument "man has dominion"? Parents have dominion over their children, yet they have no right to kill or mistreat them. Owning a car doesn't mean you can drive it on the sidewalk or through a crowded playground—not if you recognize the rights of others.

The concept of man's dominion comes to Westerners from the Bible, specifically from Genesis 1:28 in which God says:

> Be fruitful, and multiply, and replenish the earth, and subdue it: and have dominion over the fish of the sea, and over the fowl of the air, and over every living thing that moveth upon the earth.*

The Bible is thus often used by some to justify flesh eating. But vegetarian Bible students point out that there is actually more Biblical emphasis on nonmeat foods than on the supposed pleasures of flesh eating. There is the Fifth Commandment—"Thou shalt not kill"—which ethical vegetarians apply to all animals. (The Bible never says the Commandment applies only to humans.) And there is Genesis 1:29:

> And God said, Behold I have given you every herb bearing seed, which is upon the face of all the earth, and every tree, in the which is the fruit of a tree yielding seed; to you it shall be for meat.

Similar passages include Genesis 9:4, Leviticus 3:17 and 7:23, and Isaiah 66:3, respectively.

> But flesh with the life thereof, which is the blood thereof, shall ye not eat.

> It shall be a perpetual statute for your generations throughout all your dwellings, that ye eat neither fat nor blood.

> . . . Ye shall eat no manner of fat, of ox, or of sheep, or of goat.

> He that killeth an ox is as if he slew a man; he that sacrificeth a lamb, as if he cut off a dog's neck . . .

* Most of humanity has conveniently forgotten the Divine Ecological Order to "replenish the earth," concentrating mostly on subduing it.

Of course, each of these passages can be matched by a contradictory passage that seems to favor or excuse flesh eating, but vegetarian Biblicists—while not claiming that the Bible directly advocates vegetarianism—emphasize that much of the early scriptural criticisms of flesh eating were altered and amended by later Hebrew and Christian editors seeking to broaden the Bible's popular appeal. (The Roman Emperor Constantine, for example, accepted Christianity only when it allowed him to retain traditional Roman manners and morals.) And as British vegetarian Geoffrey Rudd points out: "The emphasis through all these Books is on vegetarian food—flesh foods are mentioned with loathing. Riches and rewards are expressed in terms of milk and honey, not the pitiful parts and organs of dead animals." [6]

Other ethical vegetarians are not impressed that the Bible gives humanity authority over the earth. The Bible, they suggest, is only one expression of man's search for divine guidance. There are many other holy books and teachings. Not all of them give man license to use the earth and its creatures as his personal property. In Jainism—an ancient and influential Indian religion—we find the first of founder Mahavira's "Five Great Vows."

I renounce all killing of living beings, whether movable or immovable. Nor shall I myself kill living beings nor cause others to do it, nor consent to it. [7]

Because Jain principles deeply affected the course of Hinduism and Indian culture, this principle of *ahimsa* (noninjury and compassion toward living beings) became a cornerstone of Hindu philosophy. Hinduism's epic poem, *The Mahabharata,* warns: "Those who kill and eat cows will rot in hell for as many years as there are hairs on the slaughtered cow." And: "What greater cruelty and selfishness than to increase the flesh of one's body by eating the flesh of innocent creatures?"

The first of Buddhism's Ten Precepts is, "Refrain from destroying life." Strict Buddhist laity avoid meat eating, though Buddhist monks (who traditionally beg for food) may eat meat if offered, as long as the animal was not especially killed for them.

The *Tao Teh Ching,* China's 3,000-year-old esoteric classic, though never concerned specifically with diet or food, warns of trying to dominate the earth or its processes. When it comes to humanity's relationship to the planet, Taoist philosophy is the reverse image of the Judeo-Christian heritage. Taoism suggests that the order and perfection of the universe will become apparent only when we stop trying to master and alter the world to meet our demands.

Man may indeed have dominion over the earth—an evolutionary quirk at best—but does this superiority excuse us from all ethical concerns? Does it free us to exploit and kill lesser creatures at will? Ethical vegetarianism suggests that dominion can also mean stewardship, caring for and preserving life and order whenever possible, striving to understand and harmonize with the natural world rather than constantly working to subdue or destroy it.

"Why worry so much about how animals are being treated when there is so much human suffering?"

Compassion for nonhumans and compassion for humans are not mutually exclusive. Becoming a vegetarian involves little energy. It is a nondoing—an omission of certain foods and products—not an adding on of new responsibilities. Nothing would stop a person from working to relieve human suffering while being a vegetarian. Besides, as we'll discuss later, a vegetarian diet reduces both the amount of resources used to produce food and our reliance on animals—aiding man and beast simultaneously.

"Why should we treat animals better than we treat people?"

We shouldn't. We should respect the rights of all creatures

equally. The principles of ethical vegetarianism would be a mockery if they didn't lead to an increased sensitivity to life in all its forms.

"You speak of the rights of all creatures, but only humans can have rights."

The dictionary defines a right as "something to which one has a just claim." But because nonhumans are unable to create or communicate philosophical or legal concepts, they can make no such claims. The hog riding a conveyer belt to its death can't make an impassioned plea for life and liberty. It may scream in terror, but—we are warned—to infer from this behavior that the hog thinks or understands its predicament is to treat the pig as though it had human qualities. Our call for compassion would be based on nothing more than sentimentality and anthropomorphism.

But most ethical vegetarians see their objections to slaughter as decidedly unsentimental; their objections to slaughter have nothing to do with the character or value of a given animal.

Our society is now in the throes of rethinking and expanding the entire idea of rights. In only the past ten years we've seen a blur of changes in our legal and social attitudes towards the rights of racial and ethnic minorities, women, the aged, children, homosexuals, and the mentally and physically handicapped. The issue isn't one of equality per se. The law cannot erase the real differences between people. The issue is one of equal treatment regardless of what outward differences divide us.

This reassessment, whether the resultant social upheaval and changes please you or not, is the result of both new scientific and social discoveries and a rededication to old ideas. (Women and racial minorities have, after all, been demanding equal treatment for centuries.) We used to lock the retarded and insane away, believing them to be without rights or consideration. Now, ideally, we train the retarded and allow them to participate in society at their own pace. We offer medical treatment and counseling to the mentally ill and the troubled, realizing at last that even insanity is a meaningless term.

Our laws, if not our social consciousness, no longer excuse the mistreatment of humans because they're "only slaves" or "feebleminded" or "the weaker sex." The notion of human rights —at least the right to be free of pain and deliberate mistreatment— has come to be based on something more than what an elite describes as normal or acceptable.

But if we're finally discarding the notion that rights can be doled out on the basis of one's having the right skin color or sex or IQ, are we willing also to discard the notion that one must be human to receive equal consideration? Ready or not, science may be forcing our hand.

In the late 1960s, researchers began experiments designed to teach chimpanzees the American Sign Language for the Deaf. Apes cannot make the sounds necessary for human vocal speech, but they have hands and opposable fingers. Now, more than a decade later, various projects have not only trained several chimps and a gorilla to use sign language, but the apes are able to use that language in actual conversation with humans.

Parrots learn to talk and dogs and cats can make simple desires known to their owners. But according to Harold T.P. Hayes, writing in the *New York Times Magazine,* the apes in these studies are now able to:

> . . . converse with humans for as long as 30 minutes, to combine learned words in order to describe new situations or objects, to perceive difference and sameness, to understand "if-then" concepts, to describe their moods, to lie, to select and use words in syntactical order, to express desire, to anticipate future events, to seek signed communication with others of their species. . . .[8]

Dr. Duane Rumbaugh of the Yerkes Primate Center in Atlanta emphasizes that humans haven't actually taught the apes to think or even to communicate. "All we do in these language programs is to agree with them upon a vocabulary."[9] In other words, the apes have always had cognitive abilities of which we were unaware.

What else don't we know about nonhumans? One of the most

important and poignant incidents in these language studies occurred with the first of the chimps to acquire sign language, Washoe. Washoe was bred in the hope that she'd pass her language skills on to her offspring. But Washoe's baby was unfortunately killed when it fell from a shelf. Scientists were startled to see Washoe make a sign to her dead infant, "Baby hug."

It may seem a digression to bring chimpanzees and gorillas into a discussion of ethical vegetarianism, but our changing attitude toward apes (and dolphins, who may also possess cognition) illustrates how a shift in our perceptions of nonhumans or humans almost automatically broadens the extent of our compassion. If you'd suggested ten years ago that a chimpanzee might one day hold a conversation with a human, you would have been invited to inhabit a cage yourself.

Now, psychologist Penny Patterson—who works with Koko, a female gorilla with a vocabulary of almost 500 words—says, "Just the fact that language can be taught shows people that they should rethink the rights of animals." [10]

That rethinking involves some disturbing questions: If you feel compelled to extend compassion to a gorilla or chimpanzee, realizing that they possess not only a self-concept but also the ability to express their abstract feelings, can you reasonably deny that compassion to a pig or cow or chicken or any other nonhuman animal?

Should we deny compassion to any creature just because it's less able to express its feelings in terms we can understand?

Should you deplore the killing of dolphins while your mouth is full of tuna fish? [11]

Advances in medical technology have forced us to look hard at our traditional definitions of life and death. Doctors are now able to keep people alive by using sophisticated life-support systems and so-called heroic measures. Many lives have been saved through these means, but many legal and ethical complications have also been created. We no longer speak of death as merely the absence of a heartbeat. We use terms like brain death—the point at which consciousness and awareness cease and are incapable of recovery. We are learning that a beating heart and inflated lungs alone do not constitute a meaningful existence.

Legal precedents have already been established to allow doctors to disconnect life-support systems once it becomes apparent that a patient's brain activity has stopped and is irretrievable. Notice that our courts, doctors, and the rational public do not (thank goodness) measure the value of life on the basis of the patient's skin color, IQ, bank account, or social status. We concern ourselves with specific questions: can the person respond to meaningful stimuli? Is the person aware? Can he or she feel pain?

Leaving aside the controversy over euthanasia and medical ethics, let's assume that we agree on one premise: once awareness vanishes and is irretrievable, the body kept functioning indefinitely solely by machines and external manipulation is a mere husk. Whether it's legal or moral to pull the plug in such a situation is not the question here. Our discussion must focus only on one point—that the fundamental characteristic of sentient beings is their capacity for awareness and expression. As long as a human shows the slightest ability to register emotions, our traditions and laws work to protect that individual's interests.

And what of nonhumans with interests? While you may argue, however illogically, that animals have no legal status, little or no intelligence, and no social standing, you cannot reasonably deny that animals are capable of feeling and awareness. They feel pain.

Knowing that, as Thoreau said, "The hare in its extremity cries like a child," can we refuse to consider a creature's suffering merely because it belongs to another species? This issue isn't a new one. The eighteenth century English philosopher Jeremy Bentham wrote of animals: "The question is not can they *reason?* Nor can they *talk?* But can they *suffer?*" Peter Singer, a contemporary philosopher, puts it another way.

> A stone does not have interests because it cannot suffer. Nothing that we can do to it could possibly make any difference to its welfare . . . but if a being suffers, there can be no moral

justification for refusing to take that suffering into consideration.[12]

Unfortunately, people do refuse to consider the suffering of others—human and otherwise. Our biological world is controlled by physical laws, but not our inner world—the realm of the spirit. Gravity prevents us from flying under our own power, but no similar force enjoins us to act responsibly or compassionately. If we are moved to protect or spare another being's suffering, it's because something inside, that twinge—the residue of thousands of years of cultural and spiritual evolution—tells us that it's the right thing to do.

This inner voice doesn't always speak clearly or loudly enough, as our poor treatment of each other and the planet demonstrates, but there's no doubt that our highest aspirations are toward compassion and mutual respect. And because this compassion isn't—in the best of worlds—parceled out to humans on the basis of race, ability or social status, ethical vegetarians see no logical reason why compassion shouldn't also be extended to all sentient creatures.

Humanity will always use animals in one way or another. But the way the world operates at large needn't be the way you function on a personal level. Nothing is stopping you from responding to an inner call to recognize the rights of all creatures.

"Animals have no souls. It's no sin to kill them."

This traditional justification for man's unrestricted use of animals argues that since animal lives perish totally when they die, humans are under no obligation to preserve nonhuman life. The counterargument is that if animals do indeed lack souls, we should be that much more concerned with letting them live out the only existence they will know.

Eastern philosophies like Hinduism have argued that animals have souls, but that animal souls are indistinguishable from human souls—all souls being a part of the Universal Soul (*paramatman*).

To strict Hindus, the killing of an animal carries a heavy spiritual or karmic weight, as does the killing of a human, because the act interferes with the destiny of an individual creature.

But since we can neither prove nor disprove the existence of a soul in human or beast, the question can never be resolved. We can, however, make a good case for the existence of pain. Thus our equitable treatment of other beings should be based on what we know beyond doubt—that it's morally inexcusable to needlessly cause other beings pain and suffering.

Two factors may seem to complicate this attitude: (1) Some creatures—shellfish, some crustaceans, and insects—may not register pain as do higher life forms. Can this presumption be used to justify the eating of shrimp and lobsters? And (2), what about those animals raised free of cruelty and slaughtered absolutely painlessly, as on a small farm?

Most ethical vegetarians are opposed to unnecessary killing regardless of the creature's sensibility to pain or the slaughter methods used. The fact that an animal is killed for food when alternatives exist makes the act unnecessary and, in the eyes of ethical vegetarians, unjustified. This may seem to be an extreme position, but consider: old buildings feel no pain. They are not alive. Yet many citizens howl in outrage when an ancient structure—particularly one with historical significance—is bulldozed to make way for a parking lot. Responsible people don't like to see life or property destroyed unnecessarily. (Unfortunately, these sentiments usually pertain more to inanimate objects and endangered species than to the animal residents of factory farms or packinghouses.) But while the value of a nineteenth century townhouse or a stand of redwoods is relative, the question of slaughtering animals for food is not. Neither nutrition nor society forces us to eat flesh.

We can morally justify violence and killing in certain circumstances—self-defense, destroying dangerous or destructive animals, and extraordinary behavior under survival conditions—but teachers and thinkers have cautioned for centuries that deliberate cruelty to lower life forms leads to a desensitizing of the human spirit, making it easier in the long run for humans to mistreat each other. Violence too easily becomes familiar and institutionalized. Even religions whose teachings have traditionally regarded animals as humanity's God-given property recognize that needless cruelty and slaughter are unjust. Mistreatment of animals may not be a mortal sin, says the *New Catholic Encyclopedia;* nor is killing an animal for food or some other use. But wanton cruelty or destruction of animal life is irrational, not to man's benefit, and certainly not an example of positive spiritual development.[13]

Advocates of ethical vegetarianism have claimed, in fact, that compassion towards animals can eventually produce a more sensitive ethical attitude toward humans.* As Dr. Schweitzer tells us:

> I cannot but have reverence for all that is called life. I cannot avoid compassion for every thing that is called life. That is the beginning of morality. Once a man has experienced it and continues to do so—and he who has once experienced it will continue to do so—he is ethical. He carries his morality within him and can never lose it, for it continues to develop within him. He who has never experienced this has only a set of superficial principles. These theories have no root in him, they do not belong to him, and they fall off him. . . . [R]everence for life comprises the whole ethic of love in its deepest and highest sense. It is the source of constant renewal for the individual and for mankind.[14]

Reverence for nonhuman life is often criticized and ridiculed as impractical. The traditional Hindu worship and protection of cows has, for example, been derided as wasteful and foolish. But cow-protection—as Mahatma Gandhi called it—like the principles of ethical vegetarianism in general, has a powerful and constructive symbolic value. As Gandhi wrote:

> Cow-protection is to me one of the most wonderful phenomena in human evolution. It takes the human being beyond his species. The cow to me means the entire subhuman world. Man through the cow is enjoined to realize his identity with all that lives. . . . She is the mother to millions of Indian mankind.

---

* Adolph Hitler advocated vegetarianism and apparently followed a lacto-ovo diet—with occasional lapses into meat eating—for more than half his life. This hardly disproves the idea that ethical vegetarianism may lead to greater sensitivity to human suffering. Hitler's diet was the result of philosophic and hygienic concerns, not reverence for life. In any event, as Jay Dinshah—the founder of the American Vegan Society—says, "No one has ever claimed that vegetarianism was a sure cure for insanity."

> The cow is a poem of pity. Protection of the cow means protection of the whole dumb creation of God.[15]

Even if a nonflesh diet produced no measurable emotional or spiritual benefits, ethical vegetarianism would still be valuable as a practical expression of the ancient idea of reciprocity: doing unto all creatures as you would have them do unto you. The notion of animal rights is therefore not the product of sentimentality or anthropomorphizing. The concept springs from our innate or learned notions of what constitutes moral and constructive behavior. Writer Brigid Brophy puts it this way:

> I am the very opposite of an anthropomorphizer. I don't hold animals superior or even equal to humans. The whole case for behaving decently to animals rests on the fact that we are the superior species. We are the species uniquely capable of imagination, rationality, and moral choice—and that is precisely why we are under the obligation to recognize and respect the rights of animals.[16]

Many meat eaters are admittedly uncomfortable with the origins of their diet. They laugh nervously, excusing slaughter as something beyond their control. "They didn't kill the animal specifically for me. If I didn't buy this package of meat, someone else would." This attitude isn't always generated by callousness, but by ignorance: the majority of U.S. consumers are almost totally removed from the realities of food production. Many go on eating meat only because they're protected against the sights and sounds and smells of the slaughterhouse by "the graceful distance of miles."

The meat industry, of course, has a vested interest in keeping the public insulated from the details of meat production. Industry associations like the American Meat Institute and the National Livestock and Meat Board supply the news media and public schools with so-called educational materials. Children receive various booklets describing how meat goes from farm to table. Some brochures show cartoon animals as smiling and happy candidates for the dinner plate. Meat is described as supernutritious, if not indispensable.

But nowhere in this literature are scenes of the killing floor. No mention of slaughter itself is clearly made. You are left to assume that the animals simply disassemble on cue, cleaving apart on invisible dotted lines to fall neatly into prelabeled Styrofoam cartons. By then it's too late to face the ethical implications.

If more people had to do their own killing and butchering, there would be that many more vegetarians.

More people are doing their own killing these days, however. Thousands of Americans in recent years have moved back to rural communities and farms to seek The Good Life—growing their own vegetables and raising their own cattle and chickens (though many have gone back to the land as vegetarians.) Unlike the majority of meat eaters, these people at least admit the essential truth about meat consumption. Says one:

> . . . killing warm-blooded animals that are similar in so many ways to ourselves is the least pleasant thing we do. But isn't it somehow more honest, less hypocritical, to do your own slaughtering, rather than picking out your chops or steaks . . . in the supermarket? [17]

Because they tend to raise their animals with care and affection, finally killing them as skillfully as possible, the new homesteaders believe themselves to be closer to reality than urban meat eaters, and with good reason. Their desire to be noble and compassionate while dispatching their livestock may become ludicrous, though, as when a writer suggests that a chicken may be killed by "slowly slitting its throat—a little deeper with each stroke. Well done, and the bird just looks up and smiles as it passes into oblivion." [18]

Another farmer recalls the killing of his pig.

> Shirley Pearl [was] a friendly and intelligent creature. . . . I gave her an apple to eat and, while she was placidly munching, shot her. . . . She fell over like a stone, whereupon I immediately stuck her. It sounds brutal in the telling . . . but it was a clean kill, and I felt good that I had done right by my animal. [19]

The writer may indeed feel good, but he stops short of

admitting the whole truth: that he killed a friendly and intelligent creature only because he wanted to eat her. This idea of doing right by one's animal friends raises a crucial point: no matter how well most modern homesteaders care for their livestock— providing the best in feed and shelter—they still end up killing these animals to satisfy tastes rather than actual needs. Doing your own killing may be more honest and less hypocritical, but, say ethical vegetarians, it's even more honest to admit that such slaughter isn't necessary in the first place. Saying, "We like meat," isn't the same as saying, "We have nothing to eat but meat." Can we really do right by an animal by killing it?

This brings us back to the most obvious point about slaughter: it's not pleasant. Most meat eaters shove this fact into the backs of their minds. But those who watch the blood spurt out of their Shirley Pearls know that killing animals is a miserable pastime.

But, we are told, "You'll get used to it." Can you imagine a more frightening, surrealistic phrase applied to the destruction of life than this bland assurance—you'll get used to it?

Even those hunters who shoot for fun rarely admit to enjoying the actual kill. They'll tell us they love the chase, the hike through the forest, the Great Outdoors; or, that the killing is secondary, that they eat the meat, that they're helping to maintain the balance of nature. But few will say, "Gee, I love to go out and kill animals."

Should someone admit this—that they really enjoy killing— most of us would take a giant step backward, fearing for the speaker's sanity and our personal safety. The killing of animals or people is generally regarded in this society as repulsive but acceptable when necessary.

Some people go further, believing that the killing of humans is never acceptable whether in war or self-defense. But almost everyone agrees that to enjoy killing is a sign of mental instability. Meat eaters are therefore in a curious position. While admitting the gruesomeness of the violence done by them or for them, and while admitting their disgust or displeasure with the realities of the slaughterhouse, they excuse their continued participation by arguing—invalidly—that such butchery is a necessity.

We are left with a summary of five points—a kind of *reductio ad absurdum* of flesh eating:

1. Animals other than humans, especially higher life forms, are capable of feeling pain and pleasure.

2. It is morally unjustifiable to disregard the suffering of another creature.

3. Even when pain isn't a factor, it's morally wrong to wantonly destroy or interfere with beings and processes when there are peaceful or constructive alternatives.

4. The killing of animals—even when done painlessly, as a mercy killing, or when absolutely necessary—is not normally considered an enjoyable act. Most people don't willingly engage in behavior they consider repulsive if such acts are unnecessary.

5. Flesh eating, except under survival or extraordinary conditions, is not necessary in the normal human diet when nutritious alternatives are available.

Nathaniel Altman, in *Eating for Life,* used USDA statistics to estimate that the average North American meat eater reaching the age of 70 will have eaten the bodies of:

   14 cows and steers
    2 calves
   12 lambs and sheep
   23 hogs
   35 turkeys
  840 chickens
  770 pounds of fish.[20]

The only thing missing is a partridge in a pear tree. Somebody probably ate that too.

*Chapter Ten notes.*

1. Plutarch, "On the Eating of Flesh," quoted in Janet Barkas, *The Vegetable Passion* (New York: Charles Scribner's Sons, 1975), p. 53.
2. Henry David Thoreau, *Walden,* from "Higher Laws."
3. Albert Schweitzer, *Reverence for Life* (New York: Harper and Row, 1969), pp. 115-122.
4. Oliver Goldsmith, *The Citizen of the World,* Letter XV.
5. Peter Singer, *Animal Liberation* (New York: New York Review Books, 1975), p. 254.
6. Geoffrey Rudd, *The Bible and Vegetarianism* (Cheshire, England: The Vegetarian Society) undated pamphlet, p. 4.
7. John B. Noss, *Man's Religions* (New York: Macmillan Co., 1960), p. 150.
8. Harold T.P. Hayes, "The Pursuit of Reason," *New York Times Magazine,* 17 June 1977, p. 73.
9. *Ibid.,* p. 76.
10. Arthur Lubow, "Riot in Fish Tank 11," *New Times,* 14 October 1977, p. 48.
11. Helen Jones of the Society for Animal Rights, quoted by Lubow, p. 51.
12. Singer, p. 9.
13. "Cruelty to Animals," *New Catholic Encyclopedia,* vol. 4, (New York: McGraw Hill, 1967), p. 498.
14. Schweitzer, pp. 116-177.
15. Noss, p. 260.
16. Brigid Brophy, *The Rights of Animals* (Cheshire, England: The Vegetarian Society, 1965), p. 8.
17. John Vivian, *The Manual of Practical Homesteading* (Emmaus, Pennsylvania: Rodale Press, 1975), p. 266.
18. Richard W. Langer, *Grow It!* (New York: Saturday Review Press, 1972), p. 238.
19. James B. Dekorne, "Pork By the Book," *The Mother Earth News,* 33:31-2, May 1975.
20. Nathaniel Altman, *Eating for Life* (Wheaton, Illinois: Quest Books, 1973), p. 63.

# ELEVEN

# My Gladiola Likes Bone Meal

Vegetarians shouldn't delude themselves. Some killing is necessary. Some is unavoidable. We cannot live without sometimes directly or indirectly causing the destruction of other creatures or life forms. Take a peaceful stroll in the woods and hundreds of insects may die noiselessly under your heels as you commune with nature.

Grow your own vegetables, but unless you control insect predators your garden will feed only the bugs. Be an organic gardener and use no harmful insecticides, but you'll still have to hand pick or trap or use biological controls to destroy the invaders.

And what about rabid animals, rats, and disease-bearing insects such as the anopheles mosquito and tsetse fly? To say we must never kill other creatures would be unrealistic and might cause many human deaths—a curious tradeoff. Yet few ethical vegetarians or environmentalists have ever argued that we should allow man's enemies to ravage human populations unchallenged. They have suggested instead that our controls must reflect intelligence and care for ecological balance. Better food storage facilities and sanitation measures would, for example, do more to reduce the rodent population than several tons of rat poison. So would restoring the natural balance of predators—from birds to bobcats.

Human life and safety must be protected, but not by a

scorched earth policy of indiscriminate pesticide use and destruction of the natural order. Indeed, many of our problems stem from the wholesale slaughter of pests. (Draining swamps may reduce the mosquito population, but it also destroys the habitats of countless birds, fish, reptiles, and amphibians whose disappearance then produces even more problems.) We must also recognize that humans can never be 100 percent free of all animal or insect interference. The best we can do is to reduce the damage done by these agents without wrecking the environment in the process. We must practice an economy of action, always doing the least to accomplish our ends.

This may seem contradictory, to argue for ethical vegetarianism on one hand while excusing the destruction of life on the other—especially after all I've said about reverence for life. Yet the fundamental principles of ethical vegetarianism and animal rights remain sound: because *some* killing may be unavoidable doesn't mean that *all* killing is unavoidable. Perhaps the Roman poet Ovid put it best in the first century A.D.

> Take not away the life you cannot give;
> For all things have an equal right to live.
> Kill noxious creatures where 'tis sin to save;
> This only just perogative we have;
> But nourish life with vegetable food,
> And shun the sacrilegious taste of blood.[1]

We can still avoid unnecessary slaughter. We can avoid inflicting pain whenever possible. Just how far each person may go in defining what is necessary and what is unavoidable is an open question since both terms are relative. A few ascetics will dust their paths to avoid stepping on an ant and breathe through gauze to avoid breathing in and killing even a gnat. Perhaps such heroic efforts bear witness for us all. More worldly ethical vegetarians may feel content to simply avoid flesh foods, and/or milk and eggs, and the most obvious animal by-products. No one but a saint would suggest that we might live our lives without ever killing even the smallest life form. The Japanese poet Issa wryly noted 200 years ago,

All the while
I pray to Buddha
I keep on killing
Mosquitoes.[2]

A few sentences back I used the phrase "the most obvious animal by-products." Many ethical vegetarians may successfully shun leather, fur, and feathers; but what about the invisible by-products, the ones we may not realize are animal products?

- *Bones.* Cattle shin bones are used in the production of buttons, pipestems, chessmen, dice, knife handles, electrical bushings, and crochet needles. Bones may be burned to form bone black, a charcoal used in the bleaching of white sugar and in the manufacturing of fats, waxes, oils, and pharmaceutical goods. Bones may also be burned to produce bone ash, a white calcium carbonate used to make both bone china and fertilizer.

    Veal and other bones are boiled down to produce gelatin, a colloidal protein found in desserts, ice cream, mayonnaise, as a clarifying agent in the manufacturing of beer, wine, and vinegar, and as a bacterial culturing medium in laboratory work. The widest use (nonfood) of gelatin is probably in the production of photographic film.

- *Blood.* Albumin (clarified serum) is used in the production of buttons and plywood glue, for leather finishing, as a pigment fixative in cloth, in medical products, fertilizer, and—ironically—in cattle feed.

- *Fat.* Pork fat is used in the manufacturing of lard, germicides, insecticides, machine lubricants, oils, leather processing, truck tires, and the production of stearic acid (a component of paraffin) used in candles and home jelly-making jar sealants. Glycerine, a liquid freed from animal fat, is used to make soap, medicines, and explosives.*

---

* Glycerine may also be produced from vegetable matter.

• *Hair.* Pig and horse hair is used in felt, rugs, baseball gloves, and upholstery stuffing. The shoulder and back hair of hogs is used as the pure bristle of expensive brushes.

• *Goose and duck down.* Down is the most prized stuffing for sleeping bags and cold weather clothing. While some down is harvested from live birds, most is a by-product of slaughtering.

• *Wool.* One-seventh of all U.S. wool comes from the slaughtered sheep rather than harmless shearing. Lanolin is derived from degreased wool.

• *Sheepskin.* Found as chamois, shoe linings, gloves, hat bands, and book bindings.

• *Horns.* Used to make imitation tortoise shell, knife handles, and buttons.

• *Cattle feet and shins.* Used to produce neatsfoot oil, a leather preservative and dressing.

• *Intestines.* Sheep and lamb guts are used as surgical ligatures and as strings for some musical instruments and tennis racquets. The strings on one racquet represent the intestines from 11 sheep.

• *Miscellaneous.* Bones, heads, skins, feet, connective tissues, cartilage, and sinews are rendered down to produce glue used in furniture joining, matches, sizing, sandpaper, toys, tools, billard balls, imitation rubber, gummed tape, paper boxes, auto bodies, book binding, mother-of-pearl, picture frames, and—at the last—caskets.[3]

How far must ethical vegetarians go in avoiding animal products? Must they give up photographs, films, television, newspapers, and magazines because of gelatin? Must they avoid books because the bindings may have been fastened with animal glue? And how will they know this? How will they know whether their vegetables and fruits have been fertilized with bone meal or dried blood or fish wastes?

One of the most critical uses of slaughter by-products is in medicine and surgery: the anticoagulant thromboplastin is made from cattle brains; the antihemorrhagic and heart stimulant epinephrine comes from adrenal glands; to provide insulin for one diabetic for one year takes the pancreases of 40 cattle.[4] To produce one pound of dry insulin takes 100,000 hog pancreases.[5] Similar animal by-products include adrenalin, pituitary extract, testosterone, thymoscrescin, albumin, bilirubin, and the digestive enzymes pepsin and rennin.

Yet although the source for these medical agents has traditionally been the slaughterhouse, drug manufacturers and scientists are continuing to develop synthetic substitutes. This is a blessing for both nonhuman and human animals. The anti-inflammatory drug cortisone, for instance, was once strictly a slaughterhouse product. It is now synthesized from ingredients found in yams and soybeans. And millions of diabetics, some of whom suffer allergic reactions to animal insulin, will benefit from the eventual synthesis of insulin, now being pursued by researchers using recombinant DNA. Synthetic insulin will be identical to human insulin and probably cheaper to produce than the insulin yielded by packinghouses. (The cost of insulin is tied to the increasing cost of beef.)

But until animal-source drugs are replaced by synthetics—and laboratory animals and vivisection are replaced by tissue cultures and computer models—some ethical vegetarians may have a problem squaring their moral concerns with their medical needs. Must ethical vegetarians refuse medical treatment based on animal products, avoiding even the ambulance ride to the hospital on those pork-fat tires—as some religious groups refuse blood transfusions and surgery at the risk of their lives? Or does the ethical vegetarian's dedication to preserving life also include the preservation of his or her own life?

George Bernard Shaw, an aesthetically and hygienically directed lacto-ovo-vegetarian for 70 years, was forced to use liver extracts to correct a case of pernicious anemia (the condition was not the result of his diet, however). When other vegetarians called him a phony for relying on a slaughter by-product, Shaw lashed out:

> Liver extract you would take if you developed pernicious anemia. If you were diabetic you would take insulin. If you had edema you would take thyroid. You may think you wouldn't; but you would if your diet failed to cure you. You would try any of the gland extracts, the mineral drugs, the so-called vaccines, if it were that or your death.[6]

There is no official vegetarian manifesto to tell us where to draw the line—nor should there be. Ethical vegetarianism is not a religion, though religions have traditionally been attracted to it. Each vegetarian must find his own solution to the dilemma posed by animal by-products. Some will find it enough to avoid flesh foods. Others will go all out trying to purify their lives, examining every product and process for the tiniest hint of animal contamination.

But even with a microscopic inspection of their environment, vegetarians must end up recognizing that it's flatly impossible to be totally free of all indirect contact with animal products in modern society. Is the practice of ethical vegetarianism thus inconsistent and impractical—as some critics have charged?

Of course it is. No philosophy created by humans is ever consistent. All of us wage a constant daily struggle to adjust our values and beliefs to an unpredictable and ever-changing world. All of us are subjected to lies and hate and violence, but that hardly makes impractical our individual efforts to be honest, compassionate, and respectful.

In the same way, sensible ethical vegetarians know they cannot change the world. They know they cannot close down the slaughterhouses overnight or undo society's heavy reliance on animal by-products. But they also know that they needn't kill wantonly nor tacitly accept slaughter done by surrogates. They know they can seek and support creative alternatives to animal exploitation and destruction. That they may be forced to kill noxious creatures or live with a myriad of animal derivatives doesn't mean ethical vegetarians cannot strive to practice reverence for life at every practical opportunity.

What about plants? Current popular opinion says plants can think, feel pain, respond to love and hate, and even read our minds. Are vegetarians plant murderers because they decapitate cabbages and vivisect tomatoes? Is eating plants the same as eating animals?

In 1966, Cleve Backster, a polygraph (lie detector) expert, hooked a galvanometer up to a plant in his New York office. It was an impulsive act, Backster later admitted. He wondered whether a leaf would register an electrical response when water was applied to the plant's roots. Backster's plant, a palmlike *dracaena,* reacted all right, but the lines traced by the stylus looked remarkably like the kind of emotional response Backster was used to seeing in human subjects taking a polygraph test.

Backster was fascinated. He decided to burn one of the leaves, wondering what kind of response the galvanometer would record. To Backster's surprise, his thought of injuring the *dracaena* appeared to cause the stylus to scratch out a violent reaction, indicating to Backster that the plant had perceived his hostile intentions. (Oddly, the *dracaena* and other plants in similar experiments registered less violent reactions when actually burned or injured than they did when the experimenter merely thought of inflicting damage.)

These first experiments were the birth of the current idea that "plants are like people." [7] Since then, Backster has moved on to a variety of experiments that demonstrate, according to

Backster, that awareness is shared by all living matter whether it's on a cellular or molecular level. But Backster's enthusiasm, while shared by many interested in parapsychology, hasn't made much of an impact on the conventional scientific community.

The American Society of Plant Physiologists, meeting in June, 1974, held a special session in which speakers described various unsuccessful attempts to duplicate Backster's experiments. Backster himself later appeared at an American Association for the Advancement of Science public meeting and admitted "that he had neither repeated his basic experiment . . . nor had he firmly established the existence of any new phenomena." [8] Several of Backster's other key experiments have apparently been refuted by controlled studies, leaving Yale botany professor and science writer Arthur W. Galston to observe that:

> Until a reported phenomenon can be independently confirmed by critical researchers anywhere, it must not be accepted as true. By this test Backster fails. . . .[9]

Backster's critics don't necessarily deny that plants hooked up to galvanometers register responses. But why, they ask, jump to conclusions? Why pounce on a stylus tracing as proof, rather than merely a phenomenon to be investigated? A galvanometer indicating electrical activity doesn't in itself prove that plants think and feel. Dr. Adrian Upton, a neurology professor at MacMasters University in Ontario, Canada, conducted an experiment similar to Backster's, though for entirely different reasons. Setting up a battery of paraphernalia—artificial respirator, electroencephalograph, and intravenous feeding equipment—Dr. Upton connected it to a bowl of lime gelatin "about the size of a human brain." Amazingly, Dr. Upton soon found the equipment registering responses "typical of those emitted by a living person." In fact, Dr. Upton pointed out, under current Canadian law the Jello couldn't even have been considered legally dead.[10]

Before we infer that the gelatin's activity indicates its animal past (Dr. Upton certainly didn't), that the life force in countless heads, feet, and bones lives on in a bowl of dessert, let's recall that all electronic equipment is affected by external stimuli—

fluorescent lights, radio waves, humidity, and so on—and must be carefully adjusted.

But let's assume that Backster's and similar experiments really do demonstrate that plants think and react emotionally. Let's forget for the moment that vegetable matter contains nothing remotely resembling a central nervous system. And let us also accept Backster's thesis that plants are capable of monitoring the actions of animals and people.[11] Accepting all this, let's now ask why? Nature is streamlined and economical. Life forms are generally endowed with only those abilities useful for survival and pro- creation. Pain and the ability to perceive potential enemies or environmental threats are warning devices. They allow a creature the chance to escape or adapt.

Plants are sensitive to environmental changes in air, water, light, and soil composition, and they are able to adapt to some external changes. They can droop and curl their leaves in the heat of the day, for example, to conserve fluids. Plants will also grow towards the light, follow moisture with their roots, and synthesize various toxins as defense against insect attacks. But no plant can defend itself or evade an enemy by quickly moving out of the way.

How would it profit a plant to be aware of physical danger while not being able to make use of that awareness? Should we believe that nature or God has given plants the ability to feel, think, and suffer for no reason—knowing as we do that evolutionary forces are never frivolous?

No one denies that plants are living matter, or that on a molecular level (if not a spiritual one), all life is a unity. The molecules making up a *dracaena* are the same molecules that com- prise you and me. Only the DNA/RNA blueprint determines whether a given set of particles will turn out to be vegetable or animal. It is quite likely that plant life—indeed, all sentient life—may be exquisitely sensitive to unseen and undiscovered stimuli. Cleve Backster may have demonstrated that plants act as barometers of emotional and physical changes. Human mood variations may produce as yet unmeasured chemical or electrical alterations in the immediate atmosphere. Perhaps all life from one-celled creatures to humans is in cosmic harmony, vibrating at the same pitch. Yet to propose even these theories is a long way from accepting the "fact" that plants are capable of discriminatory thought and emotion.

But plants are alive, and vegetarians who profess a reverence for life still end up killing plants. Hindu philosophers who wrestled with this question thousands of years ago resolved it by putting life on a spiritual scale. Humans were at the top, with other animals, insects, and plants arranged in a descending order. The dietary laws followed by these mystics were thus based on a simple moral principle: the higher a life form was on the scale, the greater was the responsibility involved in taking that life. Since humans had to eat something, the most reasonable course was to eat only the lowest life forms—vegetable matter. The sages recognized that plants were alive, but that the life force in them was so low in comparison to animals that killing them produced the least bad karma or spiritual repercussions. (Some more extreme vegetarians and fruitarians remain unconvinced by this rationale; they have restricted their diet to using only those fruits, nuts, and seeds that can either be harvested without destroying the plant or harvested after the parent plant dies.)

Whether carrots lie awake at night dreaming of becoming asparagus is beside the point. Plant life is part of the natural order and our moral responsibility extends to plants as well as other living matter. The major difference between eating plants and eating animals—aside from the obvious biological differences—is that while we *must* eat plant matter to maintain our lives and health, nothing compels us to slaughter higher life forms, especially those which we have no doubt are capable of suffering.

And when you think about it, you'll realize that meat eaters actually eat more plants than vegetarians. Meat production feeds tons of vegetable matter to livestock, recovering only a fraction as edible foods. Vegetarians and those on plant-based dietaries eat plant foods directly, using much less in the process. Kill plants we must, but we can still practice reverence for life by taking no more than we need.

*Chapter Eleven notes.*

1. Ovid, *Metamorphoses.*
2. Issa, *A Few Flies and I* (New York: Pantheon Books, 1969), p. 77.
3. Most of the information on by-products comes from scattered news articles and:
   Albert Levie, *The Meat Handbook,* 3rd ed. (Westport, Connecticut: AVI Publishing Co., 1970).
   Thomas P. Ziegler, *The Meat We Eat* (Danville, Illinois: Interstate Printers and Publishers, Inc., 1968).
4. Ziegler, p. 138.
5. Levie, p. 12.
6. G.B. Shaw in a letter to Symon Gould, founder of the American Vegetarian Party, quoted in Janet Barkas, *The Vegetable Passion* (New York: Charles Scribner's Sons, 1975), p. 96.
7. Backster's experiments have been well covered by the press. A concise account appears in Peter Tompkins and Christopher Bird, *The Secret Life of Plants* (New York: Harper and Row, 1973), pp. 3-16.
8. Arthur W. Galston, "Talking to Your Plants; A Yale Botanist Talks Back," *Yale Alumni Magazine,* December 1975, pp. 27-30.
9. *Ibid.*
10. "Bits and Pieces," *The Mother Earth News* 39, May 1976, p. 18.
11. Tompkins, p. 7.

# ☙TWELVE ❧

# Vegetarianism and the World Food Crisis

> Meat is the last requirement to be met. If the people must wait until pigs and cattle have sufficient food, they will die of starvation one year before they can get an abundance of meat.
> Dr. Mikkel Hindhede (1920)[1]

We can't leave the ethical questions raised by meat eating without noting that meat production on its present scale also creates hardship for humans. Most experts on world food problems have long called for a drastic reduction in global meat consumption and production. They estimate that the planet's population may reach seven billion within the next 30 years—far more than can be fed with present agricultural practices and food policies centered around meat production. But we don't have to wait 30 years to see the effects of famine. Georg Borgstrom, an expert on world resource problems, estimates that only 450 million of the world's people are presently well fed, while 2,400 million are underfed and poor.[2]

"What if everybody became a vegetarian?" The question is usually thrown out as though it contained a threat of disaster. But consider the arithmetic of meat production: if all the arable land in the world were divided up among the present population, each person would receive about one acre of land suitable for crop production. (Twice as much land is probably available, but the cost

233

to reclaim or alter it—clearcutting forests, for instance—would be too great to be practical.)

Now imagine you had to decide how best to use your personal one acre. You could graze a steer on your plot, letting it fatten on the free grass and forage, but your precious acre would be tied up for at least a year, perhaps two, all to feed one animal. You might decide instead to use the land to raise grain for feed. You could, assuming you had good weather and a reasonable harvest, even eat a little of the grain produced. The majority of it, however, would have to be used to feed your livestock. Your animals would demand from one to 16 pounds of grain for every pound of edible meat they yield.

Look at the feed-to-meat conversion ratios for various animals: to get back one pound of edible meat, you have to feed a steer 16 pounds of grain and soy, six pounds for a hog, four pounds for turkeys, and three pounds for chickens. Milk production takes about one pound of grain for each pint of milk received. If you choose beef production, then, your 1,000-pound steer—whose fattening tied up your entire acre for more than a year—would end up as only about 400 pounds of edible meat.

But supplying one person with 2,500 calories a day on a meat-based diet actually requires not one, but 3½ acres. The same person on a wheat-based diet would need only one-quarter acre, while a single acre devoted to rice and beans would supply six people with 2,500 calories each day.[3] Look at it another way: an acre of land used to raise feed for cattle, pigs, poultry, or milk would ultimately yield enough animal protein to provide a fairly active male with less than a 250-day supply of dietary protein. But the same acre used to grow edible soybeans would provide enough protein for 2,200 days.[4]

World food authority Lester Brown says that people in under-developed countries have a yearly per capita grain allotment of roughly 400 pounds. Almost all of this is eaten directly. Few people can afford the luxury of feeding grain to livestock. The average North American, however, receives an annual 2,000 pounds of grain per capita. Almost 90 percent of this is fed to animals. The rest is used in breads, pastas, and as cereals. The average North American meat eater, Brown says, uses five times the resources of the average Colombian, Indian, or Nigerian.[5]

In *Diet For A Small Planet,* author Frances Moore Lappé gives us the staggering facts of meat production's hidden costs:

The produce from one-half of all U.S. farmland is fed to animals.

About 90 percent of U.S. barley, corn, sorghum, oats, and (unexported) soybeans is fed to livestock.

The United States and other developed nations—only about one-third of the world's population—use 75 percent of the world's fish catch. Much of it is fed to livestock.

Wealthy nations import protein from poor nations for animal feed. One-third of Africa's peanut crop is used to feed dairy cattle and poultry in Western Europe.

The U.S. imports beef—half of it from Central America—in an amount roughly equivalent to the total yearly beef consumption of many underdeveloped countries, though the amount represents only about seven percent of U.S. consumption.[6]

Ms. Lappé asks us to imagine ourselves sitting down to an eight ounce steak:

. . . then imagine the room filled with 45 to 50 people with empty bowls in front of them. For the "feed cost" of your steak, each of their bowls could be filled with a full cup of cooked cereal grains.[7]

Unequal distribution of food isn't the only problem compounded by an overemphasis on meat production. Three crucial agricultural necessities are now in short supply throughout the planet: land, fertilizer, and water. Meat production not only uses an inordinate share of the first two (returning food only to the affluent), but it also uses water at a shocking rate. Vegetable production uses about 300 gallons of water per day to produce food for one person on a plant-based diet. A mixed animal-plant diet, however, uses 2,500 gallons per day—again to feed only one person.[8] To produce one pound of meat thus costs about 25 times more than what it takes to produce a pound of vegetable food— a loaf of bread, for example.

Commercial meat production also abuses the water supply. Animals in the United States alone produce about two billion tons of manure yearly. Much of that, because of irresponsible feedlot and packinghouse practices, is flushed into overloaded sewage systems or dumped directly into rivers and streams. While boasting that it uses "everything but the squeal," the meat industry dumps tons of what it doesn't use—grease, intestinal wastes, meat scraps— into municipal sewage systems. Georg Borgstrom says the production of livestock creates ten times more pollution than residential areas, and three times more than industry.[9]

What effect does a U.S. meat-centered diet have on energy supplies—particularly on dwindling world supplies of petroleum? The answer can be seen in this example: if all the petroleum reserves in the world were devoted solely to food production— none for transportation or heating—and if this production were geared to feed the world's four billion people a typical North American diet, all the world's oil would be burned up in only 13 years.[10]

Consider also the huge amounts of natural gas and petrochemicals converted to the fertilizer used to grow the grains and other products that end up in the rumens of cattle. To grow an acre of corn takes the rough equivalent of 80 gallons of gasoline. (Using manure instead of chemical fertilizer might cut this to 50 gallons.) But when the corn is harvested and used for animal feed, only a fraction of the corn's true value returns to the consumer.[11] Obviously, fuel conservation can be pursued at the dinner table as well as on the road.

Some experts say that meat production should be increased in underdeveloped countries. Yet boosts in production don't necessarily result in more protein for the masses. Meat production is now higher than ever in Central America, yet most of that beef winds up on the counters of fast food restaurants in the United States. Brazil has 97 million head of cattle—the world's third-largest cattle population after the United States and the U.S.S.R. But most of Brazil's meat is exported, with Brazilians regularly subjected to beef shortages, high prices, and reduced meat supplies available to the poor.[12]

Spokesmen for the meat industry defend cattle as efficient food producers, pointing out that steers can graze on land unsuitable for crop production. But according to Alan Berg in *The Nutrition Factor*, even when cattle feed on nonarable land, their eventual conversion to meat tends to benefit only the wealthy and already well-fed. In the United States, the majority of beef animals graze only during their first eight months of life. Cattle are then shipped to feedlots where they finish on grains that might have fed humans directly.

Don't look to the oceans for a quick solution to our food problems. To positively affect world nutrition, global fish harvests would have to be increased by six times.[13] Yet fish harvests—due in part to overfishing and pollution—have actually been declining worldwide for several years. Many marine scientists believe that most of the oceans have already been fished to their maximum.[14] Even if it were ecologically possible to increase fish yields, it would cost tens of billions of dollars and demand a revolution in fishing techniques. Of the present world fish catch, roughly one-third (20 to 25 million metric tons) ends up as animal feed in wealthy nations.[15]

What about those science fiction stories of how humanity would one day turn the oceans into farms, with dolphin boys herding millions of tons of cattle-fish into seagoing packing-houses? It's still science fiction. The more scientists learn about the complexities of sea life and fish breeding, the less it appears such dreams can be realized. Ocean and freshwater fish farming are realities, but their impact on the global food crisis can only be minimal—even allowing for an increase in their numbers. Existing fish farms now tend to produce either gourmet foods or yields of only local importance.[16]

Vegetarianism clearly makes fewer demands on our planet's strained resources than a meat-centered diet. But will your individual decision to become a vegetarian have any measurable impact on world food problems? In theory, yes. Lester Brown suggests:

> If the average U.S. citizen were to reduce his consumption of beef, pork, and poultry by ten percent . . . 12 million tons or more of grain would become available for purposes other than livestock production.[17]

Just because excess grain suddenly becomes available is no guarantee, of course, that it will find its way into the bowls and bellies of the poor. The huge grain companies, multinational corporations, and governments of wealthy nations would more likely use the surplus grain as an additional profit source—exporting it in larger amounts or storing it to create artificial price-boosting shortages.

Such greed is hardly restricted to capitalistic economies. The Soviet Union is moving toward using more grain on a per capita basis than the United States—not that the average Russian will be eating more bread and meat than his American counterpart. He may eat less, actually, because Soviet agricultural and meat production practices are less efficient than in the United States. The Russians may put an even greater strain on world food reserves than they did in 1972 by buying more grain to feed to livestock while getting less food value back in the bargain.

A widespread vegetarian conversion, in theory, should also free land that could then be used to grow more plant proteins to feed the hungry. But most of the world's arable land, like its grain, is controlled by a few corporations and governments. And they are more devoted to profit than human needs. In Colombia, a hectare (2.471 acres) of land used to raise carnations will bring in almost ten times more money than a hectare devoted to wheat or corn. Arable land is often tied up by a corporation raising a profit-making export crop, while the country must import basic foodstuffs at a higher cost to its citizens [18]—unless they can eat carnations and live on coffee.

Changes in international dietary patterns are occurring at present, but generally in the wrong direction. As developing nations move toward relative affluence, their populations tend to demand what the rich have—more meat and animal products rather than less. Much of the grain freed by our conversion to vegetarianism could ironically wind up being sold to sate the appetites of newly privileged groups in developing nations, while the poor go on scrabbling for crumbs. Shifting to a plant-based dietary might save much of the world from famine, but only if people and governments are willing to make necessary social and political changes. The most important factor contributing to the world food crisis is an unequal distribution of control over agricultural resources—an incredibly complex problem that can hardly be solved by mass vegetarian conversions.

Besides, as enthusiastic about vegetarianism or a lowered meat intake as we may be in the United States and other wealthy nations, we cannot easily sell the idea to the rest of the world. Even on a modest budget, a North American vegetarian has access to a dazzling variety of fresh fruit and vegetables and canned, frozen, and packaged foodstuffs. When we exult over a nonanimal diet we point to the numerous foods we can eat in lieu of flesh. But this is not the case in many other countries. A narrow range of local food choices and expensive imported goods may force a nonmeat eater to live on a dreary succession of sparse meals. The average Indian worker must work two hours to earn the equivalent of a liter of milk, while his Western counterpart need only work five to ten minutes to earn the same amount of money.

A quick switch to producing plant foods instead of meat won't solve world food problems overnight either. The problem is more complicated. Many plants, no matter how easily grown or in what amounts, cannot be utilized directly by humans. Other plants are low in protein or essential nutrients. Still others may contain substances that block mineral absorption in humans or produce allergies.

Given the financial and technological commitment, we could solve these food problems with improved processing techniques. Cattle can convert inedible oilseeds and roughage into usable protein, often filtering out harmful qualities. Humans can accomplish the same thing with chemistry and mechanical processing. Existing acceptable foods can be fortified with added nutrients. Legumes and grains can be converted into nutritious imitations of almost any food or texture. With enough money for intensive research and development, food technologists might eventually be able to convert all kinds of inexpensive vegetable matter into duplications of the traditional foodstuffs of any culture on earth.

Such food miracles would avoid the objections even hungry people have against strange tastes and appearances. But miracles cost money. Vegetarians and advocates of lowered meat consumption shouldn't fool themselves into thinking solutions come cheap and fast. Just because we can raise 26 tons of spinach in the same space that yields only one ton of beef doesn't mean we can get people to eat the spinach.

Meat eating isn't the cause of all the world's ills, nor would a vegetarian revolution be a magic cure-all—though you'd never know it to hear some vegetarians. But dietary customs and food policies do affect all our lives. Your decision to stop eating flesh foods may only reflect the actions of one person, but the world changes in small steps. Obviously, any dietary plan that helps to increase one's ethical awareness, that uses fewer precious resources, and that dramatizes our potential ability to feed the world is worth pursuing. A sensible vegetarian diet can't hurt you and will probably leave you healthier in body and soul.

Your shift to vegetarianism may not directly help to feed your brothers and sisters, but your personal food habits will affect those around you. Your lifestyle will demonstrate that a nonflesh diet is not only possible but preferable, nourishing, and satisfying. As a vegetarian you will at least have the satisfaction of knowing that your daily life contributes in a small, private, indirect way to the alleviation of both human and nonhuman suffering. You will know, if nothing else, that instead of being part of the problem you are part of the potential solution. As Laurence Pringle concludes in *Our Hungry Earth:*

> If we have the good sense and the will to change to a less-wasteful lifestyle, we will provide a new model for the millions of people who want to emulate us. And that, perhaps even more than surplus grain, will be a powerful force in our efforts to solve the world food crisis.[19]

*Chapter Twelve notes.*

1. Mikkel Hindhede, "The Effects of Food Restriction During War on Mortality of Copenhagen," *JAMA,* 74(6):382 (7 February 1920).

2. Georg Borgstrom, *Too Many* (New York: Macmillan Co., 1969), p. *xi.*

3. A.M. Altschul, *Proteins: Their Chemistry and Politics* (New York: Basic Books, 1965), p. 264.

4. Louis H. Bean, cited in Nathaniel Altman, *Eating for Life* (Wheaton, Illinois: Quest Books, 1973), p. 41.

5. Lester Brown, *By Bread Alone* (New York: Praeger Books, 1974), p. 6.

6. Frances Moore Lappé, *Diet for a Small Planet* (New York: Ballantine Books, 1975), pp. 12, 24, 25, 26, respectively.

7. *Ibid.,* p. 14.

8. Altschul, p. 265.

9. Georg Borgstrom cited in Lappé, p. 22.

10. David Pimental, et al., "Energy and Land Constraints," *Science,* 21 November 1975, p. 757.

11. Lawrence Pringle, *Our Hungry Earth: The World Food Crisis* (New York: Macmillan Co., 1976), p. 104.

12. Alan Berg, *The Nutrition Factor* (Washington, D.C.: The Brookings Institution, 1973), p. 66.

13. *Ibid.,* p. 68.

14. Brown, p. 160.

15. D.S. Halacy, Jr., *The Geometry of Hunger* (New York: Harper and Row, 1972), p. 151. (Borgstrom has pointed out that one-third of U.S. canned fish is used as cat food.)

16. Brown, p. 160.

17. *Ibid.,* p. 206.

18. Richard Barnet and Ronald Muller, "How Global Corporations Compound World Hunger," in C. Lerza and M. Jacobson, *Food for People, Not for Profit* (New York: Ballantine Books, 1975), p. 248.

19. Pringle, p. 108.

# ❧ THIRTEEN ❧

# No Bones about It: The Vegetarian Kitchen

This is a resource chapter. Rather than duplicate much that can be found in numerous vegetarian cook books, this chapter will discuss several foods of special interest to vegetarians, while providing some general hints and suggestions. An assortment of recipes is also included, but readers are urged to consult the reading list at the end of the book.

Vegetarian cookery isn't difficult; it's different. Don't despair if you're not familiar with many of the foods discussed in this and other chapters. Buy or borrow a few of the cookbooks listed or use a few of the recipes in this book. Take your time and experiment. You need only add one new recipe or food each week to build a repertoire of new meals and food combinations.

*Equipment.* You won't need to add much new equipment to your kitchen. You can, in fact, get rid of your meat grinder, barbecue grill, rotisserie, sausage stuffer, basting pans, and smokehouse. Keep your blender. Few kitchen devices use as little energy and do so much. As a vegetarian, you'll use a blender for most of the same tasks you perform now—making sauces, purees, salad dressings, batter, and drinks. A blender can also be used on a small scale to grind or chop nuts and seeds, though a grain mill is best for this.

If your budget is a bit larger, consider a food processor. Once a luxury wielded by gourmets, food processors are becoming as common in U.S. kitchens as toasters and blenders. The basic processor (Cuisinart is the best known, though there are almost a dozen less-expensive imitations) comes with four blades designed to chop, shred, slice, blend, and mix.

Most so-called labor-saving devices end up costing us a bundle in cash and electricity, not to mention self-respect. But the best food processors are rugged, worth their cost, and use less electrictiy than a blender (about one kilowatt hour per year or five cents worth of power.)

And they do the job fast. You'll do most cutting or shredding in bursts of one or two seconds. You can shred a series of whole carrots in less time than it took to pick them, slice a zucchini into uniform slices perfect for stir-frying, chop onions sans tears and runny nose, mix pastry dough in half-a-minute, and prepare multi-vegetable salads and fruit dishes in the proverbial wink. The food processor is to the serious cook what the power saw is to the carpenter. But even I-Hate-To Cooks and Eat-and-Runners will—armed with a processor—find themselves actually spending more time in the kitchen creating the nutritious meals they thought they didn't have time for.

Most food processors will do a satisfactory job pulverizing seeds, nuts, and beans. For larger amounts—say when bread baking—you may want a grain mill. Hand cranked and motorized mills with steel or stone burrs are widely available. Don't run right out to buy one, however. Wait until you have more experience with whole foods. Grain mills can be used to make fresh wheat, corn, rye, rice, seed, or nut flours, cereals and pancake ingredients.

Cast-iron cookware was mentioned earlier as a good way to add small amounts of iron to your diet. Iron skillets, pots, and Dutch ovens also heat more evenly than aluminum ware. And once seasoned by several weeks of cooking, ironware develops a nonstick surface and a character and aesthetic appeal all its own. Bake up a skillet full of corn bread and you'll see what I mean.

The wok has caught on in the United States, and few utensils are better suited to vegetarian cookery. Essentially a wide steel bowl, the wok makes it possible to stir-fry or sauté vegetables as many Asians do—lightly and crisply, just enough to let the vegetables "bite back." Too many people overcook vegetables, serving them up as a watery mess. Don't say you hate vegetables until you've had them prepared in a wok.

Pressure cookers are expensive but worth every penny. Although the best vegetable soup is one that simmers all day on the back of the stove, a pressure cooker enables you to make soup with that all-day flavor in less than an hour, saving time and fuel. Pressure cookers do the same speedy work in preparing grains, legumes, and fresh vegetables—sealing in most of the nutrients that might have been lost in a steaming, open pot.

Unless you plan on eating canned and frozen vegetables, you'll need a few good paring knives. Don't buy cheap ones. They won't hold an edge. Dull knives slip and cause accidents. Buy carbon steel or quality stainless steel knives. Use a cutlery steel or soft Arkansas sharpening stone to keep a good safe edge on them.

You should have several other small items: a good nonsliding cutting board of hardwood—though lucite will serve—and a hand cheese grater. Kitchen supply shops usually carry an inexpensive hand-cranked grater that comes with three different grating surfaces. Another inexpensive device useful to vegetarians is a collapsible, perforated, stainless steel gadget used to steam vegetables. Along with wok cooking, lightly steaming vegetables is one of the best ways to preserve their flavor and nutrient content. This inexpensive gadget sits on little legs inside a larger pot or skillet. You bring an inch of water to boil in the pot, put your vegetables in the steamer, and steam them for only a minute or so. The vegetables never touch the water, lose little of their vitamins, and are cooked with a minimum of energy.

There are dozens of other small and large items you might

want—everything from egg timers to crockpots—but the few items I've described will be of most use to the vegetarian cook.

*Food sources:* I don't have to tell you how popular and important the home vegetable garden has become in recent years. More than half of all U.S. households now maintain a garden. You needn't live in a rural area or the suburbs to grow your own. City gardening is possible on rooftops, in vacant lots, in small backyards, and in containers on balconies and patios. Even someone with limited time and finances can grow salad greens and cherry tomatoes. And families growing their own groceries often find that their children don't have a built-in prejudice against vegetables. Besides lowering your food bills, gardening's biggest appeal is the taste and nutritional quality of homegrown produce.

Next to growing your own, farmer's markets and small family farms are the best sources of fresh, locally grown produce. Prices tend to be lower, you can buy in bulk for canning and freezing, and you end up supporting the small farmer directly. Seek out the organically minded farmer whenever possible. Why ingest pesticidal residues if you can avoid it? You can also find out where the nearest pick-your-own farms and orchards are in your area. An hour in the fields will reward you with vine- or tree-ripened fruits and vegetables. The experience will also show your children that the whole world isn't yet plastic-wrapped.

Co-ops and buying clubs are a big help to the vegetarian interested in choosing from a wide variety of foods while buying in bulk at lower prices. Buying seeds, legumes, and grains in one-pound packages at the supermarket doesn't pay. Most co-ops and natural food stores keep their produce in bins or crocks. Customers scoop out as much as they need. Buy enough to last a week or two—no more. Refrigerate all grains and seeds to guard against mold and spoilage.

## FOODS OF SPECIAL INTEREST

**Brewer's Yeast** is called so because it was originally a by-product of the brewing industry. Brewers would skim off the head during the beer-making process, drying the residue to make a vitamin-rich powder. This powder was then sold as a food supplement. Yeast is actually a plant product. Each speck of the powder is really a one-celled plant, 1/4,000 of an inch in diameter —about the size of a human blood corpuscle. Most yeast is now produced as a primary product rather than as a derivative, and is grown on molasses or whey. Yeast is 50 percent protein, with an NPU of 67. Yeast contains the B complex,* minerals, trace minerals, and 16 amino acids.

Yeast is relatively inexpensive and generally free of additives or pesticidal residues. A variety of brands and types are available in natural food stores. Some yeasts have added minerals to boost the nutritional value or to balance yeast's naturally high phosphorus content. Brewer's yeast tablets are also available, though not recommended unless you have lots of time to kill: it takes a handful of tablets to equal just one tablespoonful of powdered yeast.

Yeast's one drawback is its taste. The flavor varies from bearable to unpalatable. But this can be successfully masked by mixing yeast with fruit juice and other foods. Yeast can also be added to soups, blender drinks, casseroles, and bread doughs. Used judiciously, yeast's flavor will not come through most foods.

Brewer's yeast or food yeast is *not* the same as baker's yeast. The latter is a live yeast in cake or powdered form. It's designed for use in baking bread, not for direct consumption.

---

* $B_{12}$ does not occur naturally in nutritional yeast as do other vitamins and minerals. If the yeast is labeled as containing $B_{12}$, it is because the manufacturer has fortified the yeast with this vitamin. Conversely, if $B_{12}$ does not appear on the label, there is none in the yeast.

Seaweed has been eaten for centuries by the peoples of Asia, Ireland, Scotland, Wales, and Denmark. There are various types of edible seaweed—all go under the collective name algae or brown seaweed. Perhaps that's why seaweed hasn't caught on in most of North America. People equate seaweed with the slime that grows on the sides of aquariums and swimming pools.

One of the most widely used seaweeds is kelp, a vigorous ocean plant that may grow 200 feet in length. Harvested by boats that shear off the tops of growing plants, kelp can grow back to its original length in two or three days. Kelp has an outstanding mineral content. Most seaweeds have an ash content of 10 to 50 percent. This means that up to one-half of the volume of seaweed is minerals—a far greater proportion than any land plants. Seaweeds contain *all* the trace minerals necessary to human nutrition.

Powdered or granular kelp is available in natural food stores. Whole seaweeds can be found there also and in Asian grocery stores. Look for hiziki, kombu, wakame, nori, and dulse. Dried seaweed may be soaked, chopped, and sautéed with other vegetables. The seaweeds agar-agar and Irish moss (carrageen) can be used to make vegetable gelatin. Powdered kelp also makes an excellent fertilizer and animal food.

Soybeans needn't be a vegetarian's sole food, but so multi-faceted is the soybean that one could live on soybean products without ever actually eating a dish of the beans themselves. In *Soybeans for Health, Longevity, and Economy,* author-scientist Phillip Chen underscores the value of this amazing legume, saying: "The Chinese nation exists today because of the use of the soybean as food."

Soybeans are justly famous for their protein content. The amino acid distribution in soybeans resembles the pattern found in animal protein more than it does that of plants. The NPU of soy flour is 61, granules and beans measure 57, and sprouts are 56. (Meat and poultry, you'll recall, measure 67.)

Soy products are rich in assimilable iron, potassium, calcium, and phosphorous. Soybeans have ten times the calcium of meat and twice that of eggs. The beans are rich in B vitamins, bearing twice as much riboflavin as eggs. Soy oil contains lecithin (which may be purchased separately), a substance some researchers believe may help to lower serum cholesterol levels. The oil also contains vitamins E and K.

Soy flour and granules may be easily and inexpensively added to all kinds of food and baked goods, boosting their nutritional value. Soy milk is available in stores and can also be made at home. It is used as a formula base for infants and for those with a lactose intolerance, and may also be fermented to make yogurt. No wonder the soybean has been called the meat that grows on vines.

Soybean derivatives are used extensively in industry, but their adaptability in the kitchen is no less great. Besides the familiar yield of flour, granules, powder, milk, oil, and sprouts, soybeans can be made into dozens of Asian staples. Two of these deserve special mention.

Tofu (also known as bean curd) is a food of infinite versatility, superior nutrition, good taste, and remarkably low cost. When made at home—and the best tofu *is* homemade—the price is about ten cents a pound. That's for a food that can be broiled, fried, freeze-dried, used as a main dish, eaten as dessert, served as an appetizer or snack, or used in salads, sauces, soups, dips, and sandwiches.

To make tofu, whole soybeans are soaked overnight, pureed, and heated. Soy milk is expressed from the pulp (which can also be used in cereals, breads, and soups) and curdled to separate the curds from the whey or clear liquid. The moist soy curds are then drained and pressed to form cakes of tofu. This off-white, delicate product neither smells nor tastes like the parent bean.

Tofu has a mild, subtle taste—so subtle that tofu readily takes on any flavor you wish. Marinate tofu in teriyaki sauce and broil it. Roll it in flour or dip it in batter and deep fry it. Blend tofu with fruit for a custardlike dessert. Cut tofu in chunks and add it to soup or vegetable stews. Crumble it into salads. Its uses are limited only by your inclination to experiment.

Tofu is easily digestible and high in protein (NPU 67).

Seven ounces of tofu will yield 25 to 30 percent of an adult's RDA for protein—at a cost of pennies. Tofu is also low in calories: each gram of usable protein is accompanied by only 12 calories, a ratio comparable to some varieties of seafood. Tofu is cholesterol-free, low in saturated fats, and high in essential linoleic acid.

But beyond its imposing nutritional qualities, tofu tastes good —so good that, given the chance, it's bound to become a staple in your kitchen. For more on tofu making and use—with 500 recipes—read *The Book of Tofu,* by William Shurtleff and Akiko Aoyagi.

Another soybean product slowly catching on in the United States is tempeh ("tem-pay"). Like yogurt, tempeh is a microbially cultured food. Cracked soybeans are cooked, inoculated with a starter culture, and held at 85 to 90 degrees for 20 to 24 hours. The heat and bacterial action transform the beans into deliciously tender, mild-flavored cakes with the texture of cheese. Deep fried, sautéed, or broiled, tempeh—like tofu—can be served as a main dish, in salads, eaten out of hand, in sandwiches, and soups.

Besides its superb flavor, tempeh is inexpensive (one cup of soybeans makes a pound of tempeh) and can be made at home. Information and supplies (starter culture and beans) can be obtained from The Farm, Summertown, TN, 38483; and from Micro Cultures, P.O. Box A, Bayville, NJ 08721. (Several pioneers in various parts of the United States have already begun commercial tempeh production as this book is being written. Tempeh may already be available in your local natural food store.)

**Wheat Germ** has an NPU of 67, ranking its protein utilization with that of meat and poultry. Two tablespoons of wheat germ will yield roughly two usable grams of protein. Wheat germ is also a good source of vitamin E, thiamin, and riboflavin. (White flour is made by refining out the bran and germ, leaving only the starchy endosperm. Refined flour is enriched by replacing only a fraction of the nutrients lost in milling.)

Purchased in bulk, wheat germ is relatively inexpensive. Keep it refrigerated to guard against rancidity—the germ has a high oil content. (Fresh wheat germ should taste sweet; it tastes sour when rancid.) Small jars of toasted wheat germ are available in supermarkets, but this is uneconomical and probably not as nutritious as buying it raw in bulk. Toasting destroys some heat-sensitive B vitamins.

Wheat germ can be eaten mixed with breakfast cereals (its low tryptophan content is complemented by milk), used instead of bread crumbs, and combined with casseroles, nut loafs, bread, and other baked goods.

**Sunflower Seeds** will keep a parrot happy and make good cattle feed, but the seeds of *Helianthus annus* are a much better food than might be supposed. Almost two-thirds of the protein in sunflower seeds is usable. Three tablespoonsful supply about four usable grams of protein. The seeds are a good source of unsaturated fatty acids, potassium, zinc, and phosphorus. Sunflower seeds offer significant amounts of magnesium and iron— their iron content (six milligrams per 100 grams) ranks close to similar portions of egg yolk or wheat germ. The seeds can be ground into meal or purchased as such (they are more easily digestible in this form) and used as you would wheat germ. Sunflower seeds should be generally free of pesticidal residues—the plants have few insect or disease enemies.

**Sesame Seeds** are one of humanity's first cultivated oilseed crops. Sesame products have long provided the people of Turkey and Syria with a basic source of fat. And sesame seeds are an amazingly good source of essential nutrients. One hundred grams (3½ ounces) contain 1,125 milligrams of calcium. (A pint of milk supplies 250 mg; a cup of cottage cheese yields 200 mg of calcium.) The seeds also contain unsaturated fatty acids, lecithin, B vitamins (principally inositol, choline, and niacin), and vitamin E. The NPU is a respectable 53.

Sesame seeds should be ground in a hand mill or blender to increase their digestibility. Their most usable form is as paste or butter, known as tahini, available in natural food stores and shops selling foods of the Near East and Mid-East. Vegans can depend on sesame products as a source of calcium—the calcium-phosphorus ratio is 2:1. Tahini can be used as salad dressing, in blender drinks, as a sandwich spread, and in mixed dishes. Sesame meal can be used as you would wheat germ.

**Pumpkin Seeds** have an approximate NPU of 60. Two tablespoonsful deliver roughly five grams of usable protein—about 12 percent of the average RDA. Unlike most seeds, pumpkin seeds contain significant amounts of the EAAs isoleucine and lysine; pumpkin meal can be used to complement lysine-weak grains. Pumpkin seeds are also rich in unsaturated fat and minerals. They are higher in phosphorus and iron than most seeds— one cup contains 26 mg of iron. Pumpkin and squash seeds are also rich in zinc. Lightly roasted pumpkin seeds make a wholesome snack.

**Rice** is a staple food, relatively low in protein but with a high NPU (70). Brown rice is the choice of most natural food enthusiasts. Unlike white rice, the brown is high in fiber and has a characteristic flavor and chewiness. The short grain variety is somewhat more glutenous than the long or medium grain.

**Tamari** is a fermented soy sauce. All soy sauces are not tamari, however. Many so-called soy sauces are little more than colored water and flavoring. Real tamari is made with wheat, sea salt, and soybeans and is aged for at least two years in wooden casks. Tamari adds flavor and some nutrients to soups, casseroles, salad dressings, and cooked vegetables.

**Miso** is a fermented soybean paste containing some B vitamins and lactobacilli similar to those found in yogurt. Use miso in various dishes as you would tamari.

**Yogurt** (unflavored) has the same NPU and mineral and caloric content of milk, but it's more valuable than straight milk. The bacteria that cause yogurt to ferment also predigest the lactose. This aids digestibility and assimilation. Make your own yogurt or buy it plain. Avoid the flavored, sugared glop. Use yogurt for breakfast with grains and fruit, as the base for salad dressing, instead of sour cream on potatoes, as a midmorning snack, and so on.

**Sprouts** are an inexpensive, nutritious, aesthetically satisfying food. Grow your own right in the kitchen. Any seed can be sprouted—the standards are mung and soybeans, lentils, alfalfa, and garbanzos. Make sure the seeds you buy are sold for sprouting and eating; garden seeds are often treated with fungicides.

Soak seeds overnight. Drain. Put them in a large jar or collander. Rinse several times every day. (You cannot overrinse.) Eat when the sprout is the length of the seed or longer. Put sprouts in the sunshine and they'll develop tiny green leaves and chlorophyll. You needn't cook sprouts. Add them just before serving soups, salads, and casseroles. Try a sprout sandwich.

**Molasses** is a mineral storehouse that can be used in bread dough and other baked goods, in baked beans and casseroles, and in blender drinks. Molasses—buy the blackstrap variety—has a strong flavor. Go easy your first time using it.

**Honey** can be used in place of table sugar. You'll have to experiment, though, if you use it in baking bread. Try cutting back on the amount of liquid called for in the recipes—honey is 75 percent water. And unlike table sugar, honey has its own characteristic flavor which varies depending on the variety. The darker the honey, the stronger the flavor.

**Meat Analogs** are vegetable proteins made to resemble flesh foods in appearance, taste, and texture. Many vegetarians and minimal meat eaters enjoy sitting down to meals of burgers, sliced chicken, and corned beef, all made of TVP—textured vegetable protein.

Meat analogs are made by taking soybeans, wheat, peanuts, or other vegetable products and converting them into a slurry. This semiliquid is then fed into spinning machines resembling those used to produce rayon and nylon. Forced through thousands of tiny holes, the slurry emerges as fine jets. The jets are fed into an acid solution and congealed into threads. These soy protein filaments may then be spun into remarkably deceptive imitations of meat texture. The crunch and chewiness of chicken, steak, hamburger, and bacon may all be duplicated to one's delight or discomfort.

To complete the illusion, the tasteless fibers are treated with a variety of flavorings, colors, sugar, salt, binders, egg albumen, gluten, oil, and additives such as monosodium glutamate (MSG). Vitamins and minerals are also added to boost or balance nutritional values. (Many TVP products contain added vitamin $B_{12}$).

One of the largest producers of meat analogs says that TVP products are made to resemble flesh foods "to help [people] identify with traditional eating patterns." But, of course, those opposed to eating flesh for ethical or aesthetic reasons are doing their best to avoid traditional eating patterns. "I don't eat corpses," said one of my vegetarian friends, "and I'll be damned if I'll eat imitation corpses."

Other vegetarians use TVP extensively, staying with the traditional main dish pattern, centering their meals around ersatz flesh foods. And some new vegetarians have discovered that the familiar textures and appearances of analogs help ease the transition from flesh to plant foods.

Objections to TVP products are largely aesthetic. Meat analogs contain no animal by-products. And, unless they contain egg protein, they are free of cholesterol. But they are a relatively expensive processed food, laced with artificial colors and additives. This may not appeal to those seeking wholly unfabricated foods.

# A Sampling
# of Good
# Meatless Recipes

HOW TO COOK BROWN RICE.

Rice triples in cooking: 1 cup of dry rice yields 3 cups of cooked rice.

Put one part rice to two parts water in a pot. Bring water and rice to a boil. Turn down heat to a simmer. Keep pot covered. Simmer 30 minutes or until water cooks away. Turn off heat. Keep pot covered and let sit for 5 to 10 minutes to steam rice thoroughly.

In a pressure cooker, use 2 parts water to 1 part rice. Bring pot up to pressure and cook rice and water for 10 minutes at 15 pounds pressure.

HUMMUS.  (Chick pea-tahini spread)

    1 cup cooked chick peas (garbanzo beans)
    1 cup tahini
    2 cloves of garlic, pressed
    2 lemons, juiced
    2 tablespoons olive, safflower, or other light oil
      powdered kelp to taste
      chopped parsley and/or chopped onions

Puree chick peas in a food mill.  Add tahini, garlic, lemon juice, oil, and kelp.  Mix or blend to a smooth paste.  Add finely chopped parsley and onion to taste.

Use as a sandwich or cracker spread.  Add more oil if the hummus is to be used as a dip.

*To cook chick peas.* Soak 1 cup of beans overnight in 3 cups of water.  Drain.  Cook beans in water until soft.  Add water if necessary.  If using a pressure cooker, *do not* soak beans.  Use 3 cups of water to 1 cup of beans.  Cook for 20 minutes at 15 pounds pressure.

FALAFEL. (A traditional Middle-Eastern food)

¾ cup of chick peas (garbanzo beans)
    seasonings: finely chopped onion or garlic; basil, marjoram, thyme, kelp, etc.
¼ cup tahini

Soak beans overnight and drain. Add to 1½ cups of boiling water. When water again comes to a boil, turn down to a simmer. Cook beans until tender (about 2 hours, less with a pressure cooker.)

Drain beans. When cool, mash or blend into a paste. Add seasonings to taste. Add ¼ cup of tahini. Mix well and form into patties 2 or 3 inches in diameter and ½-inch thick

Saute in an oiled skillet until brown on both sides; or form paste into 1-inch balls, roll in unbleached flour, and deep fry at 365°F. Balls will pop to the surface when done. Drain on absorbent paper.

Serve patties on a bun or in a sandwich with lettuce and tomato. Falafel balls make nutritious additions to boxed lunches.

## EGG ROLLS.

*Egg Roll Filling:* \*
      2 cups cooked brown rice
      1 large onion, chopped
      2 green peppers, chopped
      1 cup chopped mushrooms
      ½ cup ground sesame and pumpkin seeds
      1 tablespoon tamari
      1 tablespoon brewer's yeast

*To Make the Wrappings:*
      1 cup unbleached flour
      1 cup whole wheat flour
      2 eggs
      2¾ cups water

Combine ingredients for wrappings and beat until smooth.

Grease a small frying pan (an omelet pan works fine). Pour in approximately ¼ cup of batter. Tilt pan and spread the batter evenly over the pan bottom. Let a thin layer of batter stick to the pan bottom.

\* Any combination of grains, vegetables, and rice will work well.

Cook batter until it sets (like a pancake or crepe). Then turn pan over and flip flat wrapping onto a plate. Cooked side should be facing up.

Continue making wrappers until all the batter is used up.

Heat peanut oil in a large frying pan, add filling mixture, and stir-fry. Don't overcook. Ingredients should be heated but crisp.

Ladle out 2 tablespoonsful of filling onto a flat wrapper. Place filling on bottom half of wrapper, fold in the sides, and roll into a tight package.

Use cornstarch and water to make a paste "glue" and use to brush along egg roll ends. Do this carefully, pressing and sealing the ends securely. Repeat until all the filling is used up. (Unused wrappings can be fried and eaten as snacks.)

Deep-fry egg rolls in hot (but not smoking) oil until evenly browned on all sides. Drain on absorbent paper.

Enjoy them hot or cold.

SUNBUNS.

    1 cup ground sunflower seeds
    1 tablespoon chopped green pepper
    1 egg, beaten (optional)
    2 tablespoons chopped onion
    ½ cup minced celery
    1 tablespoon parsley, finely chopped
    ½ cup shredded raw carrot
    1 tablespoon safflower or sesame oil
    ½ teaspoon powdered kelp
    ¼ cup tomato juice
        herb seasoning to taste

Combine ingredients and mix well. "Dough" must be of the consistency to form patties that retain their shape. Place patties on a lightly greased pan or oven dish. Bake at 350°F., turning patties to brown on both sides.

You may broil the patties instead of baking. Coat patties on both sides with oil before broiling.

Serve hot with applesauce, yogurt topping, grated cheese, or a fresh tossed salad.

## A BASIC BREAD RECIPE.

4 cups water
¾ cup oil
½ cup honey
4 eggs, beaten: optional
4 tablespoons baker's yeast
6 tablespoons brewer's yeast
12 cups flour, approximately: whole wheat or a combination
      of whole wheat, unbleached white, rye, soy, corn, etc.
optional: dried fruits, chopped; ground seeds; bran;
      wheat germ; skim milk powder.

Combine warm water, oil, honey or molasses, and eggs. Allow to sit until ingredients are warm. Add yeast and enough flour to make a batter (like pancake batter). Beat well.

Allow to double in size. Stir and add any optional ingredients. Add enough flour to make dough. Knead on floured board about 10 minutes, until dough is no longer sticky.

Let dough rise. Punch down. Let it rise again. Form into loaves. Let it rise until doubled. Bake 325°F. about 1 hour. Makes 6 loaves.

## STIR-FRIED VEGETABLES.

½ to ¼ head cabbage
2 onions
2 tablespoons oil
1 small piece of minced ginger
1 clove of garlic, pressed
½ cup chopped celery
½ cup shredded carrot
1 tablespoon tamari
½ pound of bean, lentil, or alfalfa sprouts
1 tablespoon cornstarch
3 tablespoons water

Chop or slice cabbage and onions. Add oil to wok and bring to medium high heat. (Oil shouldn't smoke.) Add minced ginger and pressed garlic to oil. Add the vegetables slowly, stirring constantly to distribute them across the wok surface. Add tamari sauce.

Continue stirring vegetables. When vegetables are hot but still crisp, add sprouts and stir quickly. Don't allow the sprouts to overcook or go limp. Mix cornstarch and water and add to wok. Stir until this gravy becomes thick.

Serve stir-fried vegetables over steamed rice.

## PAT'S SOYBEAN PÂTE.

 ½ cup soybeans, soaked overnight in 2 cups of water
 ½ cup of chopped onions (or more to taste)
  1 cup cottage cheese
  garlic powder or garlic cloves to taste
  thyme and oregano

Cook until tender in soak water. Blend beans with onions, cottage cheese, garlic and herbs—adding a little milk if the blender clogs. Blend to a smooth paste. Refrigerate.

Spread on crackers, pour over rice, use as a sandwich spread. For a thicker sandwich spread, thicken with cottage cheese or tahini.

## RICE PATTIES.

¼ pound mushrooms, corn, peppers, or almost any vegetable
   of your choice
   oil
2 tablespoons butter
2 tablespoons flour
4 tablespoons milk
2 large eggs
2 teaspoons chopped parsley
2 cups cooked short-grain brown rice
   black pepper, salt, or kelp to taste
   bread crumbs

Chop vegetables or mushrooms and fry in large oiled skillet until tender. Stir in melted butter, then flour and milk. Remove pan from heat. Add beaten eggs, parsley, rice, and seasoning. Stir until mixture is uniform. Let cool. Shape into patties 3 inches in diameter by ½- to ¾-inch thick. Roll patties in bread crumbs.

Grill in oiled skillet at medium heat or until patties are golden brown on both sides. Drain on absorbent paper. Serve hot with mixed vegetables as a main dish. Rice patties are excellent as leftovers and lunch box additions. Eat them cold out of hand with a dash of homemade mayonnaise. Makes 12 patties.

## ROBIN'S RICE-VEGETABLE-MUSHROOM TART.

1½ cups short-grain brown rice
2 onions, chopped
3 tablespoons oil or butter
¾ pound mushrooms, sliced; and/or corn, tomatoes, broc-
    coli, etc. Use your imagination.
1¼ cups yogurt
4 eggs, beaten
1 pound cottage cheese
¾ pound cubed or grated cheddar cheese
    chopped parsley to taste
    paprika
    pepper and dash of salt if desired

Cook rice. When rice cools enough to handle, press into a 9-inch pie plate or a 9 x 12-inch baking dish to form a crust. Sauté chopped onions in 3 tablespoons of oil until onions become clear. Add mushrooms and other vegetables. Cook lightly until tender. Pour onions and vegetables into rice crust.

Blend yogurt, eggs, cheese, and seasonings. Pour over vegetables. Bake 45 to 50 minutes at 350°F. or until inserted knife comes out clean. Serve hot or cold.

## NUT LOAF.

    2 tablespoons butter
    1½ cups celery, chopped, braised and buttered lightly
Add:
    1½ cups chopped onions
    1 cup chopped walnuts
    1 cup chopped cashews
    ¼ cup rolled oats
    1 pound cottage cheese
    3 eggs
    ½ cup almonds, ground to flour in blender or hand mill
    ¼ cup sunflower seeds, ground as above
    ¼ cup cooked brown rice
    ¼ teaspoon each basil, thyme, and oregano

Mix all ingredients well. Turn into greased loaf pan and bake 1 hour at 375°F. Longer baking will produce a firmer loaf. Serve hot as an entrée. Refrigerate leftovers and serve as sandwiches (with ketchup or mayonnaise), in salads, or soups.

## GRILLED TOFU.

pressed tofu cakes or cubes
iron skillet, lightly oiled
*or*
charcoal grill, hibachi, or campfire reduced to coals
marinade
skewers

Marinade may be any barbecue, teriyaki, or hot sauce. Marinate tofu cakes for at least 1 hour, turning occasionally. Grill tofu to a golden brown, basting with leftover marinade. Serve hot wtih sprinkles of tamari.

*To press tofu.* Cut 1 x 2 x 3-inch blocks of tofu and spread out on a clean doubled bath towel. Leave an inch or so between cakes. Cover with another doubled towel. Place a cutting board or tray over the top towel and add a 5-pound (or heavier) weight. Press for 30 minutes to an hour.

After the first 15 minutes to a half hour, remove the top towel or replace it if soaked through. Tofu is well pressed when you can hold a single piece vertically like a playing card.

## DEEP FRIED TOFU.

tofu, well-pressed
oil for deep frying (soy, peanut, safflower, etc.)
deep skillet, wok, or deep-fryer
deep-frying thermometer
cooking tongs
absorbent paper

Heat oil to 375°F. Carefully place several tofu cakes into the oil (the temperature will drop at this point, so keep a check on the thermometer) and deep fry until the cakes turn golden brown. They will float on the oil's surface if your frying vessel is deep enough. Remove tofu and drain off excess oil.

Serve hot with tamari or miso toppings. Deep-fried tofu may also be served cold, added to soups or stews, salads, and sandwiches. You may also grill deep-fried tofu, using the previous recipe.

## VICTORY BREAKFAST.

1 banana, ripe and soft
1 apple
1 to 2 tablespoons wheat germ
1 tablespoon crushed almonds, walnuts, or sunflower seeds
2 tablespoons raisins
1 to 2 tablespoons honey or molasses
$\frac{1}{2}$ cup or more of yogurt, milk, or soy milk
1 tablespoon lemon or orange juice, fresh-squeezed

Mash banana in bowl into a puree. Grate entire apple (skin, core, and seeds) and mix with banana. Add wheat germ, nuts, raisins, honey or molasses, and milk. Add lemon or orange juice. Mix thoroughly and enjoy. Serves 1.

This is a basic recipe. Use your imagination for variations. You may delete the honey and increase the amount of dried fruit or fruit juice. Vary the kind and amount of grains. Use rolled oats, wheat flakes, cold brown rice (cooked), or ground sesame seeds. Eat as breakfast, midday snack, or dessert.

## BLENDED TOFU FRUIT TREAT.

8 to 12 ounces chilled tofu
1 to 2 tablespoons honey
1 tablespoon raisins
8 to 12 ounces fresh chilled blueberries, strawberries, peaches,
    or cantaloupe.

Blend all ingredients to a puree. Serve as a dessert or snack.
Top with crushed nutmeats, sunflower, or sesame seeds.

## FROZEN BANANAS.

Cut bananas into halves and impale on a popsicle stick. (Or
make your own sticks from ¼-inch diameter dowel rods. Cut rods
into 5-inch lengths.) Freeze bananas solid.

This is a perfect snack—a replacement for the junk-on-a-stick
most children are unfortunately addicted to. A frozen banana will
satisfy that late night hunger attack with only 50 calories—about
7 times fewer than the calories in a cup of ice cream.

(Seedless grapes may also be removed from the stem and frozen solid: a tooth-numbing snack.)

VEGETARIAN GELATIN.

   ½ cup agar-agar *
   ½ cup cold water
    2 cups fruit juice
      honey to taste
      lightly oiled gelatin mold or dessert cups

Add agar-agar to cold water. Let it sit for 5 minutes, then bring to a boil until dissolved. Remove from heat. Pour in fruit juice. Add honey. Pour mixture into mold or cups. Chill until gelatin becomes firm. (This takes less time than with true gelatin.)

If you wish to add chopped fruits, nuts, or vegetables, let jell firm slightly before pouring into mold. Turn in fruits, etc., and mix with jell. Pour mixture into mold and refrigerate until firm.

* Agar-agar is a translucent seaweed available from health and natural food stores and from Asian groceries.

## ALMOND CHUNK SNACKS.

2 cups whole shelled almonds
½ cup raisins
6 to 8 tablespoons honey
¼ teaspoon pure vanilla extract

Grind almonds in a blender or hand mill to a fine powder. Mix ground almonds and raisins in a saucepan or deep iron skillet. Add honey. Turn heat to low. Allow honey to liquefy, stirring continuously. Add vanilla. Stir until mixture is uniform.

Turn "dough" onto breadboard and roll with rolling pin until mixture is roughly ½ to 1-inch thick. You may shape mixture into a square or rectangle. Let dough cool for an hour or so. Cut into 2-inch squares. Refrigerate overnight or until hard.

Not for calorie watchers.

# Bibliography

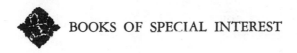 BOOKS OF SPECIAL INTEREST

Hooker, Alan. *Vegetarian Gourmet Cookery*. San Francisco: 101 Productions, 1970. Just what the title implies. Restaurant-tested recipes and a solid introduction to vegetarian cookery.

Lappé, Frances Moore. *Diet for a Small Planet*. Rev. ed. New York: Ballantine, 1975. Less about vegetarianism per se than about meatless cookery and the ecological and social problems created by eating at the top of the food chain. A basic reference book that belongs in every kitchen.

Richmond, Sonya. *International Vegetarian Cookery*. New York: Arco, 1965. Recipes from all over the world. The perfect book for putting variety in your menus.

Robertson, Laurel; Fliners, Carol; and Godfrey, Bronwen. *Laurel's Kitchen*. Berkeley: Nilgiri, 1976. Written with intelligence, love, and understanding. A most valuable cookbook and detailed nutrition guide. Superb directions for bread baking and meal planning.

Shurtleff, William, and Aoyagi, Akiko. *The Book of Tofu*. Brookline, Mass.: Autumn, 1975. The most important book on food ever published for vegetarians—if not all the world. Clear prose and beautiful illustrations take you step-by-step through tofu making at home. Five hundred recipes for preparing this versatile and nutritious food. Buy this book and a sack of soybeans and you'll be one step closer to food independence.

Thomas, Anna. *The Vegetarian Epicure*. New York: Vintage, 1972. An informal poll generally shows this book to be the favorite of experienced vegetarian cooks. But it's also a superb book for beginners. Reach for this elegant volume when your meat-eating friends (the ones who are convinced you eat a monotonous diet) drop in for dinner.

 OTHER GOOD COOKBOOKS

Brown, Edward Espe. *Tassajara Cooking*. Boulder, Colo.: Shambhala, 1973. An excellent choice for the first-time vegetarian cook.

Burgess, Mary. *Soul to Soul*. Santa Barbara, Calif.: Woodbridge, 1976. Can a vegetarian enjoy soul food? Ms. Burgess says yes.

Dinshah, Freya. *The Vegan Kitchen*. Malaga, N. J.: American Vegan Society. Meals with no animal products whatever.

Ewald, Ellen Buchman. *Recipes for a Small Planet*. New York: Ballantine, 1973. Meatless meals with balanced protein.

*The Farm Vegetarian Cookbook*. Summertown, Tenn.: The Book Publishing Co., 1975. Recipes from a vegetarian community.

*The Findhorn Cookbook: Cooking with Consciousness.* New York: Grosset & Dunlap, 1976. Food through the eyes of the famous spiritual community.

Ford, Frank. *The Simpler Life Cookbook from Arrowhead Mills.* Fort Worth, Tex.: Harvest, 1974. Good introductory paperback to whole grains and their infinite uses.

Ford, Marjorie, et al. *The Deaf Smith Country Cookbook.* New York: Collier, 1973. Down-home cooking without flesh foods.

Friedlander, Barbara. *Earth, Fire, Air, and Water.* New York: Collier, 1972. Good food as an aesthetic experience.

Hittleman, Richard. *Yoga Natural Foods Cookbook.* New York: Bantam, 1970. Food to go with whole body awareness.

Hurd, Frank and Rosalie. *Ten Talents.* Chisholm, Minn.: Hurd. A huge collection of mostly vegan recipes.

Kaufman, William I. *Three-Hundred-and-Sixty-Five Meatless Main Dishes.* New York: Doubleday, 1974. Now you'll only be at a loss in a leap year.

Lee, Gary. *The Chinese Vegetarian Cookbook.* Concord, Calif.: Nitty Gritty, 1972. Reads like Mr. Lee is standing next to you in the kitchen. Informal and to the point.

Lo, Kenneth. *Chinese Vegetarian Cooking.* New York: Pantheon, 1974. Another approach to Chinese cuisine without meat, fowl, or fish.

Sacharoff, Shanta. *Flavors of India: Recipes from the Vegetarian Hindu Cuisine.* San Francisco: 101 Productions, 1972. Another centuries-old culture shares its culinary delights.

Vithaldas, Yogi, and Roberts, Susan. *The Yogi Cookbook.* New York: Crown, 1968. You don't have to do yoga to enjoy this. The authors introduce us to various Indian foods.

 MISCELLANEOUS COOKERY

Brown, Edward Espe. *The Tassajara Bread Book.* Boulder, Colo.: Shambhala, 1970. Learning to make good bread can nourish the body and spirit.

Dworkin, Stan and Floss. *The Good Goodies: Natural Snacks n' Sweets.* Emmaus, Pa.: Rodale, 1974. Wean yourself from junk food with wholesome snacks.

Hewitt, Jean. *The New York Times Natural Foods Cookbook.* New York: Quadrangle, 1971. Not a vegetarian cookbook, but surely one of the best additions to your kitchen. A little bit of everything and how to do it well.

Hunter, Beatrice Trum. *Fact Book on Yogurt, Kefir, and Other Milk Cultures.* New Canaan, Conn.: Keats, 1973. A meticulous examination of the myths and facts about fermented milk products, plus instructions for homemade yogurt, kefir, and cheeses.

Jacobson, Michael. *Nutrition Scoreboard.* New York: Avon, 1975. The codirector of the Center for Science in the Public Interest offers a valuable book that rates foods according to their overall nutritional value. Solid nutritional information.

Kaufman, Ted and Jean. *The Complete Bread Cookbook.* Paperback Library, 1969. For the first-time baker or the experienced chef. Three hundred international recipes for breads, biscuits, rolls, and more.

Kirschmann, John D. *Nutrition Almanac.* New York: McGraw-Hill, 1975. A well-organized, readable survey of nutritional data.

Kunz-Bircher, Ruth, et al. *Eating Your Way to Health.* New York: Penguin, 1972. Dietary theory and practices from the famous Bircher-Benner clan.

Lappé, Frances Moore, and Collins, Joseph. *Food First.* Boston, Mass.: Houghton Mifflin, 1977. The *real* reasons why most of the world goes hungry and what we can do about it.

Lerza, Catherine, and Jacobson, Michael. *Food for People, Not for Profit.* New York: Ballantine, 1975. More than fifty essays on food: why some go without, why some eat too much, why it's grown the way it is, and what we can do about it.

Senate Select Committee on Nutrition and Human Needs. *Dietary Goals for the United States.* Washington, D.C.: U.S. Senate, February 1977. GPO No. 052-070-03913-2. This is the controversial booklet issued by the Nutrition Committee that calls on Americans to eat less meat, less fat, and less sugar—and to get more exercise. Buy a copy before it becomes a collector's item.

Verrett, Jacqueline, and Carper, Jean. *Eating May Be Hazardous to Your Health.* New York: Anchor, 1975. Unpleasant but true. Drugs, disease, and filth in our food and how it gets there. Don't eat with your eyes closed.

Yudkin, John. *Sweet and Dangerous.* New York: Bantam, 1973. Dr. Yudkin's analysis of sugar's dangers will help you to do what you should have done years ago: throw away that sugar bowl.

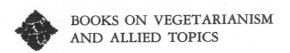 ## BOOKS ON VEGETARIANISM AND ALLIED TOPICS

Altman, Nathaniel. *Eating for Life.* Wheaton, Ill.: Quest, 1977. A concise survey of vegetarianism.

Barkas, Janet. *The Vegetable Passion*. New York: Charles Scribner's Sons, 1975. A history of vegetarianism.

Hur, Robin. *Food Reform: Our Desperate Need*. Austin, Tex.: Heidelberg, 1975. The author assembles massive documentation to support his call for a health-building vegan diet based on nutritionally balanced plant foods.

Singer, Peter. *Animal Liberation*. New York: New York Review, 1975. A carefully reasoned call for equal treatment for nonhuman animals. Takes you inside the tortured worlds of laboratory and factory farm animals.

# Index